Oliver Goldsmith

MASTERS OF WORLD LITERATURE

Published:

In Preparation:

MASTERS OF WORLD LITERATURE SERIES
LOUIS KRONENBERGER, GENERAL EDITOR

Oliver Goldsmith

A GEORGIAN STUDY

by Ricardo Quintana

The Macmillan Company, New York
Collier-Macmillan Limited, London

To Dick and Terrie

16765

First Printing

THE MACMILLAN COMPANY, NEW YORK
COLLIER-MACMILLAN CANADA LTD., TORONTO, ONTARIO

Printed in the United States of America

Contents

Preface and Acknowledgments

I AM ONLY too keenly aware that here I cannot begin to make due and full acknowledgments for all the encouragement and assistance of one sort or another which I have received while working on the present study of Goldsmith. There are, however, a few people, some of them friends or acquaintances and others personally unknown to me, to whom I must express my particular thanks. Louis Kronenberger, by providing a place for this book in his Masters of World Literature Series, gave me the right incentive at just the right time, though long before that he had already, by reason of his delight in eighteenth-century letters and the wit and grace of his own writing, given me much for which I am grateful.

In the field of scholarship, the pioneering work of Katharine C. Balderston and R. S. Crane lays a heavy debt on all students of Goldsmith. Arthur Friedman's long-awaited edition of the *Collected Works* gives us at last a reliable text, an authoritative canon, and by means of critical introductions and notes an important summary of the significant matters brought to light by modern scholarship.

So far as biography is concerned, Ralph M. Wardle's *Oliver*

Goldsmith, which upon its appearance in 1957 took its place as the finest work of its kind, has not since then been superseded nor is it likely to be for a long time. Only those who have worked closely both with the facts and the nonfacts of Goldsmith's life can fully appreciate exactly what Mr. Wardle has succeeded in doing by way of clarification and orderly presentation.

More than a little Goldsmith criticism has appeared in our time. Much of it is exciting, some of it is memorable. Here I should like to mention, more or less in the order in which I first encountered them, a few critical items which for me have proved unusually suggestive. Virginia Woolf's essay on Goldsmith, which appeared originally—and anonymously—in 1934 in the *Times Literary Supplement* of London, has all along been wonderfully reassuring. I have returned more than once both to D. W. Jefferson's important "Observations on 'The Vicar of Wakefield' " in the *Cambridge Journal* (1949–50) and to the equally important critical introduction given by Frederick W. Hilles in his edition (1951) of *The Vicar.* Finally, I owe much to A. Norman Jeffares, whose *Oliver Goldsmith* (1959) is distinguished for its critical acuity and its admirable balance.

My thanks also go to Professor Arthur Sherbo for his assistance in connection with several details concerning Goldsmith's life, and to three agencies of the University of Wisconsin, the Graduate School, the College of Letters and Science, and the Institute for Research in the Humanities, which have granted me various research leaves of absence during the course of the past five years.

The Goldsmith text which I have used throughout (save in the case of certain passages in the *History of England, in a Series of Letters* and in *Animated Nature*) is that of the *Collected Works of Oliver Goldsmith,* edited by Arthur Friedman (5 vols.; Oxford: The Clarendon Press, 1966), by permission of the Clarendon Press, Oxford. The text of Goldsmith's letters is that of *The Collected Letters of Oliver Goldsmith,* edited by Katharine C. Balderston (Cambridge: The University Press, 1928), the text of "Mrs. Hodson's Narrative" is to be found in Appendix III of the same Balderston edition of the *Collected Letters,* and references to and quotations from Goldsmith's Memorandum of his own life as dictated to Bishop Percy are to the text thereof as found on pages 12–16 of Katharine C. Balderston's *The History and Sources of Percy's Memoir of Goldsmith* (Cambridge; The University Press, 1926), all by permission of the Cambridge University Press.

Quotations from (1) *Boswell's London Journal, 1762–1763,* (2) Sir Joshua Reynolds's prose Portrait of Goldsmith, (3) Boswell's "Journal" for 1773, and (4) Boswell's "Journal" for 1775, are from, respectively, the following:

(1) *Boswell's London Journal, 1762–1763,* edited with Introduction and Notes by Frederick A. Pottle. Copyright, 1950, by Yale University. McGraw-Hill Book Co., Inc.

(2) *Portraits by Sir Joshua Reynolds,* prepared for the press with Introduction and Notes by Frederick W. Hilles. Copyright, 1952, by Yale University. McGraw-Hill Book Co., Inc.

(3) *Boswell for the Defence, 1769–1774,* edited by William K. Winsatt, Jr., and Frederick A. Pottle. Copyright, 1959, by Yale University. McGraw-Hill Book Co., Inc.

(4) *Boswell: The Ominous Years, 1774–1776,* edited by Charles Ryskamp and Frederick A. Pottle. Copyright, 1963, by Yale University. McGraw-Hill Book Co., Inc.

All these quotations are by permission of Yale University and McGraw-Hill Book Co., Inc.

Quotations, as indicated in the body of my book, from Vols. VI (1929), XIII (1932), and XVII (1937) of *The Private Papers of James Boswell from Malahide Castle,* copyright to which is now held by Yale University, are by permission of Yale University and McGraw-Hill Book Co., Inc.

I take this opportunity to thank all the above publishers and Yale University for these permissions.

R. Q.

By Way of Prologue

1

IT WAS EARLY in February, 1756, that Oliver Goldsmith, penniless after a two years' tour of Europe in the character of a philosophic vagabond, landed at Dover. Since leaving his native Ireland in the autumn of 1752 he had studied medicine—after a fashion—at Edinburgh and then at Leyden; later he had made his way across Flanders to Paris; he had been in Switzerland and perhaps in Germany, and had visited Padua and other Italian cities.

Exactly how old he was at this moment of arrival in England we do not know. When it was still possible to consult the Goldsmith family Bible, now lost, one learned only that he was born on November 10, the year having been worn or cut away. The best guess is that he was now twenty-five, but though there are good reasons for settling on 1730 as the year of his birth, we find ourselves, as a result of all the conflicting opinions on the subject delivered by Goldsmith himself and various relatives and friends, faced with a choice of dates ranging from 1728 to 1731. The matter is not in itself of great importance; there were assuredly no mysteries surrounding his parentage and birth. It is merely that here we have the first instance of the kind of comic confusion which has come to preside over so many of the details and precise circumstances of Goldsmith's life. Those who knew him at first hand or professed to have authoritative information have contributed handsomely to these biographical uncertainties through their eager but often contradictory testimony. Did Goldsmith himself sometimes add wittingly to the confusion, not so much through what he said about himself as through what he did not say? It is hard to tell, but in any case he offers little help in setting straight the actual facts at those points where they lie most in doubt.

Coming ashore that day in February, 1756, he was in effect bidding good-bye to his youth. The years of school and university were over, his European travels were at an end. Family funds had sustained him at Edinburgh and Leyden, and had held out until he had reached Italy, at which point the uncle who recently had been financing him had lapsed into incompetence through illness and advanced years, the expected remittances had stopped, and the money sent off by other relatives to meet this emergency had never reached him. He had been obliged, so he stated in a brief Memorandum of his life dictated years afterward to his friend Bishop Percy, "to return back thro France &c. on Foot, lodging at Convents chiefly of the Irish Nation."

He must have made a sorry figure as he set foot on English soil, bedraggled, unkempt, and all too obviously without a shilling to his name. He stood about five and a half feet, his hair was brown, his body well-built. But it was his head and his face one noticed— an incredible head and face. Everything was out of proportion. The bulging forehead was too big, the mouth protruded hideously, the chin looked as though it had been sheared away. His face was almost round and badly pitted with smallpox. Various people have left us their impressions. His features, one friend charitably remarked, were plain but not repulsive and took on a different cast when lighted up by conversation. In the well-known Reynolds portrait the ugliness is there but somehow transcended. On the other hand, the painter's sister, Miss Reynolds, who had little affection for Goldsmith, saw nothing to idealize; he impressed everyone at first sight, she said, with an idea of his being a low mechanic, "particularly . . . a journeyman tailor"; while a London newspaper, desiring for reasons of its own to maul *She Stoops to Conquer* shortly after the play's successful opening, could refer to the author's "grotesque Oranhotan's figure."

How he made his way from Dover to London we do not know. He may have found some kind of temporary employment before he reached the city, but it could not have been long before he arrived in the great metropolis, and found himself adrift there, living from hand to mouth. The cold indifference of the English afforded a bitter contrast to what he had known at home and what he had met with on the Continent, at least among the peasants in France and Italy. He fancied that his Irish manner and his brogue put him at a hopeless disadvantage. He was without friends, recommendations, money, or impudence—so he was afterward to describe his plight, in a letter to his brother-in-law written at the close of 1757—and in a country where being born an Irishman was sufficient to keep him unemployed. Many, he believed, would in like circumstances "have had recourse to the Friar's cord, or suicide's halter." But by the time he was writing this the worst was behind him and he could say that "by a very little practice as a Physician and a very little reputation as an author" he was making a shift to live. His commitment to letters was not yet final, but he had had a taste of Grub Street and knew now that he possessed the true gift for words. After such a discovery no person is ever quite the same again. In the end, however, it was events beyond his control which set him on the course he was to keep for the rest of his life. Had he gone out to India to seek his fortune, as he was planning to do shortly, he very likely would not have become one of the foremost professional writers of his age.

2

Goldsmith's life in an outward, chronological sense presents only two periods. The first extends from his birth to his arrival in London, a matter of slightly more than twenty-five years if 1730 is taken as the date of his birth. The second runs from 1756 to his death in April, 1774, thus covering the eighteen years of his residence in London and his entire career as a professional man of letters. It is naturally this latter, all-important period which holds most of our attention. However, the early one is not to be entirely overlooked, for it throws some light—some though not nearly so much as could be wished—upon the person known to us from the years of his achievement.

The story of Goldsmith's childhood and youth in Ireland, of his departure for Edinburgh in September, 1752, and of his subsequent travels on the Continent has been told time and again. For our purposes here, it does not call for retelling in any detail. He came of a long line of local Anglo-Irish gentry residing for the most part in counties Longford and Westmeath. Many of these, like Oliver's own father, were clergymen in the Established Church, and a few had achieved deanships. Goldsmith was the second son in a family of seven children. He grew up in a substantial house near Lissoy (since known also as Auburn), Westmeath, a house acquired at about the time of his birth when his father, the Reverend Charles Goldsmith, had succeeded his wife's uncle as curate-in-charge of the parish of Kilkenny West. The family was a curiously assorted one; indeed, the differences in personality and talent which the members displayed point unmistakably at some rather unusual genetic pattern. The father, a graduate of Trinity College, Dublin, was a good-natured man who was often aroused to glowing benevolence and imprudent generosity by fellow creatures having slight claim on him; yet on occasion and out of false pride he could be guilty of stubborn, foolish behavior. Between Oliver and his mother there was no strong bond of sympathy, and she remains a rather indistinct and not too appealing figure in the chronicle. Henry, the elder brother, studied at Trinity College, took orders, married, and at his father's death in 1747 came into a portion of the latter's clerical holdings. He remained poor and obscure, but he seems to have been a man of some intelligence and of strong character and unvarying good will. Oliver loved and respected him beyond all the others. Maurice and Charles, the two youngest brothers (John, the youngest of all, died in early youth), were seemingly possessed of much less intelligence or at any rate lacked ambition and fell into the cruder provincialities of their time and place. Of the two sisters, Catherine married well, her husband, Daniel Hodson, belonging to a good family that lived not far from Lissoy; Jane, or "poor Jenny," on the other hand, made an unfortunate marriage. And amongst them all, one ugly duckling, who had already given some evidence of exceptional talent but was more notable for his unfortunately comical appearance and his fecklessness—as though his physical person and his innate disposition were results of some prank that had been played with the biological factors of inheritance.

If Goldsmith had no reason to boast of his ancestry and immediate family, he was not ashamed of them and he never concealed or misrepresented his origin. His natural brogue remained with him. His manners to the end were those he had acquired in the rural Ireland of that time. To his English friends everything about his speech and bearing seemed to indicate a decidedly low social background—it was easy to mistake the established, traditional ways of provincial gentility for boorishness. "He had lived a great part of his life with mean people"—so wrote Reynolds in his remarkable prose Portrait of his friend. The statement, one feels, is somewhat misleading, but there is reason to believe that Goldsmith sometimes reacted to this sort of judgment on the part of his acquaintances in London by exaggerating those things in his speech and behavior which caused them to question his background. Yet such a response, if a fact, must not be taken for the heart of the matter. He despised affectation of any sort; his standard was simplicity, naturalness, in life and in art. He could remain true to himself only by living in accordance with his natural breeding. And, after all, the elegance of his writing, which escaped no one, cannot have been wholly an accident.

In order to get at the hard facts concerning the first twenty-five years of his life we are obliged to discard a great deal of the material that has attached itself in the way of legendary stories and

hearsay to the traditional accounts of this early period. Goldsmith's own letters take precedence over most of what has come
down to us, but unfortunately only six of his letters that have
been preserved antedate the London period. We knew what
schools he was sent to, and something of his unhappy life as an
undergraduate at Trinity College, Dublin, from which he was
graduated A.B. early in 1750. For almost three years thereafter
he was at home, doing nothing, or coming to grief in whatever he
undertook, and it began to look as though this ugly duckling
would never go it on his own. Finally, through the efforts of an
uncle, he was pushed forth into the wider world.

There are many questions concerning this first period and particularly about the three and a half years following his departure
from Ireland that remain largely unanswered. In the first place,
what sort of medical education did he manage to pick up, and
did he ever take a medical degree? According to his own statement
in a Memorandum dictated toward the close of his life to his
friend Bishop Thomas Percy he received the degree of bachelor
of medicine at Trinity, having stayed on there after receiving his
A.B. There is some reason to believe that the M.B. was in fact
conferred on him by his own college either at the early date specified in the Memorandum or sometime during the first London
years. There is no record of any foreign degree. Twice he set himself up as a practicing physician, in 1756 or thereabouts and
briefly in 1765; he was known as "Dr. Goldsmith"—"Doctor"
being the courtesy title for one holding the M.B.—almost from the
time he first began to be heard of as a writer, and his name appeared on the title page of *The Traveller* (1764), the first of his
notably successful works, as "Oliver Goldsmith, M.B."; and in
1769 Oxford granted him an M.B. on the strength of his supposed
degree of similar nature from Trinity College, Dublin. It is, of
course, traditional to laugh at Goldsmith's absurd presumption in
ever presenting himself as a qualified medical practitioner, but it
is possible that he was not so hopelessly unqualified as has been
assumed. Mid-eighteenth-century medical science was still rudi-
mentary at best, and he must have picked up something at Edin-

burgh and on the continent. Dr. Johnson once remarked that he would as lief pray with Christopher Smart as anyone else. Speaking retrospectively, may we not perhaps say that we would as soon have had our lives jeopardized by Goldsmith as by the next physician?

A question of really greater importance, though it has not been brought up so often, has to do with the more informal sort of education that he must have been acquiring during his stay at Edinburgh and in the course of his travels on the continent. He may or may not have taken his medical studies seriously, but in any case it stands to reason that he was meeting with all sorts of exhilarating experiences of both a social and an intellectual kind. What were they? What new interests were being awakened? Precisely how was his whole horizon being enlarged? Always alert to his immediate social environment and possessing a caricaturist's eye for the telling details, he took note (so we learn from one of his letters from Edinburgh) of the landscape of Scotland and the manners of the natives, all so amusingly different from what he was used to at home—Lien Chi Altangi, the Chinese observer of the English, had once, it seems, been an Irishman at large among the Scots. Later on, from Leyden, he wrote to his uncle about the typical Hollander, "one of the oddest figures in nature." Foreign travel at this time was often accompanied by all sorts of minor discomforts, but those who made the European tour were not looking for familiar comforts in new places. They went abroad to observe local and national customs, to study the underlying principles of foreign governments, to see buildings and monuments, to look at pictures and listen to foreign operas, to learn about the books and the ideas then in circulation. Lack of money obviously cut Goldsmith off from some of the higher pleasures, but even as a vagabond he was, we know, a philosophic one, observing, inquiring, and storing away a great deal in his mind and his eye's memory. He never directly commented on the intellectual experiences of these years, but something of their nature can be inferred from the writing he did in his early Grub Street period. It is safe to say that while in Scotland he learned about the new rhetoric then being taught at Edinburgh and Glasgow, which put genuineness of feeling before all traditional techniques of expression; and it is likely also that he was introduced to the available essays of Hume, which took up so many of the general questions then holding the attention of the intellectual world, and submitted them to much keen analysis. In France, Montesquieu, d'Alembert, Voltaire, and others were establishing a whole new complex of ideas concerning human society and history; unquestionably Goldsmith shared in the enormous excitement which this new orientation was arousing. In later life he seems to have lost interest in some of the ideas and intellectual approaches that as a younger man he found so exciting and important, but this was not, it would seem, in consequence of any great change of heart or of mind but because he was after all essentially a poet: the ideas which found lodgment in his imagination, the viable ones, were those that enabled him to give structure to deeper human experience.

His character must, of course, have been quite firmly set by the time he left Ireland, but what it was in essential respects is not made very clear by the anecdotal material that has come down to us, so much of which must be viewed with mistrust. It is in regard to certain predilections and attitudes—that cast of mind revealed in his literary art but manifesting itself long before—that the record is of chief value. The ballads he heard as a child, sung by those in and about Lissoy, made a lasting impression on him, and it is said that as an undergraduate he eked out his meager resources by writing ballads to be sung in the streets of Dublin. There was nothing distinctively Irish about the ballad as he recognized it. With Lissoy he associated traditional songs of wide dispersion like "Johnny Armstrong's Last Good Night" and "The Cruelty of Barbara Allen." His own *Edwin and Angelina,* written about 1765, indicates what in time he came to think of as the important element in the ballad. It was the story, which he himself then proceeded to fashion in accordance with the pattern found in the popular romances that were still being written and continued to delight simple readers and simple listeners—the type of story he was to adopt in his own prose fiction, characterized by an amazing plot full of unexpected turns, of hardships brought on by chance, and of revelations and reversals leading up to sudden good fortune and happiness. Silly and wonderful at the same time! As the Vicar of Wakefield observed when prosperity deigned to smile once more on the Primroses, accidents, though they happen every day, "seldom excite our surprise but upon some extraordinary occasion."

A variant on this sort of narration is the cock-and-bull story, and this seems also to have appealed to Goldsmith, for he resorted to it more than once. There was, for instance, the occasion when his family demanded an explanation of his most recent series of misadventures. Goldsmith's sister, Mrs. Hodson, gave an amusing account of this episode in the brief Narrative of her brother which she was persuaded to write after he had achieved fame. He had departed in the direction of Munster on a fine horse and with £30 in his pocket, and it was assumed that he was leaving Ireland, but to the surprise of all the family he at length reappeared, penniless and riding a broken-down nag known to him as Fiddleback. The story he proceeded to tell of his adventures was a most wonderful blend of what might have been truth and what might have been fiction. In the midst of misfortunes he had been befriended, he said, by a certain Counsellor F. G., thanks to whom he had been able to make his way home. Had he, his mother asked, written to thank the dear good man? He confessed he had not, whereupon Mrs. Goldsmith pronounced her son an ungrateful savage, a monster, and in the words of Mrs. Hodson "the whole boddy of his Friends which were present up braided him. . . ." Then, when their passions were all spent, he proceeded to inform them that he had made the whole thing up for their amusement. By way of giving a last turn to this farce, he later assured his sister that as a matter of fact everything had happened as he had described it. Goldsmith's puckish delight in the extraordinary story, the extraordinary plot, was an expression of a deeply ingrained sense of irony. Things, you say, do not happen this way. Nevertheless, the Comic Spirit assures us that our delight in such fanciful adventures is not wholly childish—that it is in some measure a recognition of a hidden reality.

3

Goldsmith's rise from obscurity to a position of prominence in the literary world was effected in remarkably short time. There is, in fact, nothing that quite matches it in the eighteenth century. Johnson, for instance, succeeded in establishing himself only after a considerably longer and possibly more difficult struggle.

Toward the close of 1756 Goldsmith had found a post as usher in a boys' school at Peckham maintained by a Dr. Milner, whose son Goldsmith had met when they were both in Edinburgh. His duties here were not the sort that left him joyful after hours, but it is doubtful whether, like the Vicar of Wakefield's son, George Primrose, also "usher at an academy" for a brief period, he was ever browbeaten by the master or hated for his ugly face by the mistress. Milner, in fact, seems to have treated his undermaster handsomely, and he was shortly offering to use his influence with the East India Company to secure for Goldsmith an appointment which would take him out to India and a fortune there. And it was at Milner's table that Goldsmith met Ralph Griffiths, the publisher-owner of the *Monthly Review*.[1] Griffiths needed someone to help with the book reviews appearing regularly in his journal, and he offered to take Goldsmith on upon Grub Street terms: quarters above the bookshop—it was The Sign of the Dunciad, Paternoster Row—board, £100 a year, and for this as much writing as could possibly be done between nine in the morning and two o'clock in the afternoon. Goldsmith accepted the offer, and in April, 1757, his reviews began to appear. They were still appearing in September, but by that time Griffiths and his wife, both domineering people, had had enough of Goldsmith, and he of them.

But he had made a place for himself in Grub Street, and al-

---

[1] It is amusing to note that it was Griffiths' apparently nonexistent brother, "Fenton Griffith," who as "G. Fenton" had in 1748 brought out Cleland's notorious *Fanny Hill*. David Foxon has an account of the matter in *The Book Collector* (Vol. XII, Winter, 1963). See also his *Libertine Literature in England, 1660–1745* (New Hyde Park, N.Y., 1965), pp. 52–63.

though he was called back to Peckham early the following year (1758) to fill in at the school during an emergency, he was back in London before the autumn and writing again, only now on his own. His letters to Ireland—we have six of them between the close of 1757 and the beginning of 1759—give us some insight into his state of mind at this time. He was excusing to his relatives his long silence, explaining the hardships he had gone through and what was now keeping him in London. Sometimes he fell into nostalgic reminiscences, and again he pattered along in the gayest style about his present way of life. There are passages of poignant emotion, but mood and tone are changing constantly. Was he writing from the heart? Not altogether. He wanted to reinstate himself in the good graces of his family, and he did have a few more favors to ask; he was assuming certain postures, he was measuring his phrases. If there is an element of calculation about this, it can be ascribed to Goldsmith's remarkable feeling for what are best described as rhetorical effects. Since turning professional writer he had come to recognize, we may believe, what it meant to use words to mold and communicate emotional experience, controlling with precision the effect on the reader. At its lower levels this sort of rhetoric is no more than skillful craftsmanship; at the highest it can be genuine art.

The last of the six letters is, however, in a markedly different key. It is addressed to his brother Henry, and though undated (it bears only an incomplete postmark), it was presumably written about mid-January, 1759. There is something close to despair here, and nothing about it suggests attitudinizing. He detests, he says, the society he is now obliged to partake of:

> I can now neither partake of the pleasure of a revel nor contribute to raise its jollity, I can neither laugh nor drink, have contracted an hesitating disagreeable manner of speaking, and a visage that looks illnature itself, in short I have thought myself into settled melancoly and an utter disgust of all that life brings with it.

He gives advice on the education of Henry's son: teach him the necessity of being selfish, teach him thrift and economy, and teach him these things—virtue alone is not enough—in order that he may not expose himself to the insidious approaches of cunning. It is only toward the end of the epistle that Goldsmith manages to write himself out of this black mood, and then he speaks cheerfully of a "Life of Voltaire" which he has finished and gives some of the couplets he has been composing for what he calls a "heroicomical poem."

What was happening at about this time seems to have been somewhat as follows. Earlier, in 1758, Goldsmith's appointment to the East India Company had been settled and he had been posted to the Coromandel Coast in India. That summer, however, the disconcerting news that the French had overrun the coast and were laying siege to Madras had reached the officers of the East India Company in London, who saw fit to keep all word of these events from the public and were obliged to resort to delaying tactics in the case of those whom they had agreed to employ in India but who had not yet left. It occurred to Goldsmith, as he awaited word to depart, that he could save passage money by signing up as hospital mate on a ship bound for the East. Late in December he presented himself at Surgeons' Hall for examination but was found unqualified. The East India Company had perhaps had a hand in the verdict, but we can only speculate.

The worst of it was that Goldsmith had managed with characteristic maladroitness to land himself in a fine mess. In order to make a good appearance at Surgeons' Hall he had had to have a new coat. This he had secured on credit, having persuaded his old employer, Ralph Griffiths, to go security. Now he owed the tailor, he was unable to clear himself with Griffiths, the coat was in pawn, the money advanced on it had somehow disappeared (given, it has been said, to a woman in great necessity), and Griffiths and the tailor were threatening arrest. Such were the circumstances behind his letter to Griffiths of January, 1759—a letter of appeal, of self-reproach, and, at the same time, of self-vindication:

> I have been some years struggling with a wretched being, with all that contempt which indigence brings with it, with all those strong passions which make contempt insupportable.

He would be able to settle all accounts in a month. He was, he granted, guilty of meannesses born of poverty, and with remorse he acknowledged his imprudence, but a villain he was not.

Stories of all kinds have come down to us concerning Goldsmith's imprudent behavior throughout his entire life. But there are two points that need to be made. Irresponsible as he was in all money matters, no professional man of letters ever worked harder and more conscientiously to fulfill his contracts with publishers. Secondly, not only was he aware of the weakness in his own character responsible for his imprudence, but he objectified his experience and generalized upon it. It was better, he was now telling his brother Henry, that a boy should be taught the necessity of selfishness than that he should be left to learn it from later experience. Soon Goldsmith was to discern in the good-natured man—the man who does not know the meaning of prudence in his worldly dealings—a clear symbol of folly, and as always the Goldsmith sense of irony came into play. He himself could not be wholly calculating, and for that reason he was a fool in the eyes of the world and to a degree in his own. But what of those who made a virtue of the necessity of selfishness? What emerged in Goldsmith's imagination was a comedy of antithetical values—a comedy, not a tragedy, for the resolution of the conflict lay in a middle position apparent all along to common sense. Those whose lives were a mixture of naivety, guilelessness, and imprudence were not admirable, nor were good-natured sentimentalists who overlooked the realistic consequences of such persistent innocence. But equally unattractive were the cynical, calculating worldlings. All shortsighted, the lot of them; all destined by the comic spirit for condign chastisement.

4

The affair involving Griffiths and the tailor passed off quickly and undramatically enough, with Goldsmith managing somehow to satisfy the claims against him. And by the time it became clear that he would not be going out to India—not just then, at any

rate—he was content to take up professional writing in earnest.
Such work of his as had thus far appeared in print was not extensive (the reviews for Griffiths, and a translation of a recent
French book—Marteilhe's *The Memoirs of a Protestant*—which
had come out early in 1758), but it had served to give him an
identity among the London publishers. For some time he had
been under contract with the Dodsleys for a book which in his
letters to Ireland he had been referring to as an "Essay on the
Present State of Taste and Literature in Europe," and at about
the time he was being threatened with arrest by Griffiths he had
been taken on as a book reviewer for Smollett's *Critical Review,*
a Tory periodical running in direct opposition to Griffiths'
Monthly Review. When on April 2, 1759, the Dodsleys brought
out his book, now entitled *An Enquiry into the Present State of
Polite Learning in Europe,* his standing was considerably enhanced even though his name was not considered important
enough to be given on the title page or anywhere else in the book.
As the year advanced, Goldsmith found himself with more and
more work on his hands. He was living now in miserable quarters
in Green Arbour Court—outrageously ironic name—and it was
here that Thomas Percy, not yet a Bishop but already evincing
that interest in letters which was shortly to lead to his great work
on the ballads, *The Reliques of Ancient English Poetry,* paid him
a call early in March. It was apparent that Goldsmith—Dr. Goldsmith as he was soon being called—was a man to know. His circle
of acquaintances was being noticeably enlarged. It may already
have included Edmund Burke, who like Goldsmith had been a
student at Trinity College, Dublin. Three more years and Goldsmith's position was no longer in doubt. His series of essays first
known as the "Chinese Letters" (January, 1760–August, 1761) and
in their collected form as *The Citizen of the World* (1762) had
scarcely been a failure. From this point on, one success followed
another: *The Traveller* (1764), *The Vicar of Wakefield* (1766),
The Deserted Village (1770), *She Stoops to Conquer* (1773). He
had been a member of the famous Club since its founding in 1764,
but before that he had become a recognized personality in the

world of Georgian London. He lived up to and beyond his means —the rooms he eventually occupied in the Temple were expensively furnished, his tailor bills were an affront to common sense— but his earnings were large, at least for an eighteenth-century writer, and he was in constant demand both as an editor who had the knack of bestowing new life on old material and as a writer of biographies and histories which were certain to become best sellers on the strength of his name. If his contemporaries were blind to his true intellectual qualities, there were few of them who disputed his distinction as a writer; his stylistic grace, his humor, his mastery of the then-recognized kinds of writing—essay, verse, prose romance, comic drama, biography, history—were fully acknowledged. Nevertheless it was chiefly in the character of one whose personal and social qualities matched his physical appearance in point of eccentricity that he was known to the public. At the time of his sudden and premature death in 1774 the Goldsmith legend was already of mature growth. What was subsequently said and written amplified and enforced the legend but did not alter it substantially.

5

The legend, it must be acknowledged, has not given rise to so distorted a view that the approximate truth concerning Goldsmith as a person and as a literary artist has ever been wholly obscured. In this respect he has not suffered to anything like the same degree or in the same manner as has Swift, for instance. The legend is unfortunate nevertheless, for it has fixed in too many minds an image of Goldsmith which makes it more difficult than it ought to be to estimate in proper terms his actual achievement. In real life—so we have been told time and again—he was charming and warmhearted yet incredibly absurd in the things he did and said, helpless in the face of all practical demands, improvident, and as envious as Satan. As a writer, it has been assumed, he is speaking in his own person and holding our interest by reason of the infinite grace with which he is revealing to us his own emotional experience. The man and the writer have both been sentimentalized. "Your love for him," declared Thackeray, "is half pity." What in the world, we may ask, is there to pity? Goldsmith had a spectacular rise to fame; he was one of the most successful professional writers of his day. That he lived beyond his means was and still ought to be his own affair—it is really high time that in this respect we stopped passing judgment upon him from a narrow, commercial point of view. Nor are the ridiculous clothes which he sometimes affected any true concern of ours—who knows in what spirit he displayed himself in his Tyrian-bloom satin and garter-blue silk breeches costing £8. 2s. 6d.? By a miracle he was a genius and the greatest master of comedy to appear during the second half of the century. That is the central fact, never to be lost sight of. His vision of human experience embraced much. It was anything but self-centered. He understood comic distance, and his art, for all its grace and apparent plasticity, has the strength and firmness of impersonal statement. It is his triumph to have expressed in imaginative art better perhaps than any of his notable contemporaries that fine equipoise of civilized thought and feeling which marked the period we think of as High Georgian. It is time that we concerned ourselves less with his ugly face, his awkward social presence, and more with the actual nature of his achievement as a writer. After all, if we reckon solely in terms of literary art, the Age of Johnson is quite as much the Age of Goldsmith.

II

The Earliest Phase:
The Philosophic Vagabond in Grub Street

1

THE EARLIEST STAGE of Goldsmith's career as a writer defines itself readily enough. It begins with his first review in the April, 1757, number of the *Monthly Review* and includes the other reviews of that year (those in the five ensuing issues of Griffiths' periodical from May through September); a translation from the French entitled *The Memoirs of a Protestant,* brought out by Griffiths in February, 1758; the "Memoirs of M. de Voltaire," finished by the close of 1758 though for some reason withheld until its appearance in monthly installments in the *Lady's Magazine* in the course of 1761; and *An Enquiry into the Present State of Polite Learning in Europe,* published by the Dodsley brothers on April 2, 1759. This body of work stands more or less by itself: all of it was done while Goldsmith still, apparently, thought of himself as a temporary resident in Grub Street and was looking forward to some kind of better living, in India or elsewhere; and it is the only record we have of his general orientation at this early period. Though only the *Enquiry* can be said to be of intrinsic importance—it is really one of Goldsmith's major works, having an acknowledged place among the notable books of the period dealing with similar matters—both it and the earlier items in the *Monthly Review* deserve careful reading because of what they tell us about Goldsmith's intellectual equipment at the outset of his career. *The Memoirs of a Protestant* is of only secondary importance; the "Memoirs of M. de Voltaire" is significant mainly for showing how great Goldsmith's admiration for Voltaire was, and because it is the earliest and a rather crude example of the kind of popular biographical sketch or profile of which he was later on to become a master.

Something of the way in which he looked upon himself as a beginning writer and upon his association with Grub Street is indicated in his letters to friends in Ireland. We find him at the end of December, 1757, writing to his brother-in-law Daniel Hodson from the Temple Exchange Coffee House, "near Temple Bar," and declaring more in pride than in resentment that with a very little practice as a physician and a very little reputation as an author "I make a shift to live." The following August, when he wrote to his cousin Jane Lawder—again from the Temple Exchange Coffee House—he romanticized his situation as he imagined himself returning at length to Ireland and forgetting in the company of friends there "that ever he starv'd in those streets where Butler and Otway starv'd before him." Two weeks later, again to Hodson, after giving the particulars of his Indian appointment, he spoke in an almost boastful tone of the advantages that were his as a professional writer in London but that he would shortly be compelled to leave behind him:

> I know you have in Ireland a very indifferent Idea of a man who writes for bread. tho Swift and Steel did so in the earlier part of their lives.

Not every author, he went on, lives in a garret, wears shabby clothes, and converses with the meanest company; the truth is that a writer of any ability lives better in London than do many in Ireland who pride themselves on their fine dress and their gentility. Even in the midst of all the discouragements and humiliations that threatened to overwhelm him at the beginning of 1759, he mentioned to his brother Henry the sketch of Voltaire, which he believed—mistakenly—was on the point of being published, and in a tone of affected modesty described it as no more than a cathpenny affair, the work of only four weeks, for which he had nevertheless received £20.

The repeated references in these letters to his forthcoming "Essay on the Present State of Taste and Literature in Europe" (i.e., *An Enquiry into the Present State of Polite Learning in Europe*) show the great importance he attached to his first full-length, original work and his hope for some profit from its sale and perhaps some measure of fame. And there is one further allusion to literary work in hand which is important for several reasons. The passage occurs in his letter of August 14, 1758, to another of his cousins, Robert Bryanton:

> If ever my works find their way to Tartary or China, I know the consequence. Suppose one of your Chinese Owanowitzers instructing one of your Tartarian Chianobacchi—you see I use Chinese names to show my own erudition, as I shall soon make our Chinese talk like an Englishman to show his. . . .

The Chinese who talks like an Englishman is of course Lien Chi Altangi of the "Chinese Letters," and though these essays did not begin to appear in the *Public Ledger,* the newspaper in which they were published serially, until January, 1760, Goldsmith obviously had them or something like them in mind fully a year and a half before.[1] Thus, in spite of his expected departure for the Coromandel Coast, he had schemes for future writing in mind. The fact is that he was always planning ahead in some such manner as this. Even his frankly second-rate works—the later potboilers in the way of history, biography, and natural science—were not executed on the spur of the moment but were given a good deal of thought well in advance of composition. In the case of the major works the planning was of a much subtler and more imaginative kind, *The Traveller* growing organically out of the *Enquiry, The Vicar of Wakefield* out of the "Chinese Letters," and the plays out of the comic presentations in the essays and fiction that pre-

[1] Here I must differ from Arthur Friedman (*Collected Works of Oliver Goldsmith,* II, ix, footnote 2), who does not believe this to be a reference to the "Chinese Letters" but merely to what follows in the letter to Bryanton.

ceded. Goldsmith may have been incapable of keeping his personal finances in order, but where his writing was concerned his competence extended to far more than actual execution. It is not overstating the facts to say that during most of his professional life he worked according to a well-thought-out schedule. It is precisely this kind of forethought and ability to organize his creative resources that has been so emphatically denied him by the legend, though the record covering his authorship tells an entirely different story.

2

Goldsmith's contributions to the periodicals—these fall mainly before 1763—have in the past constituted a veritable nightmare for conscientious scholars and critics. Because his reviews and essays appeared anonymously, one is confronted at the outset with numerous questions concerning his authorship. Over the years much work was done in an effort to establish a reliable canon, but the results remained confusing. Things once unhesitatingly credited to Goldsmith were shown to be by other hands, whereas items once never associated with him were from time to time added to the list of his certain or probable works. This nightmare has at long last been dispelled by the welcome appearance of Professor Arthur Friedman's admirable edition of the *Collected Works,* which reflects and gives order to what bibliographical and textual scholarship has brought to light concerning Goldsmith's published writings, and which presents us with a reliable canon. Continued research will undoubtedly introduce further changes, but from now on we do not have to worry ourselves unduly over problems of attribution.

In the case of the book reviews which Goldsmith wrote for the *Monthly Review* in 1757 it happens, however, that exact information has long been available, for Griffiths kept a marked copy of his periodical and noted therein the authorship of each of the printed articles. Here Goldsmith is credited with something like nineteen full-length reviews and thirty-seven shorter notices.

The *Monthly Review* was staid in tone and conscientious in its survey of new books of a serious nature. In the January, 1756, number, for instance, the works mentioned briefly or reviewed at some length included a book on anatomy, another on the elements of algebra, a treatise on scurvy, *Poems Moral and Devout,* a *Mechanical Account of the Hysteric Passion,* a *Letter from a Cobbler to the People of England,* sermons on the late earthquake at Lisbon, and the doubtless edifying *Principles of Rome Exploded.* Such a sampling, however, scarcely does credit to the genuinely intellectual character of much of the *Review.* It discussed the important books of the day as they appeared, and its notices were informed; the topics and issues of the period stood forth. Thus in the December, 1756, number there was a review of William Bell's dissertation on *What Causes Principally Contribute to Render a Nation Populous?* The question here at issue was then a foremost one, and Goldsmith's interest in it was to become apparent in time.

As we approach the period of Goldsmith's association with the *Monthly Review* we find several items which must have made a particularly strong impression on him and which may very well have sent him to the books under review. The second volume of Hume's *History of Great Britain*—dealing with the Commonwealth and the reigns of Charles II and James II—was noticed in the issue for January, 1757. In February came a survey of Hume's *Four Dissertations* ("The Natural History of Religion," "Of the Passions," "Of Tragedy," "Of the Standard of Taste"), followed by a brief analysis of a work by Guillaume—Alexandre Méhégan, *Considérations sur les révolutions des arts* (Paris, 1755). In May, John Brown's *Estimate of the Manners and Principles of the Times,* just published but already being widely discussed, came in for consideration. Clearly the atmosphere of the upstairs editorial rooms at the Sign of the Dunciad was not one that discounted ideas. Goldsmith must have brought with him a certain amount of intellectual baggage acquired from his undergraduate days onward, and to this he was now making important additions. As a writer of popular histories he was to have Hume's *History of Great Britain* constantly in mind. Hume's essay "Of the Standard of Taste" and the treatise by Méhégan on "the causes which have either produced or destroyed" the arts take up matters central to *An Enquiry into the Present State of Polite Learning in Europe.* "Estimate" Brown's theories about luxury and national morality, and the effects of commerce on manners, entered into Goldsmith's growing concern over the conflict between materialistic interests and cultural values.

3

Of Goldsmith's own reviews, the two most important are those of Burke's *Philosophical Enquiry into the Origin of Our Ideas of the Sublime and Beautiful,* in the May issue, and of the *Odes by Mr. Gray* (i.e., *The Progress of Poesy* and *The Bard*) in September. But there are others that are also interesting because, like the two just mentioned, they clearly reflect the reviewer's own ideas. We are afforded our first insight into Goldsmith's literary mind, and what we find is convincing evidence of an early maturity.

Before any of these reviews are taken up in regard to their subject matter it might be well to consider for a moment Goldsmith's prose style as exhibited in these first compositions. Like most accomplished writers, Goldsmith had more than one style at his command, and a close analysis might result in the identification of several characteristic and recurrent patterns. But for most readers it is enough to recognize a polarity: on occasion he wrote a carefully and rather elaborately structured prose, involving a constant balancing or contrasting of the members; at other times he preferred a style that is more rapid and straightforward. Neither order is really a simple thing, though we are often beguiled into believing so because of the unfailing effect of ease, an effect attributable to Goldsmith's remarkable ear for word sounds and his infallible sense of rhythm and timing. The opening paragraph of the review of Burke's *Enquiry* proves that he was already a master of the structured style:

There are limits prescribed to all human researches, beyond which if we attempt to explore, nothing but obscurity and conjecture lie before us, and doubts instead of knowledge must terminate the enquiry. The genius, not the judgment, of an Author may appear in the too abstracted speculation; he may contribute to the amusement, but seldom to the instruction of the Reader. His illustrations may perplex, but not enlighten the mind; and, like a microscope, the more he magnifies the object, he will represent it the more obscurely.

As to the content of certain of these reviews of his: his comments in the May number on John Home's famous play *Douglas,* just presented at Covent Garden Theatre, mark Goldsmith's earliest appearance as a critic of the drama. There is nothing unsophisticated about his observations; he already possessed a formulated theory of the critic's function as well as a theory of tragic drama. The true critic's province is "to direct our taste, and conduct the Poet up to perfection"; let us have done with "a mechanically exact adherence to all the rules of the Drama"; drama acquires warmth and life not from observance of the rules but from sublimity, sentiment, and passion. In the case of Home's play, its patent defects are not compensated by poetic fire and heightenings of pathetic distress. Admirable, however, are the lines given to the shepherd Norval; his native innocence is happily expressed: "it requires some art to dress the thoughts and phrases of the common people, without letting them swell into bombast, or sink into vulgarity. . . ."

The trend of such remarks as these is not, as has sometimes been assumed, in the direction of a later romanticism. There is really no rejection of neoclassicism—not, at least, of English neoclassicism —involved. Goldsmith never ceased to be essentially neoclassical in spirit and in the literary principles he adhered to. His structured prose, for instance, and his enduring sense of the distinct "kinds" of literary art—the generic differences between, e.g., tragedy, comic drama, the epic, and the nonepic varieties of poetry—are visible marks of his general accord with a tradition which in his time had not yet been undermined. The emphasis he constantly placed upon the "natural" and "simple" in art is actually more classical than otherwise, as Joseph Addison's stated preference in the *Spectator* (No. 62) for "that natural way of writ-

ing" which allows a thought to "shine in its own natural beauties"
should convince us. Nor are Goldsmith's references to the emotionalism of tragedy at all out of line with English dramaturgic
theory and practice as found in the plays of Otway and Nicholas
Rowe, for instance, and in much Augustan criticism.

Another of his reviews in the May issue, one in that for July,
and three in August may also be noted. The first of these is a
short comment on the essay serial the *Connoisseur,* by Thornton
and George Colman, which had come to an end at the close of
September, 1756, and had now appeared in a collected edition.
The author of these essays—Goldsmith is referring to the imagi-
nary Mr. Town, the Connoisseur, the supposed writer of the
series—is one who instead of dictating to the reader with an affected superiority converses with him "with all the ease of a
chearful companion"; in consequence he is the first essay writer
since Addison and Steele "who has been perfectly satirical, yet
perfectly good-natured," who never for rhetorical effect represents
simple folly as downright criminal. It would be difficult to find a
better characterization than this of what Goldsmith himself was
to be as an essay writer—an easy, cheerful companion, a satirist
whose ridicule remained good-natured, a tolerant observer of
human folly.

The item in the July issue contains an observation which really
goes to the heart of Goldsmith's concept of literary art. The writer
under review—a certain Jonas Hanway, whose *Journal* concerning
his travels in England had recently appeared—does not, we are
told, know how to place trite material in new and striking lights:
"Novelty of thought, and elegance of expression, are what we
chiefly require, in treating on topics with which the public are
already acquainted. . . ." It is clear what Goldsmith means by
"novelty of thought." It is an imaginative rather than a strictly
intellectual matter; it places the familiar in a new perspective and
by thus vitalizing our common experiences extends our awareness
of life. In Johnson's critical writing we find a similar emphasis
upon exactly this same kind of novelty of thought, so-called.

Three items in the August number contain passing observations on humorous and satirical writing, and these remarks show convincingly that Goldsmith was already taking soundings for what eventually became his own "Chinese Letters." Apropos of Voltaire's *Essai sur l'histoire général* (the seven-volume edition of 1756), there is a quotation from Voltaire on the subject of Montesquieu's *Persian Letters*: their success arose from the delicacy of the satire; "satire which in the mouth of an Asiatic is poignant, would lose all its force when coming from an European." A recent book, *Letters from an Armenian in Ireland,* similar in plan to Montesquieu's satire, draws from Goldsmith the observation that a writer "who would inform, or improve, his countrymen, under the assumed character of an Eastern Traveller, should be careful to let nothing escape him which might betray the imposture"; he must preserve the fictitious character he has assumed. And in his comments on Rabener's *Satirical Letters,* just translated from the German, Goldsmith shows familiarity with that critical line of thought which in England from the Restoration onward had been concerned with the nature of humor. In the 1690s Sir William Temple had asserted that English comic drama was admirable and distinctive by reason of its humor, which truthfully reflected the eccentricities characteristic of the English as a nation—a nation blessed with independence and cursed with a climate all its own. Goldsmith, speaking of Rabener, also emphasizes the nationalistic element in humor: "There is a cast of humour, as well as of manners, peculiar to each country. . . ."

But, as has been said, the two most interesting and most important of the pieces in the *Monthly Review* are the ones devoted to the new volume of Gray's verse—*Odes by Mr. Gray*—and to Burke's *Philosophical Enquiry into the Origin of Our Ideas of the Sublime and Beautiful.* Goldsmith's ideas on poetry are best taken up in connection with his own verse. Suffice it now to say that these ideas constituted a very definite poetic which, together with Samuel Johnson's, marked a mid-eighteenth-century reaffirmation of that classical line running from certain of the Elizabethan poets through Jonson to Dryden and beyond. It was not against this line but certainly in contrast with it that there had appeared, in the mid-decades of the eighteenth century, a poetic style distinguished by conscious aestheticism of intent and effect. Goldsmith and Johnson were at one in rejecting this style, which both found repellently arty; this was verse written in a forced language, addressed to an inner circle; it was not open, vigorous public speech. Goldsmith was fully aware that Gray was indeed an authentic poet, and he would never have taken exception to verse as traditional in character—traditional, i.e., in subject matter, imagery, diction, and general tone—as the *Elegy*. But he could not accept the new manner and style of Gray's recently published Pindaric odes. Here was artificiality of the most pronounced sort; here was an esoteric language calculated to exclude the ordinary reader. It was because of Gray's natural endowment that Goldsmith, as he said, beheld with some regret "those talents so capable of giving pleasure to all, exerted in efforts that, at best, can amuse only the few . . ."; Gray should heed the advice of Isocrates —the Greek writer and educationalist—and "Study the People."

The most illuminating of all the reviews insofar as Goldsmith's own thinking is concerned is that of Burke's *Philosophical Enquiry*. Burke's treatise was an important one, and is recognized today as occupying a central place among eighteenth-century works devoted to the analysis of aesthetic values and the nature of aesthetic experience. In the century and a half lying between Hobbes and Immanuel Kant aesthetics emerged as an independent field of investigation, with English writers taking the lead, followed by the French. Broadly speaking, the English line of development stemmed from English empiricism and was concerned chiefly to account in psychological terms for the individual's reactions to aesthetic objects in nature and to the representation of natural objects in art. The French writers—e.g., Montesquieu, Voltaire, d'Alembert—exhibited more of a sociological than a narrowly psychological interest and directed their inquiries first of all to the factors responsible for the rise and fall of the cultural level of European nations and for changes in taste. Hume, in essays such as "Of the Rise and Progress of the Arts and Sciences" (1742), "Of Refinement in the Arts" (1752), and "Of the Standard of Taste" (1757), showed keen awareness of both approaches. The importance of Goldsmith's rather lengthy commentary on Burke is at least twofold: it establishes beyond any doubt his genuine interest in contemporary aesthetic theorizing, and it furnishes convincing evidence of his competence in this field as he analyses and summarizes Burke and offers certain objections which arise, we feel, out of a set of aesthetic principles of his own. As an aesthetician Burke was, in the fashion of the English empirical school, a thoroughgoing sensationalist, assigning all our "passions" either to the pain we experience in moments of personal danger, or to the pleasures that are ours through the society of women and, in a broader sense, of our fellow men. The pain brought on by immediate danger is pain pure and simple, but when we have the idea of pain and danger without being actually in peril ourselves we feel a certain delight, which can be analyzed as an unnatural tension of the nerves. This delight is the sublime, and it is occasioned by objects in nature which cause astonishment because of their greatness or vagueness (they are objects possessed, we say, of sublimity). On the other hand, beauty is a sense of positive pleasure. Burke's "pleasure" is a different thing from the "delight" which he associated with the sublime; it acts through a relaxation of the nervous system, and is occasioned by the smallness, smoothness, variety, delicate frame, etc., of certain objects.

Goldsmith was to show in *An Enquiry into the Present State of Polite Learning in Europe* that his chief concern lay with the sociology rather than the psychology of taste, but in his comments on Burke he was perfectly willing to accept the latter's psychological approach. In doing so he makes more than Burke does of the factor of self-interest. Why, Goldsmith asks, may not self-interest be present not only in fear but also in those passions occasioned by certain kinds of beauty and described by Burke as being free from any "lust"? And he goes on to say that "a great part of our perceptions of beauty, arises . . . from a rational inference drawn with an eye to self-interest. . . ." This latter phrase should be noted carefully—"a rational inference drawn with an eye to self-interest." Goldsmith had nothing of the visionary about him. He was English—eighteenth-century English—through and through in his insistence that in all our speculation we start from experience and keep it in view at all times. He was likewise of his time in the way in which he thought instinctively in terms of antithesis and balance, placing softhearted benevolism against a selfishness so narrow that it lost sight of a great segment of human experience. The mean, the balance, lay in nature itself— the world of experience molded by rational inferences. It was not Plato's world, but it was a poet's world nevertheless—a place of light, direct and clear, of instinctual pleasures, a place where a healing power was constantly at work, seeking to rectify the immoderations of folly and evil.

It was a world, too, from which Burke's sublimity of the obscure and terrifying was absent. Is it true, as Burke would have it, that terror is the sole source of the sublime? Can we not have "the most sublime ideas of the Deity, without imagining him a God of terror"? And must poetry, in order to give us the sublime, create the impression of obscurity through indistinctness of imagery? On the contrary, asserts Goldsmith, "Distinctness of imagery has ever been held productive of the sublime"; nor is Burke correct in assuming that poetic images are of sight alone—"sounds, tastes, feeling, all conspire to complete a poetical picture." The natural world, in short, did not offer itself to us solely through the optic nerve.

4

An Enquiry into the Present State of Polite Learning in Europe was published early in April, 1759. Written for the well-known publishers the brothers Robert and James Dodsley, it had probably been begun at about the time Goldsmith left Griffiths in September, 1757. By August of the following year he was sending off letters to Ireland—to Hodson, his brother-in-law, and to several cousins—announcing the coming publication of what he was then calling his "Essay on the Present State of Taste and Literature in Europe," and asking the help of his friends at home in securing subscriptions to the book. (These relatives, alas, showed complete indifference to his request. Only his brother Henry, to whom he also seems to have written, appears to have been responsive.)

The *Enquiry* deserves to rank as Goldsmith's first major work. It is not difficult to understand, however, why its true importance has not always been recognized even by his better-informed critics, for it is a youthful performance exhibiting in several places an only too obtrusive immaturity of thought and presentation and occasionally of style. Furthermore, the eighteenth-century intellectual context in which it stands can easily be overlooked if one regards the work less as an enquiry than as a protest—Goldsmith's protest, voiced on the eve of his anticipated departure for India, against the prevailing conditions of authorship in London. The note of protest is clear enough, but it is by no means dominant. The *Enquiry* is a highly intellectual work which orders and gives emphatic meaning to a whole group of ideas—ideas then in the air, ideas encountered by Goldsmith during his student days in Ireland and later in Edinburgh and on the continent, and more recently brought directly to his attention by the books he had had access to as one of Griffiths's reviewers. By the 1750s a whole new area of investigation had defined itself in European thought and was attracting some of the best minds of the age. Here questions of aesthetics, as in Burke's *Enquiry,* converged with broader questions concerning the history and sociological implications of what was then termed "taste." Goldsmith, when he came to write his own *Enquiry,* was well up in his subject. He was conversant with other men's views, and he went on to fashion a surprisingly comprehensive statement—one might almost call it a system—of his own. His treatise is much more than a protest against the state of affairs then known as Grub Street. It is Goldsmith's manifesto in defense of what is known to us today as Western civilization. Johnson's repeated statements to the effect that Goldsmith knew nothing, that he had no settled notions upon any subject, are here effectively refuted. That he did not again engage in systematic philosophic discourse—though, as we shall see, *The Citizen of the World* contains a most subtle statement but a curiously masked one—can be attributed to some extent to his reluctance to bore his readers with what might have seemed tiresome speculations to them, but chiefly to his ultimate concern as a poet—he seems always to have thought of himself as a poet, even in his role of prose writer—with supervening aspects of human experience grasped at the imaginative and emotional levels.

The *Enquiry*, published without the author's name, may have brought Goldsmith to the attention of a few knowledgeable readers, but it created no great stir. Indeed, from the point of view of Goldsmith's later literary career, its chief effect was to antagonize the most powerful man in the London theatrical establishment. Following, perhaps, the line then just taken by a James Ralph in a book published in 1758 entitled *The Case of Authors by Profession,* Goldsmith proceeded to attack the English theater as then constituted and in particular the arrogance of actors and managers. The reference to David Garrick was unmistakable. The two men were to become friends of a sort in time, but there were always reservations on both sides.

The *Critical Review* for April, 1759, contained a notice of the *Enquiry* which mixed a certain amount of praise with an equal amount of adverse commentary: the author is ingenious; his essay is written in a genteel strain and shows a politeness far above most authors; but in speaking of British universities he has fallen into gross mistakes, and he could throughout have written with less elegance while thinking with more precision and energy. It was the *Monthly Review* that did the real mauling. The article in question, appearing in November, was the work of the infamous William Kenrick, a writer who specialized in abusing those who came within his journalistic line of fire, and who was to savage Goldsmith repeatedly. The author of the *Enquiry*, we are assured, is totally ignorant of the real state of learning, having relied entirely on books for his material; his work is little else "than the trite commonplace remarks and observations, that have been, for some years past, repeatedly echoed from Writer to Writer. . . ."

Goldsmith for his part, having as it were rid himself of the book when he turned it over to the public, evinced little further interest in it until shortly before his death, when he prepared a second edition, which appeared posthumously in 1774. His revisions were considerable, the most significant one being the rejection *in toto* of the original seventh chapter, containing the heart of his own theory of taste. His suppression of this entire section probably indicates merely his fear that it was all too fine-spun for the reading public he had acquired since the first publication of the *Enquiry* and who now looked to him for writing of a much less theoretical kind.

5

The *Enquiry* is not an easy book to summarize. It strikes out in many different directions, and the various lines along which it moves radiate not from one but several axial points. Yet, as is frequently the case with Goldsmith's important works, it leaves a central impression betokening the presence throughout of a subtle kind of organizing logic.

It leads off with the flat assertion that learning and letters are in a state of corruption and decline, and we are reminded that our interest in discovering the causes should be more than merely speculative curiosity, for true learning and true morality are closely connected. By the second chapter [2] the theme of cultural decline has become the focal point. This theme is first treated in a theoretical way: the causes are stated, the stages of declination are defined. In Chapters III through V the same theme is taken up historically, learning in the "obscure ages" being reviewed and the present-day cultural situation in the different European countries being examined. This idea of the decline of literary culture

[2] All my references are to the text of the first edition (that of 1759), as given by Friedman in the *Collected Works* (Vol. I).

was not new. It had been advanced time and again in the seventeenth century, and Hume had recently considered it in his influential essay "Of the Rise and Progress of the Arts and Sciences" (1742). Much had likewise been written about the distinguishable stages through which this decline could be plotted. According to Goldsmith there are three such periods: the age of poets, the age of philosophers, and finally the age of critics. He insists, however, that the steadily downward course apparent here, from poetic imagination, to philosophic inquiry, to the wholly unimaginative pedantry of critics and commentators, is not something in nature, is not inevitable. The fault lies in ourselves; it is corrigible.

What distinguishes Goldsmith's statement is the vehemence with which he attacks those he calls critics, whom he holds largely responsible for bringing in the final phase of degeneration. Here too he was following a tradition. Baiting the critics, the unimaginative ones, the dull scholars and commentators, had long been the fashion among witty men of letters. Renaissance satirists had engaged in the sport with gusto; the young Swift had had his fling at it in the *Battle of the Books;* Samuel Johnson in the third paper of his *Rambler* (March, 1750) had described "a certain race of men, that either imagine it their duty, or make it their amusement, to hinder the reception of every work of learning or genius, who stand as sentinels in the avenues of fame, and value themselves upon giving Ignorance and Envy the first notion of a prey." The critic, says Goldsmith, judges merely by rules—not, as we should always do, by feeling. Does such emphasis upon feeling indicate an abandonment on Goldsmith's part of the neoclassical point of view? Not really. The eighteenth century in England witnessed, it is true, a marked rise in emotional temper, but we tend to forget that a certain kind of emotionalism had been present all along in English literary art—especially the drama— and had been recognized in literary criticism. If not specifically Aristotelian it was nevertheless an outgrowth of peripatetic principles stressing the importance of the emotional impact of a work of literature, and in this regard associating the writer of plays and poems with the orator who knowingly plays upon the feelings of his auditors. Especially in Scotland, both at the University of Edinburgh and at Glasgow, this affective side of literature was brought into the foreground by a new generation of rhetoricians and aestheticians. Adam Smith, for instance, whose earlier interests were with letters rather than the wealth of nations, was delivering lectures on rhetoric and belles lettres at Edinburgh during the 1740s and at Glasgow beginning in 1752. These discourses were never published, but the notes taken down by one of his students in 1762 and 1763 have recently been published (1963). Smith took up the usual subjects covered in the standard treatises on rhetoric, but was at pains to point out that good writing does not after all demand strict observance of the rhetorical rules and principles: "When the sentiment of the speaker is expressed in a neat, clear, plain, and clever manner, and the passions or affections he is possessed of and intends, *by sympathy,* to communicate to his hearer, is plainly and cleverly hit off, then and then only the expression has all the force and beauty that language can give it. . . ." It seems entirely possible that while at Edinburgh Goldsmith acquired through the people he conversed with certain views similar to Smith's. If so this fact outweighs in importance all his medical studies. Smith's reference to sympathy, to communication by sympathy, does, to be sure, look forward toward a newer aesthetic psychology which, largely through the influence of Hume, was to center on sympathy explained by reference to an underlying association of ideas. Goldsmith was not averse to Hume,[3] but it would scarcely be accurate to say that he ever consciously enrolled himself in any of the newer schools. He merely accepted the principle, thoroughly established in eighteenth-century criti-

[3] He did, it is true, tell Boswell, not long after the two had first met, that "David Hume was one of those, who, seeing the first place occupied on the right side, rather than take a second, wants to have a first in what is wrong" (Boswell, *London Journal, 1762–1763,* under June 26, 1763). Goldsmith could not, under any circumstances, have condoned what was generally thought to be Hume's irreligious tendency, and very likely under Johnson's influence his disapproval of this side of Hume had recently been increased. But he knew and was undoubtedly influenced by many of Hume's essays devoted to general topics, and in his own writing as historian he was to rely heavily on Hume's *History of England.*

cism and stressed by no one more emphatically than Samuel Johnson, that certain kinds of literature—more especially dramatic literature—work upon us through the pathos aroused by the action being unfolded before us. And always, for Goldsmith, successful communication between writer and reader was best achieved by directness and simplicity of style. We should remind ourselves, however, that this kind of expression, defined as direct and simple, was nevertheless a highly contrived thing. The "natural" sentiment and the "natural" style were triumphs of conscious artistry.

By the fifth chapter a second theme, interwoven with the theme of cultural decay, comes into the foreground as the European nations are examined and compared in regard to prevailing cultural conditions. Goldsmith had a lively sense of national peculiarities, and he had undoubtedly exercised it to the full during his travels, in the course of which he must have been storing away and refining the materials which were to find their ultimate resting place in his poem *The Traveller,* where one nation after another is analyzed and its "character" portrayed in a formulary manner. But the sharp antitheses and their resolution in a balancing compromise—factors contributing vitally to the poem's imaginative triumph—are lacking from the *Enquiry.* In the fifth chapter he writes hurriedly and superficially about the state of learning in Italy, Germany, Holland, Spain, Sweden, and Denmark, making to be sure a clever show of scattered information but achieving very little. However, when he finally comes to France (Chapter VIII) and to England (Chapter IX and following) he writes out of a much fuller knowledge and to a definite and unmistakable purpose.

Chapter VII is a pivotal one. In the opening paragraphs our attention is directed to France and England, now preeminent among the nations in both power and learning but incapable of comparison in respect of culture because of their fundamental differences. Whereas the French exhibit a "universal sameness of character," particularly in their fools and coxcombs, the English produce natural characters exhibiting all the varied peculiarities of an insular country. By and large England has triumphed in philosophy, France in taste: "We [i.e., the English] are allowed the honour of striking out sentiments, they of dressing them in the most pleasing form." And truth is an absolute excellence, whereas taste is relative.

From this point on the chapter is given over to a disquisition on taste, and here is to be found the fullest statement Goldsmith ever gave of the aesthetic principles he had worked out for himself. His review of Burke's *Philosophical Enquiry* had demonstrated not only his very real interest in current aesthetics but his knowledgeability, and here in his *Enquiry* he had occasion to systematize his own views. These can be fully assessed only in the light of the numerous books and essays in which eighteenth-century writers, English and French chiefly, were exploring the whole area of what they referred to as Taste, but such an appraisal would require a treatise devoted wholly to this field. A careful reading of Goldsmith's seventh chapter will make sufficiently clear, however, the main lines along which his thought moved and the strategy behind his thinking.

The modern reader should bear this in mind: an immutable and universal standard of taste had often been asserted—a veritable Ark of the Covenant for traditionalist guardians of a closed universe. This universality of aesthetic qualities and aesthetic experiences was now coming under attack, chiefly from the sociological wing of the eighteenth-century students of aesthetics. The history of European taste and the comparative study of national cultures seemed to reveal mostly change and nonuniformity. Those who, like Burke, took the empirical and psychological approach could retain the principle of universality by insisting upon the uniformity of the human physiological responses. But there were those who asked whether such a uniformity of response was indicated when national characters revealed such wide disparities. We find Hume, for instance, in his essay "Of the Standard of Taste," moving in and out and around these problems with a facility that has behind it wonderful penetration and intellectual candor.

Goldsmith's chain of reasoning is as follows. National differences are readily apparent—differences in the way of habitual temperament, these differences being reflected in literary art. Thus, French comic characters have a sameness about them, whereas the comic characters in English letters are individualistic, eccentric humorists. (Such, at any rate, may be said to be the drift of the opening statements of the chapter.) And since every particular country has its own standard of taste, it follows that "the critics of one country, will not be proper guides to the writer of another. . . ." This conclusion, reinforced repeatedly in the passages that follow, carries the main thrust of his whole argument concerning the function of criticism. He is saying, explicitly, that literary criticism must cease passing judgment by means of rigid formulae. What he does not say openly, but what is implied, what comes through by indirection, is that literature is vital, that it grows organically out of a particular social culture, that it must by all means be encouraged to be indigenous. He goes on to defend himself against the charge that in "setting up a particular standard of taste in every country" he is removing that universal standard "which has hitherto united the armies and enforced the commands of criticism." Taste concerns such objects as affect us with pleasure, and aesthetic pleasure has two sources, "natural" and "artificial." "Natural" pleasure is caused by the immediate gratification of the senses and is uniform in human experience. "Artificial" pleasure is given by such things as we have learned through experience to be direct contributors to natural pleasure, and these things differ, according to use, from time to time and from place to place. Taste in writing combines the two sorts of pleasure: it is "the exhibition of the greatest quantity of beauty and of use, that may be admitted into any description without counteracting each other." Criticism, which professes to direct our taste, can in no way affect our instinctive sense of natural beauty; it can only improve our taste in the useful ("useful" in the context of Goldsmith's analysis comes to mean everything that excites our interest as a result of some original utilitarian significance) and to do so it must respect natural habitude. The *Enquiry* is usually noticed in the history of eighteenth-century writings on aesthetics because of this extreme emphasis on national character in literature and general culture.

Having thus set forth his theory of taste, Goldsmith proceeds in the remaining chapters to turn the discussion into somewhat different channels. Chapters IX and X are primarily sociological in direction; Chapters XI and XII are more nearly in the nature of literary criticism proper. Chapters IX and X contain what is Goldsmith's bitterest protest against the conditions of authorship in the England of that day. The writing here is not his best; it has an abrasive quality that reduces its effectiveness, and the headlong pace may seem to indicate the release of much personal rancor. Yet the protest was in fact a brave one, and Goldsmith's vision was never clearer or more impersonal. Civilization *is* literature; or, translated into our own present-day terms, we are to regard the arts—all the artifices of the imagination—as that which bestows meaning on human existence. A society in which letters are slightly regarded, in which genius is not properly encouraged, is in a state of decline. The man of letters—whether creative genius or scholar—experiences a double frustration. On the one hand he is oppressed by the weight of tradition, by the mass of cumulative learning and achievement; on the other he finds indifference on the part of those in a position to give moral encouragement and financial assistance. Goldsmith appeals to the Man of Taste, whom he defines as one standing between the writer and the world, to protect and aid the genius and the scholar, and to interpret their work to the larger public. In effect, Goldsmith has devised his own graduated system of society: he has assigned the highest level to the genius and the scholar, the next to the Man of Taste, the third to the informed public, and the fourth and lowest to the tribe of critics, living in outer darkness. Swift would surely have bestowed his blessing on such a scheme, for it merely puts in a different way what he had expressed in his own fashion in the *Battle of the Books*.

Chapters XI and XII are the most adept in the *Enquiry*. They are packed with critical observations on literature in general, on

poetry, and on the London theater and the dramatic offerings of
the time, and while they go no deeper than the two chapters
which precede them they are more sharply focused. Goldsmith is
not one of the notable English critics, and if he had ever set out
to do the sort of concentrated critical writing that Johnson ex-
celled in he would very likely have botched the job. His instinctive perceptions as an artist and his informed judgments were
subtle, but they did not lend themselves to effective translation
into the terms of critical discourse as it was currently practiced.
However, he entertained the most definite critical opinions, and
these rested on consistent principles.

Chapter XI, "Upon Criticism," opens with an admonition to
modern poets to disregard the critics and write what they think.
They will then avoid the errors so prominent in present-day compositions: odes marked by affected obscurity; blank verse, tuneless
by nature; pompous epithets, labored diction, and all the devia-
tions from common sense applauded by the connoisseurs of the
moment. Goldsmith is here amplifying what he had already expressed in his earlier review of Gray's *Odes*. The new aesthetic
style, prominent in the poetry of the middle decades, held as little
appeal for him as for Johnson. Nor did he respond favorably to
the kind of verse which too many people have since assumed was
the only kind that was ever written or could be written in the
eighteenth century—namely, the long blank-verse poem, moralizing its theme (characteristically quite unexciting) in exaggerated
poetic diction. Goldsmith refers contemptuously to "a disgusting
solemnity of manners" in both the poetry and prose then being
written, and with this solemnity as a point of departure he
launches into a discussion of comic humor.

The observations which he proceeds to make are central to an
understanding of his own comic art and the angle of perception
controlling it. Wit and humor, he writes, as they are employed in
the depiction of fictional characters, are different things. Wit is
clever, it is astonishing, it creates an unusual atmosphere, its
presentations are above the level of actual life. The critics favor
witty writing out of their contempt for the purely natural, which

they dismiss as being disgustingly vulgar or, as they say, "low." (Such is Goldsmith's general meaning, though his words and his ordering of them have, for conciseness, been treated freely.) Humor, on the other hand, directs our attention to the natural in human life, or rather to what, by virtue of the absurdities and idiosyncracies of real people, is below nature. The witty work of art excites our admiration for the author's cleverness; the humorous portrayal causes us to measure ourselves against absurdity and folly. "We triumph in our conscious superiority," says Goldsmith, referring to the effect on us of humor. It would be interesting to analyze all the perceptions and concepts which have been telescoped in this portion of Chapter XI. One of them is the principle laid down by Fielding—and by Aristotle—that true humor does not depict those who, like cripples, are abnormal through no fault of their own. Another, however, is the insistence that the comic *is* satiric representation; it is not compassionate but corrective; it does not invite identification with the characters who are being represented but rather causes us to hold them at a distance for critical inspection. "Triumphing in our conscious superiority" has, nevertheless, a too harsh sound so far as Goldsmith's own position is concerned, for he stood far removed from any purely selfish, egocentric theory of the comic (according to Hobbes, the passion which maketh those *grimaces* called LAUGHTER" springs from our sense of "sudden glory"). Comedy, for Goldsmith, was not cruel. However, it remained the satiric discernment of the faults and shortcomings of man in general. As he matured, it also came to include the discovery on our part, after many errors, of our own true, "natural" selves; but from first to last he made war against the sentimentalization of comedy taking place in the eighteenth century. The function of comedy was, he insisted, to excite laughter, not to awaken sympathy and draw tears for erring fellow creatures. "On my conscience, I believe we have all forgot to laugh in these days." Goldsmith's motto, appropriate to all the seasons of his genius, might well have been this: Let us have comedy—true comedy!

Chapter XII, "Of the Stage," is in substance a further development of his discussion of wit and humor. It was not until he had established himself as an essayist, poet, and novelist that Goldsmith finally turned to playwriting, yet from the start he had had the liveliest interest in the theater, and the truth is that he was a born dramatist, the pity being that he did not discover the fact or that circumstances did not allow him to demonstrate it until so late in his career. His interest in the English stage was again, like his interest in nondramatic literature, a double one, aesthetic—what is good drama?—and social—what are the conditions favorable to a healthy theater? Chapter XII takes up the social aspects. The English stage is "more magnificent than any other in Europe, and the people in general fonder of theatrical entertainment." But alas, what with the managers to please and the critics to overcome, the poor playwright finds himself in a sorry plight:

> Our poet's performance must undergo a process truly chymical before it is presented to the public. It must be tried in the manager's fire, strained through a licenser, and purified in the Review, or the news-paper of the day. At this rate, before it can come to a private table, it may be a mere caput mortuum. . . .

We need new plays to combat new follies and vices. Instead, we get revivals of old plays, for the reason that these give the favorite actors of the day, those idols worshipped by a public uninformed in taste, a chance to shine; hence the popularity of those scenes, "which have been ascribed to Shakespeare," full of "forced humour, far-fetch'd conceit, and unnatural hyperbole. . . ." It is not the play that matters now but the actors, who have risen so high in the public esteem that they can assume "all that state off the stage which they do on it. . . ." Garrick, then the supreme actor-manager, is the unmistakable target of such remarks, and is thus cast in the role, previously reserved by Goldsmith for the critics, of despoiler of taste. It is doubtful whether Goldsmith ever came to think differently of Garrick, though in the revised edition he did tone these passages down. And who knows that he may not have been partly right in his judgment? Here at least it can scarcely be said that Goldsmith was motivated by envy!

The concluding chapter (XIV) is a brief restatement of the central sociological theme, placing it now in the widest possible frame of reference. Our minds are subject by turns to reason and to our appetites: we look toward higher forms of consciousness, or we are content to live like the brutes. In a sense it is pleasure either way, but "in the pursuit of intellectual pleasures, lies every virtue; of sensual, every vice." Therefore our chiefest luxury should be the refinement of reason, reason guided by Taste, Taste being the link between science and common sense, "the medium through which learning should ever be seen by society."

Goldsmith saw—or better, perhaps, felt—so clearly the organic connection between art and society. In his *Enquiry* he was writing in terms proper to logical discourse. Elsewhere he was to make his affirmation in the manner of imaginative statement, drawing directly on man's vital experiences.

III

The Laborer's Hire:
Exploiting the Essay

1

THE *Enquiry* appeared, as we have seen, on April 2, 1759. Some two weeks previously England had learned at last, via Paris, of the French operations in India against the English along the coast of Coromandel, and any expectations which Goldsmith might still have been cherishing of going out to India had been quite dissipated. By this time, however, he was ready to accept what circumstances had combined to thrust upon him. He was now a professional writer without appeal or escape; his future depended on his ability to win the favor of the middle-class reading public. His first step, apparently, was to establish himself as a regular contributor to Smollett's *Critical Review,* in the January number of which two of his book reviews had already appeared. His new contributions—all book reviews—ran from the March issue through that for September, and there were a few more in the early numbers for 1760.[1]

For the most part his critiques in the *Critical Review* are of a piece with those done for Griffiths in 1757. They touch upon a variety of matters, chiefly literary—poetry, fiction, the prose *char-*

[1] Two reviews appeared still later: in August and October, 1763.

acters and observations of Samuel Butler, rhetoric, and the drama.
One article—for January, 1759, concerning a new English translation of Ovid's *Epistles*—is the occasion for observations on taste
and criticism which parallel the comments in the *Enquiry*. And
if the article apropos of *A Review of the Works of the Rev. Mr.
W. Hawkins,* appearing in March, 1760, is Goldsmith's—the attribution is not certain—it gives us one of his few direct statements
having to do with religion: the immortality of the soul, the reviewer writes, cannot be proved by reason; "we are obliged to
revelation alone for any evidence. . . ." Everything we know about
Goldsmith shows him to have been one for whom the reason-
versus-faith debate held little interest. He had been brought up
in the Anglican Church, his religious convictions were of the
simplest but deeply rooted, and like many eighteenth-century men
of intelligence he was content to believe that Anglican reasonableness had long since defined the cooperative claims of reason
and faith. Goldsmith's religion, unlike Johnson's, for instance,
had none of the elements of tense, often tragic drama. Rather, it
afforded him a willing, a graceful, albeit an ironic, acceptance of
life.

There is one further point concerning these items in the *Critical Review* which ought not to be passed over. This has to do with
Goldsmith's practice here and frequently in his subsequent work
of drawing extensively upon other writers, often without acknowledgment. During the period of his association with the *Critical
Review* he is known to have had Diderot's *Encyclopédie* at hand
and to have borrowed from it freely and sometimes at length,
particularly from the fifth volume. At least two different questions
arise. The first and more important is this: How are we to take
substantively those passages which turn out to be largely derivative? To what degree do they speak for Goldsmith himself? Consider his review of Ward's *A System of Oratory* (April, 1759).
Much of this has been shown to come directly from articles in the
fifth volume of the *Encyclopédie*. Oratory, we are told, "is nothing
more, than the being able to imprint on others, with rapidity and
force, the sentiments of which we are possessed ourselves. . . ."

This is entirely consistent with that principle of simple and direct and hence effective literary communication which Goldsmith stressed consistently. Here, clearly enough, his quotation is a reinforcement of his own views. He had, in short, the capacity to make his own anything which he himself might have written, and he was never at a loss where to find in other men's work congenial ideas and sentiments.

The question of ethics involves several factors—the practices of the times among professional writers, Goldsmith's various indirect but nonetheless frank acknowledgments of extensive indebtedness, and the extraordinary ease with which he assimilated source material and in doing so accorded it a felicity of setting and presentation all his own.

2

From book reviewing, it was a short step to essay writing, and before the close of 1759 Goldsmith had become a recognized essayist, not indeed in the public mind, since as yet his name was unattached to any of his compositions, but among the publishers of the current periodicals. By September, 1759, he had been entrusted by the bookseller John Wilkie with the editorship of the *Bee,* a weekly periodical which ran for eight numbers until expiring at the end of November. Goldsmith bore sole responsibility for this publication, either writing or selecting from sources sometimes indicated and sometimes not, all the forty-odd items which made up the eight issues.

From this time on, for more than two years, his chief occupation was essay writing, and during this period he is known to have contributed to at least seven periodicals in addition to the *Bee.* With that adroitness which was to characterize his entire career in letters he had caught perfectly the temper and the pace of the English essay as the eighteenth century knew it. He was frankly exploiting this established form and in doing so he cut a good many corners since some of what he allowed to be published was not strictly his own writing. Yet in the end, as his lasting distinction among essay writers testifies, he gave more than full measure.

In any event his laborer's hire enabled him to live, and to live better than at any time since the beginning of his London adventures. Thus he was able to move from his miserable quarters in Green Arbour Court, sometime near the middle of 1760, to two rooms in 6 Wine Office Court, just off Fleet Street and only a short distance from the house in Gough Square where Johnson had formerly lived and where the *Dictionary* had taken shape. The fact that his new landlady was a Mrs. Carnan, related to Mrs. Newbery, the publisher's wife, by the latter's first marriage, suggests that Newbery, to whose *Public Ledger* Goldsmith was then contributing his "Chinese Letters," had begun to take a hand in the personal affairs of his valuable writer. It would seem that Goldsmith had already come to be accepted by his friends as an original, a character of humor of the right line, generous to a degree and hopelessly irresponsible in all worldly affairs. And the larger world—London, that is—was beginning to hear amusing stories about the odd Dr. Goldsmith, one of the coming writers.

His circle of acquaintances was widening markedly. In May, 1761, Thomas Percy introduced him to Johnson. Not long afterward he met Joshua Reynolds, already the most fashionable of the portrait painters, and the two were soon warm friends. In December, Goldsmith was mentioned in the *Court Magazine* as one of the distinguished authors of the time—a writer of "taste and understanding," and in the following year a brief but flattering notice concerning his work was included by William Rider in his *Historical and Critical Account of . . . the Living Authors of Great-Britain.*

Goldsmith's most successful single effort proved to be his long series of "Chinese Letters"—one hundred and nineteen of them, appearing in Newbery's paper, the *Public Ledger,* from January, 1760, into August, 1761. By 1762, when these appeared in collected form as *The Citizen of the World,* his concentrated work as an essayist was coming to an end. He had achieved an identity despite the anonymity of all his publications.

3

What has been written in the past about Goldsmith's achievement as an essayist has for the most part been based, understand-
ably enough, upon the items found in the *Bee, The Citizen of
the World,* and the *Essays by Oliver Goldsmith,*[2] this latter the
collection of twenty-seven prose pieces and two poems which
Goldsmith himself selected from his previously published material. These three groups of essays, by virtue of the kind of con-
centration each possesses, stand out from the mass of work which
he did for the periodicals during these years. We may peruse them
as we please without being disturbed by too many bibliographical
questions, feeling as we read that Goldsmith is probably the easi-
est of all the eighteenth-century essayists to live with. He is
warmer than Addison, not so warm as Steele, and he has none of
Johnson's austerity and massive weight. We may well go on to say
that if his essays are not much read today, this, if not as it should
be, is understandable in view of his journalistic skill in reporting
the passing London scene and in touching on topics of ephemeral
interest just long enough to be agreeably provocative to his contemporaries. His manner and voice are wonderfully easy and informal, his prose is always unexceptionable, flowing—to use the
florid language of no less an authority than William Godwin—
"with such ease, copiousness, and grace that it resembles the Song
of the Siren." The variety of his material is pleasing—the story;
the serious drama; the vision; sketches of daily life in London;
showpieces like the well-known "Reverie at the Boar's-Head-Tavern in Eastcheap" and "A City Night-Piece." There are characters
touched with different humors and exhibited with a restrained
irony. The tonal shadings and variations, permitting an occasional personal note or an expression of personal nostalgia, seem
always right. Goldsmith pleases and entertains, and not least for

---

[2] *Essays by Mr. Goldsmith* (1765) contained twenty-five essays and two
poems. This was reprinted, with revisions and the addition of two essays, as
Essays by Oliver Goldsmith (1766).

the reason that his wit is never pointed, never epigrammatic, but instead a kind of comic anti-wit, as in some of his flat endings which are masterpieces of effective timing. Among more recent commentators Virginia Woolf is notable for having laid stress on Goldsmith's impersonal air—something which others have often failed to observe in their preoccupation with what they take to be the strain of self-revelation. There is a detached attitude here, she pointed out; other writers bring us closer to themselves, whereas Goldsmith is standing somewhat apart from the humorous people and events he is describing.

Another approach is possible, however, as we realize when we are confronted with Goldsmith's entire work as an essayist as it is now set forth in Professor Friedman's edition of the *Collected Works*. If the *Bee, The Citizen of the World,* and *Essays by Oliver Goldsmith* tell what is perhaps the important part of the story, it is only a part. From the time of his first essays in the *Bee* in September, 1759, down through the one which appeared in June, 1762, in *Lloyd's Evening Post,* over two hundred separate items of his found their way into print.[3] It is obvious that the full record has to be kept in mind if we are to understand something of the factors which governed Goldsmith's work as a journalist-essayist and compelled him to trim to the public taste. A compre-

[3] It is difficult to arrive at a fixed figure, since there are different ways of counting these items. To the *Bee* I assign 33 essays, which figure excludes 4 articles stated to be from Voltaire and 5 poems; to *The Citizen of the World,* 122 (i.e., the original 119 "Chinese Letters" plus CXXI and CXXII, written expressly for *The Citizen,* and CXIX, "The Distresses of a Common Soldier," which had originally appeared in the *British Magazine* in June, 1760, but which, in accordance with Friedman's arrangement in the *Collected Works,* is assigned to *The Citizen* rather than to the *British Magazine.* A fourth essay added in *The Citizen* to the 119 "Chinese Letters" is CXVII, "A City Night-Piece," revised from the *Bee,* No. IV, to which in my present reckoning it is assigned); I count the "Memoirs of M. de Voltaire," given serially in the *Lady's Magazine,* as 10; and there were 41 in the following 7 periodicals: 2 in the *Busy-Body* (in 1759), 8 in the *Weekly Magazine* (in 1759–60), 5 in the *Royal Magazine* (in 1759–60), 10 in the *British Magazine* (in 1760), 3 in the *Lady's Magazine* (in 1760; these being in addition to the "Memoirs of Voltaire," appearing here in 1761), 8 in the *Public Ledger* (in 1761; these being in addition to the "Chinese Letters," appearing here in 1760–61), and 5 in *Lloyd's Evening Post* (in 1762). This would make a total of 206.

hensive examination of all the essays is here out of the question. In lieu of such a study it is proposed that we first page through the *Bee,* which really sets the tone for much of the ensuing work, then through the essays not included in any of the three well-known gatherings, glancing lastly at what was probably most familiar to Goldsmith's contemporaries, the *Essays by Oliver Goldsmith. The Citizen of the World,* which really constitutes Goldsmith's second major book, the *Enquiry* being his first, deserves separate treatment and will be taken up in the chapter that follows.

4

Goldsmith's earliest venture as independent essayist shows a marked advance in literary maturity over the earlier *Enquiry.* In the *Bee* he has acquired adaptability. He has not given over any of his previous concern with problems of taste and civilization—indeed, he has widened his field to include the much-debated question of luxury. But his touch is lighter, his style surer, and he moves quickly over a great variety of topics, serious and otherwise. And there is a difference in tone. The note of pessimism audible throughout the *Enquiry* has not entirely disappeared, but it is no longer dominant; all is not right with the world, but there is less that is flagitious and more that is humorous. Goldsmith has decided, as it were, to take up residence in this England, this London, and he has caught something of the good spirits characteristic of the golden era now beginning—the era lying between the Seven Years War and the disruptions brought on by the Revolution in France.

His approach to the reader in the opening "Introduction" of his first number is artful in its manner of address. A persona is established—the "I" who purports to be writing. He is at your service, and he hopes you will enjoy what he has to offer. If, however, you don't care for his first paper try a second, or a third, or even a fourth in case of extremity. This informality of tone is heightened by such phrasing as "a dab at an index" and a "promising plan to smooth up our readers a little," by a reference like the one to the Cat and Bagpipes in St. Giles's, and to the possibility of the author's being censured as "vastly low." Yet all the time the larger units of the prose, the paragraphs, are being molded in accordance with highly formal structural principles, often pivoting, for instance, about a middle sentence. The following is Goldsmith's first paragraph (in, that is, its revised form):

> There is not, perhaps, a more whimsical figure in nature, than a man of real modesty who assumes an air of imprudence; who, while his heart beats with anxiety, studies ease, and affects good humour. In this situation, however, every unexperienced writer, as I am, finds himself. Impressed with the terrors of the tribunal before which he is going to appear, his natural humour turns to pertness, and for real wit he is obliged to substitute vivacity.

"Like the BEE . . . I would rove from flower to flower. . . ." Such is the statement in the original version of the "Introduction," and Goldsmith's borrowings in the course of the eight numbers of his periodical are indeed many: his verse pieces are all translations or adaptations, three and probably all four of his short narratives have been taken over wholly or in part from other writers, four articles are marked as by Voltaire, twice as many as that are presented as coming from other, definite sources, and even more have been lifted without acknowledgment. But after all the *Bee* is in part and frankly a florilegium, and it is not necessary to tax Goldsmith too severely. Besides, he manages so frequently to confer his own quality on what he borrows—a fact well illustrated by the verses entitled "The Gift," in which the rather neutral language of the French original is transformed into a high negligence worthy of Matthew Prior.

But the best of the *Bee* is genuine Goldsmith, as in the case of the three essays which stand out from the others. "A City Night-Piece"—in No. IV, and later included in *The Citizen of the World*—is a genre piece, a frankly pathetic description. "A Resverie"—in No. V—is literary commentary amusingly turned out as a kind of dream allegory. But even better than these is "On Dress" —in No. II—in which Goldsmith provides us for the first time with the kind of comedy he is shortly, in *The Citizen of the World*, to make his own. The scene is the Mall and the Park, the protagonists the writer himself and his cousin Hannah, he sixty-two and she four years older, he in his best wig, no longer fashionable, she in clothes only too much so. The laughter which they excite each blames on the other, and "like two mice on a string" they endeavor "to revenge the impertinence of the spectators upon each other." There are four simultaneous points of view: that of the passers-by, of cousin Hannah, of the writer as a participant, and of the writer as he describes the episode after the fact. The comic distance upon which the entire effect depends is deftly concealed.

As things turned out, the *Bee* did not prove to be a successful venture. Why it failed to achieve popularity is difficult to say. Could it have been that Goldsmith was too various in his subjects and in his manner of treating them? As a periodical essayist he might, perhaps, have gained a greater number of regular readers if he had chosen to stay within a narrow and clearly defined range—when he shifted, in the "Chinese Letters," to a scheme which called for the introduction of certain unifying and repetitious elements, he drew an immediate and enthusiastic response from the public. But apparently it had been his hope that the variety of the *Bee* would be its chief attraction. Various, in any case, it certainly is. There are the three essays already mentioned —the showpieces of the entire series—there is verse, there are pieces on the theater, short narratives, letters and articles from Voltaire and others, and discussions of such general topics as happiness, the use of language, justice, genius, frugality, and luxury. It is all interesting enough in one way or another, but there are a few matters that are especially noteworthy.

Thus, the four narratives which are introduced call attention to themselves because all of them are stories in which the protagonists are plunged from prosperity into misery but—save in the grim "History of Hypasia"—live to experience deliverance from their

misfortunes. The ballads he had known in boyhood he had somehow come to associate with the kind of story which, following the
pattern of the popular romance, leads up to some extraordinary
reversal of fortunes. In "A Flemish Tradition" we are told that
every country has its popular traditions, and as the English have
their adventures "of Robin Hood, the hunting of Chevy-chace,
and the bravery of Johnny Armstrong," so the Flemish have the
vengeance of one Bidderman. Then follows a story which turns
upon a complete reversal of circumstances. For Goldsmith such
irony—the irony implicit in such time-honored devices as the discovery scene, wherein some all-important revelation occurs, and
the peripeteia or reversal—held a fascination which was in itself
ironic. The fortunate ending is a game we play at, reminding ourselves of the world we believed in when we were children. Can
we ever recover such a world? Though we cannot go back to it,
we are never able wholly to forget it so long as we retain the
courage to live. Goldsmith ends his "Story of Alcander and Septimius" with a moral: "No circumstances are so desperate, which
providence may not relieve." As we read this we think of the
preposterous ending of *The Vicar of Wakefield*—preposterous
but also subtly ambiguous.

The prospectus of the *Bee* had promised, among other things,
"Remarks on Theatrical Exhibitions," but only four of the essays are given over to dramatic criticism. One can only wish that
Goldsmith had fulfilled this part of his agreement somewhat more
generously, for his comments on the theater are always interesting
both in themselves and by reason of his own eventual achievement as a dramatist. On many other matters Goldsmith may well
strike the casual reader as annoyingly inconsistent but surely not
in the things he has to say about the English theater of his time
and the drama generally. And sooner or later he has a good deal
to say—in his early reviews, in the *Enquiry*, in various essays, in
The Citizen of the World, and in the episode of the traveling
players in *The Vicar of Wakefield*. It is apparent that the theater
always fascinated him. He knew something about the continental
theater, or at least the French theater, and he kept up with cur-

rent events at the London playhouses. His standards, as to the plays themselves as well as the acting and production, were high, and he found much that drew his fire. The managers were too willing to make do with inferior plays, the audience was too ready to be hoodwinked by mere elaborateness of production, the actors were often less concerned about interpreting the play intelligently than in getting applause. But it was chiefly comedy that he was interested in, and the best of the four theatrical pieces in the *Bee* is the one occasioned by the opening, in October, 1759, of James Townley's farce, *High Life Below Stairs*, which was quickly to take its place in the Georgian theatrical repertoire. The play concerns the goings-on among the servants in a certain well-to-do household, and it attempts to reproduce the actual speech of such people. It is this naturalness of speech that Goldsmith takes exception to. The playwright, he comments, "has sacrificed all the vivacity of the dialogue to nature"; his characters talk like servants, but they "are seldom absurd enough, or lively enough, to make us merry"; the author is always natural but "happens seldom to be humorous." Goldsmith is content to make his point rapidly, but he might easily have expanded what was in his mind into a much fuller discussion of the natural, the humorous, and the difference between the two in terms of comic writing. Implicit here is a theory of comic art: it must always be "natural" in the sense that it must always be a representation—of people, of events, of the world—that accords with our actual experience; but it should never sink to the dead level of uneventful commonplaceness, for it deals with the ridiculous, which is always off center and for that reason surprising.

We note, finally, the appearance in the *Bee* of a theme which is henceforth to appear repeatedly in his writing. It is a theme which lends itself to many modulations. Pity, benevolence, frugality, luxury—these are the basic terms, the various arrangements of which give rise to statements by Goldsmith which perhaps seem to indicate irreconcilable views on his part. But before pronouncing him confused, we ought to take into account some of the things which must have entered into his thinking on these matters and helped in a measure to shape it. Contrast, antithesis are implicit in the kind of language and discursive speculation present in much of the English verse throughout what we call not too accurately the neoclassical age. One idea, one principle suggests some other, and the two are placed alongside one another through a figure of parallelism, or they are set against each other antithetically. Frequently when contrariety occurs, a resolution is at hand in the form of a mediating principle affording a balance between two opposites. A logic of sorts, a conventionalized idiom, and the established pattern of the couplet all work together. Here is a manner of every-day speaking—every-day on the part of the poets, that is. But it is also a way of thinking which conditioned to a surprising degree the speculation of the age in areas other than literary—in political theory, in morals, and especially in the sort of theorizing which resulted when sociological, economic, and behavioral factors were brought together. What was sound economic policy? Should it be based on frugality, or should it encourage "luxury"? What was best for a nation, simplicity and meagerness in private and public life or "opulence"? What was the nature of pity and benevolence as experienced by individual man, and what were the social effects of acts prompted by compassion? The answers differed widely, but more frequently than not they were formulated in terms of antithesis and often through antithesis arriving at mediating, balancing principles.

Goldsmith's preoccupation with such questions begins to be apparent in the *Bee*, and although many of the essays in which these matters turn up consist largely or wholly of borrowings they are evidence nonetheless of a genuine involvement on his part. Pity, we are told, is a short-lived passion, which "seldom affords distress more than transitory assistance...." ("On the Use of Language," No. III). True generosity is a duty imposed on us by reason, but it "does not consist in obeying every impulse of humanity, in following blind passion for our guide, and impairing our circumstances by present benefactions, so as to render us incapable of future ones" ("On Justice and Generosity," No. III). A man "who has taken his ideas of mankind from study alone, generally comes into the world with an heart melting at every fictitious distress" (*Ibid.*). True economy, unknown alike to the prodigal and the avaricious, "seems to be a just mean between both extremes; and to a transgression of this . . . it is to that we attribute a great part of the evils which infest society" ("Upon Political Frugality," No. V).

What lies in sight here is the war which Goldsmith was to wage against the sentimentalism of his age. He would not accept the moral theory lying behind sentimentalism—the theory that exalted the compassionate emotions, which it was insisted were innate in man; that dwelt upon the exquisite pleasure to be found in every benevolent act; that held that in the presence of noble emotions evil and selfishness cured themselves. And he was revolted by sentimentalism in its literary form, particularly by the sentimental drama, where moral emotionalism at the lowest level of popular apprehension was given expression in an insufferable idiom. He saw a basic antithesis between the selfish theory of behavior and the theory that found man a veritable machine of benevolent, altruistic instincts and emotions. He saw an antithesis between, on the one hand, literary art that was all soft emotion and, at the opposite extreme, art that had, through a false sophistication or a too-contrived aestheticism, forsaken emotion altogether. These extremes were to be balanced against one another. There was a mean in both morals and art: common-sense behavior; emotion reasonably grounded and controlled; comedy that emphasized the ridiculous and at the same time the corrective healing power of Nature.

5

The *Bee*, considered in its entirety, is the best introduction there is to Goldsmith's methods as an essayist. *The Citizen of the World* shows him at the top of his form, raising the traditional medium of the essay serial to a comic level attained by no other eighteenth-century essay writer. As for his other essays (forty-one, contributed to seven different publications),[4] which appeared between October, 1759, and June, 1762—these have their own im-

4 See footnote 3.

portance. They include some of his finest pieces, as well as several that are of unusual interest because of what they anticipate in his later work. Taken all together, they bear witness to the remarkable resourcefulness which he displayed throughout the more than two and a half years he devoted largely to essay writing. They should rightly be considered as a body, for otherwise something of his professional strategy as he sought to sustain the public's interest is lost sight of. Ten of these pieces, however, were republished in *Essays by Oliver Goldsmith,* and these have always been associated with that collection. Here they will accordingly be regarded as component parts of that later grouping to be treated in the section that follows. So for the moment let us confine our attention to some of those thirty-one essays that did not receive the kind of second life conferred on the ten others. In these thirty-one we find Goldsmith, as in the *Bee,* constantly seeking variety in the way of theme and treatment. There are essays on literature and the theater, sketches—what we are now calling profiles—of well-known men, studies of the Irish and the Anglo-Irish, and observations on matters of national policy.

The liveliest items are the four or five in which the comic tone prevails, as it does whenever the London scene is being described. At the time of Goldsmith's arrival in England in 1756 the Seven Years War was just getting under way. It began badly enough for the English—for a time there was fear of a French invasion—and to protect the native soil hired troops were brought in from Hesse and Hanover. But gradually events took on an entirely different turn, and in consequence of the great victories of 1759 England was emerging from the war with an empire, with new wealth, and with a sudden rush of national pride and self-confidence. Modern Britain lay directly ahead. On October 17, 1759, the capture of Quebec and other recent victories were celebrated in high style throughout London. Three days later Goldsmith's account "On Public Rejoicings for Victory" appeared in the *Busy Body.* It is comic reporting of the first order on the part of our observer as he tells how he proceeded from Ludgate to Charing Cross, taking note of the illuminations, the noisy, good-natured mob, flying rockets, and the more earnest celebrations at places like Ashley's Punch-house and Slaughter's Coffee-house in St. Martin's Lane. Outwardly our friend kept his distance; inwardly he was feeling a new pride and dignity in being part of this "glorious political society"—until his elevating meditations were interrupted when a squib, placed in one of the tails of his wig by some freedom-loving Englishman, began to shoot fire. The essay ends, though, on a serious note, and it is Goldsmith himself rather than the reporter with fire dashing from his right ear who is now speaking. Let us use our victory to establish peace. Let us not prescribe too harsh terms of settlement. Let us remember that it is very possible "for a country to be very victorious and very wretched." Instinctively Goldsmith distrusted those who had clamored for war, had backed Pitt, the architect of England's triumph, and were now demanding material gains from the victory of arms. Every man, he wrote, "who is enriched by the trade of war, is only rewarded from the spoils of some unhappy member of society. . . ." These observations he followed up in an essay which appeared at the close of the year in the *Weekly Magazine*, entitled "Some Thoughts Preliminary to a General Peace."

Looking through this group of essays, we find three short series: one of four items, "A Comparative View of Races and Nations" (*Royal Magazine*, 1760); one of eight numbers, "A Series of Literary Essays" (*The Public Ledger*,1761); and again one of four numbers, "The Indigent Philosopher" (*Lloyd's Evening Post*, 1762). If Goldsmith began these series in the hope that they would prove as popular as his "Chinese Letters" he must surely have been deeply disappointed, for all three were short-lived. However, he might never have intended them to be anything more than what they turned out to be—three briefly sustained essay serials. As to content, at least the two earlier series are of decidedly limited interest today; for us they are significant chiefly in showing Goldsmith in the role of a popularizer of scientific theories and technical accomplishments. The four numbers of his "Comparative View of Races and Nations" have something in common with the earlier *Enquiry*. Goldsmith is again engaged in analyzing the cultural aspects of human society. Different climates, we see, have different effects on the human race, and we are asked to consider the people bordering on the arctic circle, those inhabiting the southern regions, then the Russians, and finally the "polite inhabitants of the temperate zone." In the last essay of this series the Irish, the Scots, and the English are characterized in turn, and in the description of the English we recognize an early prose version of the great *character* of England given in *The Traveller*. But it is Goldsmith's natural history that obtrudes, for here as he was later to do in his *History of the Earth, and Animated Nature* he has borrowed freely and uncritically from various sources, notably Buffon, and the result is scarcely impressive. In the second of these short serials, "A Series of Literary Essays," he is again the popularizer of science. Having in his opening paper—"A Preface to a Series of Literary Essays"—frankly assured his readers that it is his intention to be superficial, he goes on in the next essay—"New Fashions in Learning"—to justify the popularization of science. "The connexion between the polite arts and the sciences, is at present closer than formerly. . . ." and the present age exceeds the former in respect of the kind of writing which brings science down to the capacities of the multitude. Though Goldsmith was himself turning to such writing for personal reasons, he undoubtedly believed quite sincerely that one of the important functions of the man of letters in modern society was to interpret the results of scientific inquiry with accuracy and grace. The eighteenth-century public, buying in quantities the various digests of history and natural science which in the years that lay ahead he was to compile so dexterously, were surely no worse off if not much better. One feels that Goldsmith might perfectly well have proceeded from the *Enquiry* to further and possibly still more original work of a predominantly intellectual kind. He was, however, forced to turn to essay writing for a living. In doing so he discovered for one thing his comic powers, and for another his facility in the way of the popular digest. His deepest convictions and his theories and ideas continued to reverberate in those of his writings where his serious imagination had play. In the rest of his work, the work done solely for hire, he aimed chiefly at readability.

There is a further matter too important to be passed over. Two of these thirty-one essays tell us that Goldsmith's imagination was already at work on themes which were to find lodgment, one in *The Vicar of Wakefield*, one in *The Deserted Village*. "The History of Miss Staunton" (*The British Magazine*, July, 1760) is another story with a far-fetched peripeteia at the close. The father, a clergyman, fights a duel with the plausible scoundrel who has debauched his daughter. At the discharge of the pistols the father falls to the ground. The villainous Mr. Dawson breaks down under emotion, offers marriage to the ruined girl, and "the old man, who had only pretended to be dead, now rising up, claimed the performance of his promise. . . ." Something resembling an episode in *The Vicar of Wakefield* is discernible here, as are the lineaments of Parson Primrose, Olivia, and Squire Thornhill. "The Revolution in Low Life" (*Lloyd's Evening Post*, June 14–16, 1762) has, with reason, been called "*The Deserted Village* in prose." The scene is a village some fifty miles from town, but this peaceful, pastoral community has now been doomed to be wiped out of existence, the estate of which it is a part having been purchased by a wealthy London merchant who intends to level the cottages in order to create a great pleasure park. The essayist's comments on this situation are far-reaching: our foreign conquests and the resulting increase in foreign commerce have introduced new wealth, and new wealth accumulating in the hands of a few is not calculated "to make the aggregate happy" but swallows up the liberties of all. The essay, with its moving description of the villagers as they await displacement, its echoes of Virgilian pastoralism, its socio-economic analysis, and the clear implication it carries that the right balance between too little and too great luxury is being upset, allows us to observe the way in which Goldsmith's poetic mind was already shaping the materials of his great poem concerned, like this earlier essay, with the social injustice attendant on enclosure.

6

How free a hand Goldsmith had in the choice of materials for the collection put out in 1765 and republished the following year

under the title of *Essays by Oliver Goldsmith* we do not know.
If artistic considerations were foremost, there might also have
been the practical one of the availability of various pieces. Certainly it is not an unrepresentative selection. Whether it is the
best possible one is perhaps questionable. The two poems which
are positioned at the end (XXVIII and XXIX), suggestive of some
of Swift's less rigorous verses, serve to point up the comic vein
that runs through the whole collection. And the best comedy, as
is so frequently true of the run of his essays, is the London comedy. Thus item IV, from the *Busy Body*, is the amusing "Description of Various Clubs." Number XV, "On Dress," is that little
masterpiece discussed above in connection with the *Bee*, where
it first appeared. Selections XXVI and XXVII, from the *Public
Ledger*, are quite as good as the essay in the *Busy Body* describing the celebration after the fall of Quebec, the chief difference
being that the date has been advanced from 1759 to 1761 and the
occasion shifted to the coronation of George III and Queen
Charlotte. A common-council-man has happily taken it into his
head to communicate to readers of the *Public Ledger* his thoughts
about the ceremonies under way. There are, he feels, altogether
too many Addresses being presented to the King—"what can we
tell his Majesty in all we say on these occasions, but what he
knows perfectly well already?" He is persuaded, however, to see
the coronation, and he takes two-guinea places on one of the
stands for himself and his wife and daughter. "There we sat,
penned up in our scaffolding, like sheep upon a market day in
Smithfield. . . ." But he does not see the procession after all. When
it passes he is sound asleep.

Of those essays providing more than average interest three more
may be mentioned. "The Adventures of a Strolling Player" (XXI),
though much of it has been taken from Marivaux, is nevertheless
a worthy addition to Goldsmith's theatrical commentary. It does
not seem too far-fetched to find in his itinerant actor, always a
wanderer and always an impersonator of other people, a figure
symbolizing homelessness in a double sense.

"Some Remarks on the Modern Manner of Preaching" (XVII)
shows how far Goldsmith had moved away from that older theory

of pulpit oratory which had been upheld by Swift, for instance, and which lay behind the completely unemotional sermons characteristic of rational divines in the time of Tillotson. Swift insisted that it was not the preacher's function to be moving but instead to set forth Christian precepts in a simple, direct, unmistakable manner. Typical of his generation, he had been strongly conditioned against "enthusiasm," identified as a kind of madness possessing all those intent on upsetting established, regulated order in religion, society, and the realm of scholarly and intellectual endeavor. Actually Goldsmith has much in common with Swift, but not where the pathetic in art is concerned. Whether it was that in this latter respect he went back directly to the classical rhetoricians, or drew from articles like those on eloquence and elocution contributed to the *Encyclopédie* by Voltaire and d'-Alembert, or from an essay like Hume's "Of Eloquence," or from eighteenth-century Scottish rhetoricians, who had begun to place the emotional in a new light, Goldsmith entertained an entirely different theory of communication from the austerely rational one once in favor with Anglican sermon writers. In "Some Remarks on . . . Preaching" he is specific in rejecting the rational method, "by some called an address to the reason and not to the passions." Reason "is but a weak antagonist when headlong passion dictates; in all such cases we should arm one passion against another; it is with the human mind as in nature, from the mixture of two opposites the result is most frequently neutral tranquility." Clearly, this is not a theory of emotionalism pure and simple. It is primarily rhetorical in point of view: emotion is to be aroused and directed knowingly. And the most pronouncedly emotional of his own writings—even a poem like *The Deserted Village*—show this kind of purposeful control. Goldsmith himself, Goldsmith the writer, stands always at a distance.

Essay XXIV, "The Distresses of a Common Soldier," had appeared originally in the *British Magazine* and had afterward been inserted in *The Citizen of the World* (Letter CXIX according to today's numbering; it had not been one of the original "Chinese Letters"). It is a powerful indictment of the nation's indifference toward many of her common soldiers and sailors who, having served faithfully in the wars, frequently receiving disabling wounds, had no choice but to turn beggars after their discharge from service. These creatures "are obliged to wander, without a friend to comfort or to assist them," finding "enmity in every law, and ... too poor to obtain even justice." Goldsmith was perhaps no more sensitive than many of his contemporaries to the evils present in the Georgian world. What distinguished him was the way he voiced his protests. He did not fall back upon the easy theories advanced by those benevolists who professed to believe that as soon as pity melts the heart all is at once put to rights, and he was repelled by sentimentalism as a literary fashion. He did not hesitate to employ emotion in the cause of social justice, but he was specific, as here in this essay and later in *The Deserted Village*, as to the wrongs in question; a change of heart meant a fundamental reform in social attitudes and practices.

This discussion of the *Essays* may best be closed with a few words about the two showpieces of the volume, "The Proceedings of Providence Vindicated" (XVI), and "A Reverie at the Boar's-Head-Tavern in Eastcheap" (XIX). They are quite different from one another. "The Proceedings" is another vision-essay in the manner made popular by Addison's "Vision of Mirzah." It embodies one of Goldsmith's most extreme statements concerning the necessary presence in human affairs of the self-seeking drives; aiming at reducing the theory of an uncritical benevolence to absurdity, at the same time it is intent on demonstrating that divine wisdom has designed a best-of-all-possible worlds. Goldsmith's defense of cannibalism among the animals is based on the principle of plenitude. According to this, God's goodness realizes itself in filling up to the full each possible grade of life in the chain of being; there is overflowing life, and in consequence the animals do and must prey continuously upon one another. It is better that such cruelty should be a part of things than that God should limit his creativity. Goldsmith's argument is neither original nor impressive. Yet his celebration of the rightness of the kind of world we find ourselves in is not really, it becomes apparent from the body of his writings, a celebration of the *status quo* save in the sense that the sanity of Nature is felt to be a balance holding antithetical forces in equilibrium. The bald manner in which Goldsmith is here setting forth certain popular and not very profound propositions that he is urging upon us as universal truths may give the essay its weight, but it certainly does not do justice to the true subtility of Goldsmith's mind when intellect and imagination were working together.

"A Reverie at the Boar's-Head-Tavern" is probably the best known of all the essays in the collection—it is at any rate the one most frequently anthologized. It can be read in different ways. If it is taken as a vision of life in Old England—a vision brought upon us by thoughts of Falstaff and his companions as we sit dozing in the tavern he once honored with his presence, "still kept at East-cheap"—it is antiquarianism of the liveliest kind, thanks to the chief narrator, the apparitional Dame Quickly, whose speech proves wonderfully salty once she drops, when commanded, the silly *whiloms* and *eftsoons* which at first she feels obliged to use, out of deference no doubt to the doctored language heard on the stage in Shakespearean revivals. Thanks to her manner of telling it, her survey of the historical epochs she and the Eastcheap tavern have lived through is constantly amusing. If we choose to look more closely at the essay, we shall discover Goldsmith's sly irony. For this is a vision with a difference. "The Proceedings of Providence" is also a vision, but there everything is building up to a set of rational principles. It is scarcely the region of dreams. But we really do feel asleep in the "Reverie." Is the world always the same, or was it better of old? Mr. Rigmarole is now of one opinion, now of another, and Dame Quickly seems likewise of different minds about this all-important question, which somehow becomes merely comical as the past is made to unfold before us. "This only may be remarked in general, that whenever taverns flourish most, the times are the most extravagent and luxurious." An eminently acceptable conclusion, indeed.

IV

Scenic Comedy:
The Citizen of the World

1

IF THERE ARE individual essays that are possibly better than anything in *The Citizen of the World*, the latter, taken as a whole,
unquestionably deserves first place. In its way it is superb. There
is no other essay serial quite like it. Here for the first time Goldsmith had the opportunity to give free rein to his inventive capacities, and the result is to be seen in the brilliant variety of the
materials making up the work. The London scene has rarely been
portrayed with richer comic effect, though from time to time
the comedy yields to harsher satire. There is the framed story,
preposterous enough to please both the naive and the sophisticated reader. There are amusing characters—Lien Chi Altangi, the
Chinese visitor in London and master of ceremonies; the Man in
Black; the pawnbroker's widow; Beau Tibbs and his wife. There
are commentaries, serious and otherwise, on literary topics. There
are disquisitions on philosophic matters and problems of civilization. And running through it all, giving to it a peculiar kind of
imaginative unity, is Goldsmith's irony—an irony of contrasting
values, of multiple viewpoints. Irony is, in fact, central to this
entire series of letters, and it is from an ironic point of view that

Goldsmith is here examining those broad questions of civilization previously taken up in the *Enquiry*.

2

The *Public Ledger*, a daily newspaper owned by the publisher John Newbery, made its initial appearance on January 12, 1760. Goldsmith's first two "Chinese Letters" appeared in the issue of January 24. Newbery, we are told, desired to add a dash of humor to his paper and entered into an agreement with Goldsmith, who for £100 a year was to supply two "Chinese Letters" a week. Once the series got under way it proved to be highly popular and was accordingly featured by the editors. It ran through 1760 and well into 1761, coming to an end on August 14 of the latter year. There had been in all one hundred and nineteen of the "Letters." These, with the addition of four "Letters" not in the original series, were brought out in a collected edition of two volumes on May 1, 1762, under the title of *The Citizen of the World*.[1]

3

That the *Public Ledger* should run a semi-weekly column of the essay type was perhaps Newbery's idea. It was probably Goldsmith, however, who suggested that his contributions take the form of an essay serial, and there is every reason to believe that it was he who proposed that such a serial, cast in a form similar to that of Montesquieu's famous *Persian Letters* (1721; English

---

[1] In this collected edition Letter CXVII, "A City Night-Piece," had appeared in the *Bee*, No. IV; Letter CXIX, "On the Distresses of the Poor," had appeared as "The Distresses of a Common Soldier" in the *British Magazine* for June, 1760; Letters CXXI and CXXII were apparently new items. See Chapter III, footnote 3.

Anyone using a modern edition of *The Citizen of the World* should bear in mind that the numbering now used corrects previous confusions and for that reason does not coincide with either the original numbering found in the *Public Ledger* or the numbering given in the collected edition of 1762.

tr. 1730), should consist of pseudo-letters written by a Chinese visitor in London.

It was a genre—this of the pseudo-letter or series of letters purportedly containing an Oriental traveler's observations on European customs—which was now well-established. Several generations of readers had been enjoying the *Letters Writ by a Turkish Spy*. Addison's essay—*Spectator* No. 50—describing the behavior of four American Indian "Kings" during a visit to London was still giving amusement. Montesquieu's *Persian Letters,* the recognized masterpiece of this kind, had been imitated by Lord Lyttlelton in his *Letters from a Persian in England to his Friend at Ispahan* (1735). The *Lettres Chinoises* by the Marquis d'Argens dated from 1739, and had appeared in an English translation under the title of *The Chinese Spy.* The most recent addition to the genre, the *Letters from an Armenian In Ireland* (1756), which Goldsmith had noticed in the *Monthly Review,* and a clever little satire by Horace Walpole, *A Letter from Xo Ho, a Chinese Philosopher* (1757), where Goldsmith found the name Lien Chi, were proof that its popularity had not declined.

There was of course no law of comic logic which demanded that the central figure in these pseudo-letters of satiric commentary be an Oriental. An Englishman in Paris could perfectly well be equipped with the necessary bifocal vision, or an Irishman in Edinburgh, and there were Addison's Iroquois Indians in London. But Europe had long regarded China as that fabulous Land of Cathay, the creation of the imagination working freely with the materials supplied, since the time of Marco Polo, by the accounts of travelers, traders, and Franciscan and Jesuit missionaries. What was more natural than that the commentator from another country be an Oriental, preferably a Chinese? The doubleness of vision which was a necessary part of the comedy corresponded perfectly with that paradoxical quality which was such an exciting part of the whole China myth. The Chinese were wise, their civilization superior, yet they and everything about them, especially their decorative arts and their architecture, were engagingly quaint, improbable as things are in any Utopia. And in England the 1750s and 1760s were witnessing the culmination of the Chinese fad. There were books about China, plays with Chinese characters, and Chinese textiles, porcelains, lacquer ware, furniture, wallpaper, screens, gardens, bridges, and pagodas. The writer of an essay "On the Taste or Whim for Chinese Architecture and Furniture," appearing in the *World* in March, 1753, had observed that whereas a few years before everything had been Gothic, according "to the present prevailing whim every thing is Chinese, or in the Chinese taste; ... chairs, tables, chimney-pieces, frames for looking-glasses, and even our most vulgar utensils, are all reduced to this new-fangled standard. ...." In 1757 Sir William Chambers published his *Designs of Chinese Buildings, Furniture, Dresses, Machines, Utensils, etc.*, and soon he was at work supervising the construction of the surprising pagoda at Kew which, along with contrasting buildings, one in Moorish, the other in the classical style, had been commissioned by the Princess Dowager of Wales. When the strikingly handsome Rector of Easton Maudit, Thomas Percy, called on Goldsmith early in 1759, he had but recently finished his English translation of a Chinese novel, *Hau Kiou Choaan* (published in 1761). Arthur Murphy's play, *The Orphan of China*, similar to Voltaire's earlier *L' Orphelin de la Chine* and produced by Garrick at Drury Lane, had been reviewed by Goldsmith in the *Critical Review* for May, 1759. Half a year later, in the *Bee* (No. VI), Goldsmith was speaking of a Chinese who "once took it into his head to travel into Europe, and observe the customs" of the people there. It was only a short time after this that he introduced Lien Chi Altangi to the readers of the *Public Ledger*.

4

Goldsmith must have entered upon his new journalistic venture in the highest of spirits. He was now a thoroughly practiced hand at the essay, adept in his touch and tonal command. The scheme he was committed to was something that had been taking shape in his imagination over a long period, gradually exciting his enthusiasm and bringing his invention into full play. And the public was ready for just such a comic diversion. In short, few literary projects were ever launched under more favorable auspices than these "Chinese Letters" commissioned by John Newbery.

The thing that might have deterred another writer proved no difficulty at all for Goldsmith. His Chinese who talked like an Englishman was not to be too palpably a fraud. He would, of course, not be Chinese—that was part of the joke. How, then, was Lien Chi to be equipped with a fairly plausible knowledge of his native land? There were several works known to Goldsmith which made readily available exactly the kind of material that was needed: J. B. Du Halde's *Description of the Empire of China* (an English translation published in 1738–41); Louis Le Comte's *Nouveaux mémoires sur l'état présent de la Chine* (3rd ed., Paris, 1697); and the *Lettres chinoises* by the Marquis d'Argens (ed. of 1755). The sources Goldsmith drew upon in the course of his hundred and twenty-three "Letters" have long been known. In addition to the three just mentioned, which are the principal ones, they include the *Turkish Spy*, Montesquieu's *Persian Letters*, Lord Lyttelton's *Letters from a Persian*, and Walpole's *Letter from Xo Ho*. Professor Friedman's notes in his edition of *The Citizen of the World* (*Collected Works*, II) trace Goldsmith's borrowings and the way in which he used this material. What, however, needs to be said about Goldsmith's method of work here, and said as emphatically as possible, is that it was not plagiarism —not in the accepted sense. The literary artist takes his materials where he finds them, but he transmutes them. The dynamics are his. Observe, for instance, how Goldsmith has managed his incomparable story of the Chinese matron (Letter XVIII). Du Halde is the source, but of what? Not of the wonderfully executed comic shading, not of the ironic intonations, and not of the perfectly modulated ending, all of which make the Goldsmith version a masterpiece of short, humorous narration. Choang, suddenly a widower after an unexpected return to life, marries—suddenly and

quite prudently—a widow with a large fan, who has set the whole
train of events in motion. In the version found in Du Halde,
Choang does not marry again; tamely, he sets forth on his travels.
In the important respects Letter XVIII is clearly Goldsmith.
Furthermore, the complete *Citizen of the World* turns out to be
a skillfully unified work, as we shall see. Once it is recognized as
such, once it is perceived to be something more than a series of
short compositions loosely strung together, its imaginative originality assumes an importance which completely overshadows its
derivative elements.

5

It may be, as has sometimes been suggested, that the readers of
the *Public Ledger* began by accepting the "Chinese Letters" as
the genuine correspondence of a real Chinese visitor. If they did—
though this is difficult to believe—they must have realized their
error before very long, and they certainly took the deception with
good grace, for they continued to read Goldsmith's column with
zest. The fame of Lien Altangi, some of which was now rubbing
off onto his creator, began to spread. The "Letters" were widely
discussed; they were soon being reprinted in other publications,
and parodies were appearing. They were regarded as a novelty,
however, and by the time the collected edition appeared in 1762
public interest had begun to fall off. *The Citizen of the World* enjoyed no spectacular sale. The notices appearing in the *Critical
Review* and the *Monthly Review* were not on the whole un-
favorable, but they were certainly sorry criticism. The *Critical Review* found the "Letters" lacking in originality, but confessed
their merit when viewed "with regard to utility." The *Monthly
Review* pointed out that as a philosopher Lien Chi Altangi was
not Asiatic at all; he was European and as wide of the mark as
England's own Hobbes. It is to the credit of William Rider, whose
*Historical and Critical Account . . . of the Living Authors of
Great-Britain* appeared in 1762, that he recognized something of

the true quality of the work: of all Goldsmith's productions, he wrote, this did "the highest Honour to his Genius. . . ."

No further edition of *The Citizen of the World* was brought out during Goldsmith's lifetime. A second one appeared, however, shortly after his death, and from this time on the book rose steadily in popularity. Contemporary criticism reveals that it has not yet lost its appeal. F. L. Lucas, in his well-considered *Search for Good Sense*, is persuaded that Goldsmith never perhaps wrote anything better than the best parts of *The Citizen of the World*. And in her memorable essay on Goldsmith, Virginia Woolf [2] expressed her keen delight, observing that Goldsmith could hardly have hit upon a better method for making the new middle class of his time aware of itself. Nevertheless, our acquaintance with the *Citizen of the World* is today usually limited to a few of the "Letters," selected more or less at random and read casually. This is understandable. It would be an unreasonable person who would expect us to have a fuller acquaintance, and it must be said that however much is lost as a result of this informal approach some of the best things come through.

No one, for instance, can miss the exhilarating comedy in Lien Chi Altangi's accounts of the strange and astonishing things he meets as he diligently pursues his travels about London, taking note of places and events, people, and such venerable institutions as English funerals and visitation dinners. Irony plays steadily over all these descriptions, but it is delicately controlled. Goldsmith makes sure that humor, not sharp wit, prevails, even when the role of Lien Chi is altered and he is turned into a downright satirist, taking aim at critics, sham doctors, booksellers, pretenders to knowledge, religious enthusiasts, the fear of mad dogs, and —how strange coming from a Chinese—even chinoiserie as it flourishes among the more sophisticated of the English.

There are a few individual essays, exceptional in quality and able to stand more or less by themselves, which have found their

[2] Her "Oliver Goldsmith" first appeared in the *Times* (London) *Literary Supplement* (March 1, 1934), and has been reprinted in *The Captain's Death Bed and Other Essays* (1950).

way into most anthologies of eighteenth-century prose and for
that reason are better known. One is "A City Night-Piece" (Letter CXVII), taken from the *Bee*. Another—already mentioned in
the preceding chapter—is "On the distresses of the poor, ex-
emplified in the life of a private centinel" (Letter CXIX), that
had originally appeared in the *British Magazine*. The first is a
descriptive piece, a mood piece we might call it, giving an image
of the city as it was in Goldsmith's time, with an affective power
like that experienced in our dreams. "On the distresses of the
poor" is one of the memorable bits of sociological writing to appear in this period. How strongly developed Goldsmith's consciousness of social conditions and social problems was when he
departed from Ireland it is impossible to say, but it is apparent
that by the time of his arrival in London he was viewing European
culture from a sociological point of view similar to that established by Voltaire and his fellows. He had a sense of the forces
making for cultural differences and social change, and along with
this a profound hatred of social injustices. Eighteenth-century
England was fast learning the meaning of humanitarianism, and
reform movements of all sorts, together with organized charities,
were well under way. Goldsmith unquestionably articulated the
awakening conscience of the average Englishman. But his vision
was sharper and broader than many of his contemporaries. The
intellectuals were not, as a rule, unresponsive to the new spirit
that was arising, as witness Henry Fielding, but some showed
mainly indifference, and few of them altogether understood what
was in Goldsmith's mind. Crabbe, for instance, disputed what he
took to be the false idealization of the life of the poor in *The
Deserted Village*, and before that there had been many who denied
that anything like the conditions and events described by Goldsmith in his famous poem existed or had taken place. Jeremy
Bentham, who was once at the Mitre tavern with Johnson, Goldsmith, and Company, later mentioned his anger at Goldsmith for
writing the poem. "On the distresses of the poor," with its account of the disabled soldier forced to beg at the town's end,
warrants close reading. Swift used statistics with devastating irony

in pieces like the *Modest Proposal* and the *Drapier's Letters*. Goldsmith chose to work in quite a different manner. There are no statistics, there is no irony. Instead, there is what we accept as a kind of realism, but as in the case of the "City Night-Piece" it is a realism made unforgettable by reason of a strongly affective quality. There is no sentimentalism here, but there *is* sentiment —emotionalism consciously aroused and controlled with an express purpose in view.

But it is the characters we are introduced to which are probably the best-known thing about the "Letters": the Man in Black and his lady, the pawnbroker's widow; Mr. Fudge, the bookseller; shabby Beau Tibbs and his enduring wife. As Austin Dobson pointed out many years ago, Goldsmith was here disclosing for the first time his true gift for character delineation, in which respect he can be seen as the forerunner of Dickens, though there was no direct influence. It is, however, the Goldsmith legend which has really fixed the usual response to someone like the Man in Black. According to the legend the best things in Goldsmith's work come directly out of his own life and are for that reason so heartwarming. The Man in Black, it has been said time and again, is Goldsmith himself, or his father, or a mixture of both. Of course recollections of places and people he had known and of events in his own life enter into his writing. They enter, inevitably, into all creative work. The question is, how? Goldsmith was no more at the mercy of his private experience than of the material he found in books. He controlled both, using them, shaping them, as the genuine artist has always done, distancing them and thereby giving them a fresh and wider significance and value. The Man in Black belongs to a good eighteenth-century tradition; as Lien Chi observes, "he may be justly termed an humourist in a nation of humourists" (Letter XXVI), and we may add that he is in fact a not-too-distant relative of other well-known humor characters like Sir Roger de Coverley and Parson Adams. Sir William Temple, with his theory of the humor character, had long since prevailed over Ben Jonson, appreciative laughter over ridicule. The Man in Black is a humorist—a figure of humor—by reason of his eccentricities, but it is amusement we feel, not scorn, as we recognize the sterling qualities lying underneath, which he tries unsuccessfully to hide. He is also a figure of symbolic significance in the Goldsmith system of ideas. His history, as he tells it (Letter XXVII), is that of one who has learned from hard experience how unsound are the advertised doctrines of universal benevolence. He has, true enough, lost none of his instinctive sympathy for his fellow creatures, and he is continually doing charitable deeds, which he tries eccentrically to conceal; but his conversion from false sentimentality to the informed realism of the morally mature has been radical and lasting.

Other common misapprehensions concern the framed story—the romantic adventures of Lien Chi's son, Hingpo, and the beautiful Zelis, who as it turns out is the Man in Black's niece—and the discussions, including the defense of luxury and the decline of civilization, occurring at intervals throughout the book. The framed story is usually put down as a tiresome and ineffective imitation of the narrative element in Montesquieu's *Persian Letters*, while the recurring discourses are sometimes dismissed as merely so much incidental space-filling. It is only when we have convinced ourselves that *The Citizen of the World* is, as a matter of fact, much more of a structured whole than has usually been assumed that we begin to see how, for instance, both the framed story and the various discussions of philosophic matters and questions then in the public mind serve a definite purpose.

6

The "Letters" reflect Goldsmith's sound journalistic sense. A newspaper column of this sort, appearing regularly, is most successful when it proceeds in much the same fashion day after day but manages to be always different, providing as it were variety within a familiar, expected setting. Thus, though our friend Lien Chi Altangi is always, or almost always, with us, and we are in London most of the time, observing its life through his eyes, nothing is static. London affords an endless succession of new scenes, people of widely different appearances and behavior cross our line of vision, and the letters Lien Chi receives from abroad bring us news of strange events in exotic places.

Reasons of sound journalism, however, do not fully account for the variety of material and subjects, which is far greater than necessary. The scenes of every-day social life predominate, it is true, but how much else there is! Memorable events of the period are noted: the execution of Earl Ferrers, the death of George II, the coronation of his successor, the appearance of Charles Churchill's sensational *Rosciad* and Sterne's no less sensational *Tristram Shandy*. Satiric commentary sometimes supervenes. There are episodes involving characters like the Man in Black and Beau Tibbs. The framed story of Hingpo and Zelis is gradually unwound. We are given a number of short narrative pieces. The wanderer motif—Lien Chi, like others, has left home behind him—appears and then recedes. There is literary and theatrical criticism. It is only natural, too, that as a citizen of the world Lien Chi should from time to time enter into discussions with his friends about various aspects and problems of civilization. And so luxury is defended, democracy, oligarchy, and despotism are compared, the influence of climate and soil is investigated, beauty and utility are analyzed, and the question whether the arts and sciences are more useful or harmful to mankind is taken up. Goldsmith's imaginative resourcefulness in finding themes and supporting material is great.

If the entire series of "Letters" is vitalized by this rich diversity, it is also in a manner unified, for we see that the ultimate effect is something which has been carefully gauged. But there is another factor which also serves—perhaps more obviously—to give a shape to the work as a whole. This is the masterly control of tone. With Goldsmith tone is not everything, to be sure, but it is probably the most important single constituent in his art. No prose writer of the century commanded a wider register of tonal values—indeed, the variations of voice are in his case sometimes so extreme as to result in wholly different styles of prose. Compare, for instance, Beau Tibbs's eloquent description of the approaching coronation of George III, Lien Chi's commentary thereon (both in Letter CV), and in the independent essay on the same topic appearing in the *Public Ledger* ("To the Printer"), the common-council-man's account of his sufferings while waiting for a glimpse of the coronation procession. The upshot in all these cases may be the same, but the different points of view result in greatly varied comic effects. Beau Tibbs's enthusiasm is unbounded. To Lien Chi the spectacle is a thing "at once replete with burlesque and the sublime"—another example of the surprising way Europeans have of concocting a mixture of the solemn and the fantastic. The common-council-man, penned up sheeplike all night long in his seat in the scaffolding, falls asleep and misses the show when it passes.

But a more striking example of this kind of tonal control comes to light when four of the short narratives found in the "Letters" are placed side by side. The "Authentic history of Catharina Alexowna, wife of Peter the Great" (Letter LXII) is the kind of story which held such fascination for Goldsmith. Catharina as a girl is reduced to poverty; thereafter, she marries a subaltern officer, becomes a widow the very same day, and is finally taken in marriage by none less than Peter the Great. The manner throughout all this is factual. Is it not history, after all?

On the other hand the "History of the beautiful captive" (Letter LX), which is romance too but even more far-fetched, is given in a different style altogether. The heroine, the beautiful Zelis, who is here telling her own history, turns out to be a master of all the clichés established in romantic narration. An "insidious wretch" uses "a thousand arts" in pursuit of "his base design," but the innocent Zelis looks upon him "as a guardian and a friend." She never loved him, yet she esteemed him. At length her father discovers the wretch's villainy, challenges him to a duel, and is mortally wounded. The death scene is standard pathos: "Why, my dear, my only Pappa, why could you ruin me thus, and yourself for ever! O pity, and return, since there is none but you to comfort me."

Now turn, if you will, to the fairy tale about the Prince of Bonbobbin, his princess, and the white mouse with green eyes (Letters XLVIII and XLIX). We are never made to feel that this is parody, and yet from start to finish it is ironic in a wonderfully light and gay manner. The prince, inconsolable over the disappearance of the green-eyed mouse, regards his princess "with a stern air, for which his family was remarkable." There are many animals— assorted mice, a blue cat, porcupines who serve as train-bearers, and snails drawing a fiery chariot through the air. It takes skill to manage little fishes, whether they talk or not.

The fourth story, and in still another narrative style, concerns Choang, his wife Hansi, and the widow with the large fan (Letter XVIII). Here the irony, which is everything, arises from the mat-ter-of-fact tone, in comic counterpoint to the actual incidents, and from the bland suppression of motivation.

With four such narratives before us and their four distinguish-able styles we should pause before dismissing on the grounds of absurdity the most important story of all, the framed story of Hingpo and Zelis. If we trust Goldsmith's artistry, we can assume that this incredible narration is here for a purpose and is doing what Goldsmith intended it to do. It is—to anticipate a bit—the broadest kind of irony, and as such it stands in amusing contrast with the other ironies running through the "Letters" but not so close to the surface.

7

Irony may be said to be the key element in the "Letters," con-stituting a distinctive environment enfolding the entire series. It is irony, however, of more than one sort, irony which operates at different levels. At its simplest and most apparent it is the comic doubleness which we are kept constantly aware of throughout Lien Chi's adventures—the comic doubleness which results when what is familiar is presented from a surprising angle of percep-tion. London has two appearances, our London and Lien Chi's. And who is to say which is the right one?

And what *is* "right"? Lien Chi the persona—the purported

speaker or writer traditionally present in the eighteenth-century essay serial—is more than a mere distorting mirror. He is a traveler —The Traveller, in fact: the one who has left home and has ever since been exposed to changes of perspective. Does any traveler such as he believe that he will ever find the way back to that place, that scene, that ineffable climate of his origin? Were he to do so, would it still be home?

Lien Chi is, furthermore, a manner of speaking or writing. In the Preface added in 1762 when the "Letters" appeared together as *The Citizen of the World* Goldsmith amusingly called attention to just this aspect: "in the intimacy between my author and me," he observed, "he has usually given me a lift of his Easter sublimity, and I have sometimes given him a return of my colloquial ease." And so, we are told, the metaphors and allusions in the "Letters" are all drawn from the East. The formality of the East has been carefully preserved by Lien Chi, "our author":

> many . . . favorite [Chinese] tenets in morals are illustrated. The Chinese are always concise, so is he. Simple, so is he. The Chinese are always grave and sententious, so is he. But in one particular, the resemblance is peculiarly striking: the Chinese are often dull; and so is he.

Lien Chi the observer, who finds our London such a curious spectacle; Lien Chi the traveler, the Citizen of the World, to whom all places are equally familiar and equally strange; Lien Chi, the Chinese who talks like an Englishman in the Eastern manner and ridicules chinoiserie—the irony has many surfaces reflecting in different degrees the comic light.

Always there is awareness of the ambiguous nature of things and events, awareness of the fact that our estimates and judgments vary from person to person, from place to place. And if our reactions to the more superficial aspects of daily social life are ambiguous, so also, and to a more marked degree, are our views regarding the nature and operating principles of our civilization taken as a whole. In his *Enquiry into the Present State of Polite Learning In Europe* Goldsmith had admitted nothing to his discussion which contradicted the theories which he was expounding with dogmatic emphasis. But with his extraordinary sensitiveness to style—to style as tone, rhythm, syntactic structure, and a way of arranging one's thoughts—he was not long in learning the art of discussion as understood by writers of the neoclassical age. Since the Restoration, English poets had fashioned their verse according to parallel constructions alternating with antithetical ones, the former setting similar matters alongside one another, the latter placing two things in opposition. The antithetical manner, by extension, could become a sort of dialogue between opposites, with the result that the discursive verse so typical of the period often resolves itself into a debate, implicit or formal, between opposing sides. By the time he was writing the "Chinese Letters" Goldsmith had been imbued in this kind of rhetoric, which was also a way of thinking. It was a rhetoric which could easily enough be carried over into the medium of prose. One principle stands against a contrary one, the polarities made insistent through sustained, articulated opposition. Increasingly Goldsmith saw human experience in terms of some such formula, and likewise our generalizations about man and society. The innocently naive person arouses only the contempt of the sophisticate; the sophisticate is seen in all of his shortsighted egoism by one who still retains the guilelessness of inexperience. But with Goldsmith the ironic ambiguity is not held forever in suspense. There is always resolution. Both extremes are right, both are wrong, as appears when informed reason, common sense, and that moderation which is Nature herself are allowed to prevail.

In the "Letters" the doctrine of the middle way is voiced repeatedly. Is happiness purely sensual pleasure, or is it wholly intellectual? The answer to this question, given by Fum Hoam, one of Lien Chi's correspondents, is that we must not separate sensual and mental enjoyments: "There are two extremes in this respect; the savage who swallows down the draught of pleasure without staying to reflect on happiness, and the sage who passeth the cup while he reflects on the conveniences of drinking" (Letter VI). The middle way, once we understand it, is seen to be a positive principle of enduring strength and viability. "A mind rightly

instituted in the school of philosophy, acquires at once the sta-
bility of the oak, and the flexibility of the osier" (Letter XLVII).
Lien Chi discerns in the English constitution a similar moderation: it is "at present possessed of the strength of its native oak,
and the flexibility of the bending tamarisk," a wonderful compromise between the two extremes of, on the one hand political
freedom defeating itself for lack of discipline, and on the other,
oppressive rule (Letter L). The most eloquent statement of this
principle of strong flexibility as seen in operation in the English
political tradition occurs in Letter CXXI (one of the letters added
in 1762). Since the English govern themselves by reason every
man's voice counts, different courses are urged, and in the presence
of this variety of counsel our minds become confused:

> The man who examines a complicated subject on every side, and
> calls in reason to his assistance, will frequently change; will find him-
> self distracted by opposing probabilities and contending proofs: every
> alteration of place will diversify the prospect, will give some latent
> argument new force, and contribute to maintain an anarchy in the
> mind.

But it is not on any note of anarchy that the "Letters" close.
There is always something beyond opposing probabilities and
contending proofs, and Lien Chi's last words to us are these:
"They must often change says Confucius, who would be constant
in happiness or wisdom."

One by one, questions of great moment to the mid-century intellectuals—questions of the sort which Hume, for instance, had
been taking up in his short essays—make their appearance in the
"Letters." Are the arts and sciences more serviceable or prejudicial
to mankind? (Letter LXXXII.) Are love and beauty merely names,
or are they substantive realities? (Letter CXVI.) What is the influence of climate and soil on the culture of a particular society?
And what of luxury? Is it beneficial in its effects or the cause of a
nation's decay? In his handling of these topics in the course of the
"Letters" Goldsmith allows himself his subtlest form of irony. His
own position formulates itself out of the varied opinions that are
voiced and the formal debates which sometimes—as in Letter
CXVI—take place. It lies medially between the opposing views.

This is notably the case in regard to the question of luxury. One has only to follow the continuing debate which the eighteenth century engaged in, one side proclaiming the vast benefits arising from luxury, the other warning strongly against its evil effects, to see that Goldsmith was not playing an eccentric game of his own as he weighed the pros and the cons of the matter. In 1734 a French writer, Jean-François Melon, had come out vigorously in defense of luxury. His treatise, *Essai politique sur le commerce,* influenced Voltaire, who in *Le Mondain* (1736) and in *La Défense du Mondain* (1739) took a similar position, which he confirmed much later in his article on "Le Luxe" in the *Dictionnaire philosophique* (1764), where he argued that luxury is best for small nations. But fear of the corrupting power of luxury was deeply implanted; it did not vanish before the middle-class scorn of a Voltaire. William Bell, a fellow of Magdalen College, won a prize in 1756 with a Dissertation *(What causes principally contribute to render a Nation Populous?)* expressing the traditional distrust of any apparent benefits, such as an increased population, accruing from the "commercial and refined arts," which arts will always, sooner or later, destroy "whatsoever multitudes they may have raised." Two years later he was answered by I——B——, M.D., in *A Vindication of Commerce and the Arts; Proving that they are the Source of the Greatness, Power, Riches and Populousness of a State.* But the balancing formula had by now been put forward, and nowhere more effectively than by Hume in his essay "Of Refinement in the Arts" (in his *Political Discourses,* 1752), concerned with luxury, in which he concluded, after summarizing the case against luxury, that any degree of luxury may be innocent or blamable, according to age, country, condition. Such in effect was also the position reached by John Brown in his sometimes rather hysterical *Estimate of the Manners and Principles of the Times* (1757): though we are "rolling to the Brink of a Precipice"; though our sons suffer from "vein, luxurious, and selfish EFFEMINACY"; though "every gaudy *Chinese* Crudity, either in Colour, Form, Attitude, or Grouping, is adopted into fashionable Use, and becomes a Standard of Taste and Elegance"; though "our present exorbitant Degree of Trade and Wealth ... naturally tends to produce luxurious and effeminate Manners in the higher Ranks"; nonetheless there are occasions and degrees governing the operation of luxury. A state exhibits three phases of development, early, middle, and late. In the first two, trade and wealth are advantageous, making a nation strong because they increase the population. But the benefits disappear when the nation passes into the third and fully developed stage. Thus we see trade and wealth, conquest and opulence at one period polishing and strengthening a people, at another, refining, corrupting, weakening, destroying.

Sooner or later, Goldsmith expressed himself many times on the subject of luxury, sometimes defending it, again condemning it. His most forthright defense is found in No. XI of the "Chinese Letters": "Examine the history of any country remarkable for opulence and wisdom, you will find they would never have been wise had they not been first luxurious. . . ." So he wrote early in 1760. But two and a half years later, in his essay "The Revolution in Low Life," appearing in *Lloyd's Evening Post,* he had changed his ground: "Let others felicitate their country upon the encrease of foreign commerce and the extension of our foreign conquest; but for my part, this new introduction of wealth gives me but very little satisfaction." However, before we take these shifting opinions as proof of his inability to make up his mind about anything, we should understand how such statements stand in relation to one another. In Letter XI it is not Goldsmith but Lien Chi who is assuring us that our knowledge and our virtues are improved by luxury. Not that Goldsmith could not, and did not under certain circumstances, assent. Letter XI, however, is to be seen as part of a debate which develops in the course of the "Chinese Letters"—a debate which becomes explicit in Letter LXXXII and leads to an emphatic statement of the principle of compromise: "They who insist that the sciences are useful in *refined* society are certainly right, and they who maintain that *barbarous* nations are more happy without them are right also. . . ."

The middle way to which the intellectual ironies of the "Chinese Letters" are all pointing may not seem impressive to us today. Was it not essentially a rhetorical stance? Did it provide any truly useful answers? We like to think that because our own investigations of sociocultural phenomena are scientifically controlled they furnish us, through accurate, impersonal data, with clear directives to action. Some of the time they do, and to the extent that they do they would receive the enthusiastic approval of a Voltaire, a Hume, an Estimate Brown. Goldsmith would also have appreciated their instrumental value—more quickly, one guesses, than many of his circle. But we today also know that human experience escapes statistics, that the course of human history is not predictable. We still engage in not altogether meaningless debate over matters of moral, social, economic, and political significance. We do so with greater expertise than did the eighteenth century, and certainly with a greater sense of urgency. But we have lost something of that sheer delight in the play of intellect which the age of reason possessed. There is something to be said after all for the ironic wisdom of a Georgian like Lien Chi Altangi.

V

The *Étourdi*:
Goldsmith among the Georgians

1

WHAT LIEN CHI ALTANGI thinks of the English men and women
who chance to come under his observation is amply clear. In this
respect the "Chinese Letters" is a one-way street. We who are not
under observation, we who are merely readers, do of course form
an opinion—an image—of our Citizen of the World, and an amusing one it is, but how Lien Chi is regarded by those he is writing
about we scarcely learn. To all intents and purposes he remains,
as far as the people among whom he moves are concerned, a veritable nonperson.

How different the case of Lien Chi's creator and doppleganger!
In Goldsmith the Georgians found a person whom they could and
did transform into one of the personalities of their time. Here
was a genuine eccentric, at once amusing, irritating, and amazing.
They talked about him endlessly; they included the latest stories
about him in their letters to their friends; they conscientiously
noted in their memoirs what they knew of him at first and second
hand. Of the men of letters of the period only Johnson, one sup-
poses, excited greater interest and more extensive commentary.
From one point of view, indeed, the record concerning Goldsmith
—the things said to have been said about him, the judgments

passed on his character, the countless anecdotal reminiscences on the part of friend and acquaintance—is too voluminous. It has overwhelmed many of his later biographers and critics, who have sometimes been too impressed to think clearly for themselves. And for all its apparent authenticity it is open to challenge at many points, not so much as to the actual facts as to the coloring and emphasis given them.

But though we no longer feel any obligation to accept unquestioningly all that has been recorded or to assent meekly to those critics who have done so, we could not wish the chronicle less copious than it is. By virtue of its very bulk, the Matter of Oliver Goldsmith exists alongside, often overlapping, the Matter of Samuel Johnson. It has an imaginative dimension. Boswell and all the others who have noted in such detail the words and acts of these two preeminent writers have created for us a world that is partly real history, and like the best history partly invention— a world in time, yet a timeless one. The Club still sits at the Turk's Head in Gerrard Street, Soho. Johnson—Boswell's Socrates —still converses and disputes. Goldsmith forever makes a fool of himself as he endeavors to shine in this company of eminent men. Meanwhile, all London is listening in.

Such, at least, is the illusion. But let us remember that this is not all our own pleasing fancy. The Georgian world was a small, compact one. Middle-class civilization was reaching for a brief period the highest point of civility. Art and letters were widely appreciated, and artists, architects, and especially men of letters were quickly recognized for their achievements and accorded the kind of interest which our own century has reserved for the personalities of stage, screen, and television. George III conversing with Johnson in the library at Buckingham House proved in his dignified way that he was an eighteenth-century man of taste, and in his fine courtesy he was expressing that deference which the more aristocratic members of this society not infrequently showed toward distinguished literary men. In his *Life of Reynolds,* James Northcote tells of "a certain nobleman," one of Reynold's intimate friends, who had conceived in his mind such a formidable idea of all those persons who had gained fame as literary characters, that I have heard Sir Joshua say, he verily believed he could no more have prevailed upon this noble person to dine at the same table table with Johnson and Goldsmith, than with two tygers.

Goldsmith, we may rest assured, would have protested neither his presence in this half-mythical world nor the role traditionally assigned him in this human comedy. Had he not himself defined his part? He was the dessert, the "goosbery fool," at this feast. His metaphor is characteristically ironic: awkward clown though he was, he was also a delightful surprise.

2

Goldsmith's progress through the world of Georgian London could, if necessary, be set forth at great length. Though there are certain gaps in the record, we have otherwise a superabundance of details, which can however be reduced to a single and straight-forward enough story spanning eighteen years and falling with a singular precision into two almost equal parts, the close of 1764 marking not only the midpoint between his coming to London and his death but likewise his first resounding literary triumph and the beginning of his widespread reputation.

How he fared during his earliest weeks in London in 1756 we have only a vague idea. Living, it would seem, "among the beggars in Axe Lane," to use his own words, he may ultimately have found employment as a proofreader at Samuel Richardson's establishment in Salisbury Square. In the course of the two following years came his sojourn at John Milner's school at Peckham, his term of service for Griffiths on the *Monthly Review,* the composition of the *Enquiry,* and on December 21, 1768, his failure at Surgeons' Hall.

The latter incident turned out to be something other than a catastrophe, for in 1759 his fortunes picked up noticeably and before the close of that year he was on his way to becoming a successful essayist. He had taken lodgings in Green Arbour Court,

near the Old Bailey, and it was here that Thomas Percy, only
recently introduced to him, paid him a visit (March 3, 1759).
Percy was to recount the event in one of the most vivid passages
in his "Life of Goldsmith":

> The Doctor was writing his Enquiry, &c. in a wretched dirty room,
> in which there was but one chair, and when he, from civility, offered
> it to his visitant, himself was obliged to sit in the window. While
> they were conversing, some one gently rapped at the door, and being
> desired to come in, a poor ragged little girl, of very decent behaviour,
> entered, who, dropping a curtsey, said, "My mamma sends her com-
> pliments, and begs the favour of you to lend her a chamber-pot full
> of coals."

It is now that Goldsmith is beginning to emerge into full view.
His work as an essayist continued, yielding in 1760 and 1761 the
great series of "Chinese Letters" for the *Public Ledger*. He was
already being called Dr. Goldsmith, and amusing stories about
his feckless ways had begun to circulate. Sometime in mid-1760 he
moved to much more respectable quarters in No. 6 Wine Office
Court, which opened on to Fleet Street at the south. So far as we
know the first meeting between him and Johnson occurred here
on May 31, 1761, when Percy took Johnson to an entertainment
Goldsmith was giving in his rooms for a large group of friends.

By 1762 his work as an essayist was drawing to a close and he
was turning to other things. What must have been making the
greatest demand on his time and energy was the novel which was
at this time taking shape. Though *The Vicar of Wakefield* did not
reach the public until 1766, it is a matter of record that a third
share of it was sold to a Salisbury bookseller on October 28, 1762,
and it would have been shortly before this that Johnson, as Boswell tells the story, hastened to Goldsmith's lodgings in answer to
a frantic appeal for help, found that Goldsmith's landlady had
arrested him for rent, and effected a deliverance by promptly
negotiating the sale of *The Vicar*—or at least the sale of a part
interest in the novel—to a bookseller, presumably Newbery,
for £60.

Before the end of 1762 Goldsmith had moved again, this time
to accommodations in Canonbury House, Islington, where New-

bery and his wife sometimes lived in the summer and where the publisher now made arrangements for one of the ablest of his writers to be lodged and boarded. It was only a matter of minutes from Islington into London proper and Goldsmith was not cut off from his favorite haunts in the city. It was on Christmas day, 1762, at the house of Thomas Davies the bookseller, in Russel Street, Covenant Garden, that he and Boswell, as we know from the latter's *London Journal,* had their first sight of one another. Boswell had not yet met Johnson, but was stalking the great man and had in fact gone to Davies's on this particular day in hopes of meeting him. Johnson was not there, but Goldsmith unfortunately was and the first impression he made on the young Scotsman from Edinburgh was not a happy one. Half a year later, however, Boswell was walking out to Canonbury House to call on Goldsmith, probably because on the preceding day—June 25, 1763 —Johnson, whom he had finally snared, had remarked to him that "Dr. Goldsmith is one of the first men we now have as an author, and he is a very worthy man too."

In the course of 1764 Goldsmith came into his own. The odd jobs he had been doing for Newbery and others of the trade may have added little to his stature, but his first *History of England* (June, 1764), though anonymous, was a solid success. He and Joshua Reynolds, portrait painter to the Georgians, had become fast friends and were constantly in one another's company, as all London knew. The Club was formed in this year, and Goldsmith's presence in it as one of the ten charter members was a matter of course. By autumn he was no longer living in Islington but at the Temple in No. 2 Garden Court. But the signal event was the publication on December 19 of his poem *The Traveller.* None of his compositions, verse or prose, was more perfectly attuned to contemporary sensibility. He found himself famous. His great period had begun.

The final nine years were filled with work and more work, too much of it, unfortunately, mere journeyman's writing done on commission for all sorts of publishers. But there were also achievements of the highest order, such as *The Deserted Village* (1770), as successful as *The Traveller,* and his dramatic triumph, *She*

Stoops to Conquer (1773). These are the years too when we hear
most about him from his contemporaries. From Garden Court he
has proceeded to No. 3 King's Bench Walk in the Temple, and
still later to No. 2 Brick Court in the Temple with which he is
now chiefly associated. His friends included the members of the
Club, publishers, writers, and men associated with the theater. He
was known to Blue-stocking Ladies like Mrs. Montagu and Mrs.
Vesey, and to Horace Walpole, who knew or at least knew about
everyone. For Mrs. Horneck, a widow and a friend of Sir Joshua's,
and her two beautiful daughters, Mary and Catherine, he had the
warmest affection, which was returned in full. Frances Reynolds,
Sir Joshua's sister; Laetitia Hawkins, daughter of Sir John, the
"unclubbable" member of the Club and one of Johnson's biographers; and Johnson's special friend, Mrs. Thrale—all had impressions and opinions of him formed at first hand. It was indeed a
small world in which Goldsmith lived out his life. Anything like
a complete list of those whose paths crossed his would make a
veritable London *Who's Who* for the years in question. And all
the Georgians, it sometimes seems to one attempting to keep track
of these matters, had something to say about the strange personality in their midst.

3

Exactly what opinions did Goldsmith's contemporaries form of
him? What were their various reactions to the man as they saw
him in life, and to his work? Do we find any consistency of impression here? It is Boswell, to be sure, who in the *Life of Johnson*
has left us the most elaborately documented assessment, but Boswell is only one of a host of people, men, women, and children,
whose views and judgments we have.

There is general agreement, in the first place, as to his striking
eccentricities. The novelists and dramatists of this time were creating a notable gallery of "humorists"—characters marked, each
one, by certain special oddities and relished for their peculiarities.
Oliver Goldsmith was a "humorist" come to life; he was almost

too good to be true. Boswell in his way and Mrs. Thrale in hers both succeeded in expressing in all brevity the thing which everyone felt. "He was very much what the French call *un étourdi. . . .*" Thus Boswell. And Mrs. Thrale: "Poor Doctor Goldsmith! Lord bless us what an anomalous Character was his. . . ."

If it was an age that produced "humorists" in fiction and in fact, it was also one that, ever since the Restoration, had been accustomed to analyze human character in terms of sharply antithetical qualities. In *Absalom and Achitophel* Dryden had worked up his unforgettable *character* of Shaftesbury in such a fashion:

> When the Waves went high
> He sought the Storms; but for a Calm unfit,
> Would steer too nigh the Sands, to boast his Wit.

And Pope in his *Epistle to Dr. Arnuthnot* had depicted Sporus as "one vile Antithesis," an "amphibious Thing" responding now to the "trifling Head" and again to the "corrupted Heart." Despite the undisputed contrast between Goldsmith the writer and Goldsmith the conversationalist, the figure which the Georgians discerned so readily—the man who wrote like an angel but talked like poor Poll—was to a degree a traditional one. The antithesis into which his characteristics were made to fall so neatly was ready to hand. His genius was accepted without dispute. The evidence of it was assumed to lie partly in his essays but chiefly in *The Traveller, The Deserted Village,* and *She Stoops to Conquer.* Little was said of the *Enquiry,* and *The Vicar of Wakefield* was generally overlooked; *The Good Natur'd Man* was commonly regarded as unsuccessful playwriting. But beyond all doubt his place in literature was among the great. That was one side. On the other were displayed his social maladroitness, his envy, his deplorable desire to shine in all company, his gambling, his debts, his ugly, pock-marked face, his loose ways with women of the town. "No man," said Johnson (as recorded under 1780 in the *Life*), "was more foolish when he had not a pen in his hand, or more wise when he had." And Boswell echoed this (*Life,* May 7, 1773): "Goldsmith's incessant desire of being conspicuous in company, was the occasion of his sometimes appearing to such disadvantage as one should hardly have supposed possible in a man of his genius." The genius and the fool. Not a vile antithesis; rather a "humorous" one.

Mrs. Thrale's picture of Goldsmith as pieced together from the things to be found in her *Anecdotes of Johnson* and in her *Diary* is among the cruelest of the contemporary sketches. Johnson contributed probably more than anyone else to the antithetical pattern referred to above. Dwelling constantly upon his friend's literary achievement, he found the moving and definitive words of summary: Oliver Goldsmith, who left no kind of writing untouched, and who touched nothing which he did not adorn. Yet no one carried on more than Johnson, year after year and long after Goldsmith's death, about his unfortunate ways and his weaknesses of character. He was obsessed by the man's clumsiness, by his irritating ways and his shortcomings. Boswell has left us, as all the evidence now available shows, a faithful report of Johnson on Goldsmith, and the treatment of Goldsmith in the *Life* is to be seen as essentially a very skillful dramatization of Johnson's attitude. There were some, however, who found in Goldsmith a somewhat different person from the one depicted by Mrs. Thrale, Johnson, or Boswell. These others knew him under essentially different conditions, when he was not on exhibition as it were, when he was completely at ease with the people about him and under no strain to prove himself. What they seem to have felt above everything else was the warmth of his personality and his unforced charm. The glimpses they afford us are of a Goldsmith freed from the tyranny of the antithetical myth. Hester Milner remembered the good-natured young man who had served as tutor at her father's academy in Peckham. Another woman, related to Goldsmith's landlady at Green Arbour Court, recalled the time when as a little girl she and her friends used to enjoy Goldsmith's treats of cakes and sweetmeats. Goldsmith's own verse letters apropos of informal social affairs involving the Hornecks and their friends—one letter, of uncertain date, is the "Verses In Reply To An Invitation At Sir George Baker's"; the other, of December, 1773, is the Letter to Mrs. Bunbury—are delightful things, reflecting a social relationship undisturbed by any reservations on either side; and many years later Mary Horneck, the younger of the two sisters, who became Mrs. Gwynne, described, for the benefit of Sir James Prior, the biographer, the Goldsmith she remembered. It was impossible, she said, "not to love and respect his goodness of heart, which broke out upon every occasion"; and she disputed some of the unflattering stories concerning him which had been put about. Mrs. Gwatkin, Sir Joshua's niece, who as a little girl had encountered both Johnson and Goldsmith at her uncle's house, remembered the great Cham as thundering out at her and scolding her for showing him insufficient respect, whereas Goldsmith proved to be "the most delightful man." And George Colman the younger, in a passage in his *Random Records* (1830) known to all Goldsmithians, described how he once out of sheer petulance slapped the Doctor on the face—Colman was only "a peevish brat" of five at the time—and was promptly punished by his father by being locked up. It was Goldsmith, lighted candle in hand, who rescued the boy and proceeded to comfort him by giving an exhibition of the old shell game as played with three hats and three shillings:

> "Hey, presto, cockolorum!" cried the Doctor, and, lo! on uncovering the shillings which had been dispersed, each beneath a separate hat, they were all found congregated under one.

Accomplishments of this order were not, apparently, appreciated in the Club.

4

Obviously there were many Goldsmiths. No single characterization of him succeeds in catching all sides of his complex personality. The figure with which the majority of readers are most familiar is the one that moves through the pages of the *Life of Johnson,* and Boswell's Goldsmith is an unforgettable creation, as convincing—while we are under the immediate spell of the great biographer—as his Johnson. Whether it is a truthful likeness is another matter, and one which has been under dispute from the time the *Life* originally appeared in 1791. Many of the men who had known Goldsmith, including Burke, Reynolds, and Bishop Percy, voiced strong protests against what they declared to be Boswell's misrepresentation of their friend. One of them observed that "it is not unusual for a man who has much genius to be censured by one who has none." It was felt, furthermore, that a lawyer was not one to give a rational opinion of a poet, nor a Scot of an Irishman.

We today, however, thanks to the extensive Boswell materials which have become available in the course of our own century,[1] know more about Boswell's thoughts outside the *Life* than most of his contemporaries ever did, and for this reason we are in a better position to judge how he really felt about Goldsmith—how he felt, that is, when not on duty as Johnsonian biographer. Boswell's first meeting with Goldsmith took place, as we have seen, on December 25, 1762, and it is evident from the *London Journal*[2] that Boswell was not at the time much taken with "Mr. Goldsmith, a curious, odd, pedantic fellow with some genius." As mentioned earlier they also saw one another again on June 26 of the following year, and before Boswell left for the continent early in August he, Johnson, and Goldsmith were together several times, as duly recorded in the *Life*. Boswell returned in 1766, and thereafter, in the course of his periodic visits to London, there were frequent encounters between him and Goldsmith, as we know from the *Life*. The *Life*, however, omits certain things that bear on Goldsmith. In the "Journal" he kept of his trip to London in 1772,[3] Boswell described, for instance, his feeling of complete happiness as he found himself, on April 10 dining at General

[1] These materials include the 1924 edition of his *Letters;* the 1936 edition, from the original manuscript, of Boswell's *Tour to the Hebrides* (first printed, but with deletions, in 1785); the eighteen volumes of the Isham Papers (*The Private Papers of James Boswell from Malahide Castle.* Privately printed: 1928–1934); and the ten volumes of the *Yale Edition of the Private Papers of James Boswell* which have thus far appeared (i.e., between 1950 and 1966). And associated with these *Yale Editions* we now have Frederick A. Pottle's *James Boswell: The Earlier Years, 1740–1769* (1966).

[2] *Boswell's London Journal: 1762–1763 (The Yale Editions of . . . Boswell,* 1950).

[3] *Boswell For the Defence: 1769–1774 (The Yale Editions of . . . Boswell,* 1959).

Oglethorpe's where the only guests besides himself were Johnson and Goldsmith, the former so vast in character, the latter so eminent in letters. And in the "Journal" for 1773 [4] we have the wonderful account of his first meeting with Goldsmith subsequent to the triumphant opening of *She Stoops to Conquer*. It was on April 7 that Boswell, who had arrived in London the previous week, called at Goldsmith's room in Brick Court. Goldsmith, still in bed, roared out a welcome, and the two embraced each other. Goldsmith's pleasure at seeing Boswell again could only have been disinterested. But what of Boswell's manifestation of joy? It is easy to accuse Boswell of snobbery on this occasion, and to say that he was merely expressing his own gratification at being on embracing terms with one who was at that moment the toast of the town. But that would not be quite fair. Surely there was nothing of snobbery in what he entered in his "Journal" for April 10, 1775. Again he was in London, again he was dining at General Oglethorpe's. The dinner and the wine were both good, and Johnson, Langton, and others were also there. "But I missed poor Goldsmith." [5] And some years still later Boswell attended a Club dinner, but noted in his "Journal" (June 12, 1787) that "there was no force, no brilliancy, nothing as when Johnson, Goldsmith, or Garrick were with us." [6] What we find in the "Journals" in the way of Boswell's own remarks on Goldsmith shows that there was no deep-lying bitterness on Boswell's part. What we find in the "Journals" and in the *Tour to the Hebrides* in the way of Johnson's running commentary on Goldsmith establishes the fact that the *Life* reproduces this commentary, in spirit if not in complete detail, with remarkable fidelity. The Goldsmith of the *Life* is really a representation by Johnson, not a misrepresentation by Boswell.

To Boswell, of course, goes sole credit for the masterful arrangement of the materials present in the *Life*. The book has a shape and dimensions of its own which are to a degree independent of,

---

[4] *Boswell For the Defence: 1769–1774.*

[5] *Boswell: The Ominous Years: 1774–1776 (The Yale Editions of . . . Boswell,* 1963).

[6] "Journal" for 1787 *(The Private Papers of James Boswell from Malahide Castle,* XVII, 37).

though they do not destroy, the chronology of actual events. Goldsmith is not the central figure, yet his role in the unfolding conversation piece has been controlled in a way that seems to structure the first part of the *Life*. His appearances have been so handled as to fall into what may be thought of as five acts and a long afterpiece. We may be permitted to give the play its obvious title: *The Étourdi*. Johnson is of course present throughout most of the scenes comprising this play, and he never ceases to be the all-important character, but it is Goldsmith's presence and the timing of his entrances and exits which account for a good deal of the tensional quality found in the earlier half of the biography.

Goldsmith is first introduced into the *Life* in accordance with well-proved dramatic technique. Before he is allowed to make his personal appearance he is discussed by those already on stage. The first mention is made by Johnson, who pronounces Dr. Goldsmith to be "one of the first men we have as an author." The date is June 25, 1763, and the first act of *The Étourdi* is under way. Boswell now takes up a position downstage front and in a long address to the audience—effective dramaturgy, as our modern theater has more than once demonstrated—describes the singular character who is to appear so often in what is to follow. Shortly Boswell, Johnson, and Goldsmith are supping together at the Mitre (July 1) and a few days after this Boswell is entertaining the two men along with other acquaintances at the same tavern. On both occasions Goldsmith's unhappy behavior bears out what we have been led to expect of him. Act I comes to a close as Boswell leaves for the continent.

The second act, in some three or four different scenes, starts with Boswell's return to London early in 1766 and stretches over events of the four following years. During Boswell's absence *The Traveller* has been published and Goldsmith is now a famous man. Later—in 1768—*The Good Natur'd Man* is produced. Act II of *The Étourdi* closes brilliantly with the dinner party Boswell gives on October 16, 1769, in his lodgings in Old Bond Street. It is a famous group that crowds the stage: Johnson, Reynolds, Garrick, Arthur Murphy, Tom Davies. And in the midst of all these, to divert them, struts Goldsmith in an amazing bloom-colored coat, tailored for him, he announces, by John Filby at the Harrow in Water Lane.

The third act, taking place in 1772, is something of a letdown. Boswell is now in London again. He meets Goldsmith at General Oglethorpe's dinner party on April 10, and there is conversation between Johnson and Goldsmith. For the rest of the time, however, Goldsmith does not appear in person. Instead, we listen to Johnson as on at least two occasions he dwells upon Goldsmith's shortcomings. He is, says Johnson, "so much afraid of being unnoticed, that he often talks merely lest you should forget that he is in the company" (April 11). Again: it is Goldsmith's misfortune in conversation that "he goes on without knowing how he is to get off. His genius is great, but his knowledge is small" (May 9). Johnson's attitude has altered since the beginning of the play, as though he had now come round to the view expressed at the very start by Boswell. At every turn he acknowledges Goldsmith's achievement, but he is increasingly irritated by him. Despite his genius Goldsmith knows nothing, he is always talking—talking at random merely to remind you of his presence.

If the third act is thin, Act IV more than makes up for this. It is the longest of all and the richest in material. Early April, 1773, finds Boswell at the beginning of another London visit. *She Stoops to Conquer,* having opened at Covent Garden on March 15, is still enjoying frequent performances. Its author is much in the news, both because of his play and because he has just caned the publisher of the *London Packet,* that paper having recently published a scurrilous article attacking "the *great* Goldsmith" and bringing in a reference to Mary Horneck. Goldsmith, charged with assault, has been forced to settle by paying £50 to a Welsh charity. To cap it all he has written a letter in explanation and self-defense to the *Daily Advertiser.* Boswell mentions the letter to Johnson, who pronounces it "a foolish thing well done." Through April Boswell is constantly on the go. He is with Johnson frequently, with Johnson when Goldsmith is also present, with Johnson and others when Goldsmith is absent. There is famous talk, with Johnson and Goldsmith taking the lead. There are comments and disquisitions on the anomalous Goldsmith when he is not of the company. The climactic scene comes on May 7 during and after a dinner given by Edward and Charles Dilly, the publishers. Johnson is in his most expansive conversational mood. Goldsmith, trying to break in, is overpowered, and throwing down his hat in a passion cries, "Take it!" There are further words between the two, but as the scene ends Johnson is asking pardon and Goldsmith is answering that "It must be much from you, Sir, that I take ill." Two days later Boswell, on the point of departing for Scotland, takes leave of Goldsmith. He is not to see him again.

Our play ends with a sharply curtailed fifth act followed by a rather lengthy afterpiece. Act V differs from the preceding scenes in being laid not in London but Edinburgh. The time is 1774. News of Goldsmith's sudden, unexpected death on April 4 of this year has reached Boswell, and on June 25 he writes to Johnson. "You have said nothing to me about poor Goldsmith," he remarks. Johnson replies on July 4:

> Of poor dear Dr. Goldsmith there is little to be told, more than the papers have made public. He died of a fever, made, I am afraid, more violent by uneasiness of mind. His debts began to be heavy, and all his resources were exhausted. Sir Joshua is of opinion that he owed not less than two thousand pounds. Was ever poet so trusted before?

On the following day Johnson writes similarly to Bennet Langton. Boswell gives both of Johnson's letters in the *Life*. The pertinent passage in the one of July 5 is this:

> [Poor Goldsmith] died of a fever, exasperated, as I believe, by the fear of distress. He had raised money and squandered it, by every artifice of acquisition, and folly of expense. But let not his frailities be remembered; he was a very great man.

And with this the curtain falls.

The afterpiece is retrospective, consisting of remarks on Goldsmith made for the most part by Johnson and for the most part dating from the years subsequent to his friend's death. Some of these remarks are essentially factual. Johnson talks of Dr. Turton's attendance on Goldsmith during the final illness (September 19, 1777); he observes that Goldsmith "was as a plant that flowered late" (*ibid.*), and that it was long before his merit came to be acknowledged (April 9, 1778). But many of the comments are pronouncements on his personality and achievement, and they add up to a kind of spoken *"character* of Dr. Goldsmith." It is a *character* based upon the antithetical principle. Repeatedly, Johnson describes emphatically and concisely the unpleasant qualities. Goldsmith referred everything to vanity; he was not a social man; he "never exchanged mind with you" (April 11, 1776). He was not an agreeable companion; "he talked always for fame" (April 7, 1778). He had no settled notions upon any subject, and for that reason always talked at random; he had been at no pains to fill his mind with knowledge, merely transplanting it from one place to another (April 9, 1778). He had so much envy he could not conceal it; he was so full of it "that he overflowed" (April 12, 1778). And yet . . . Johnson is always ready with the counterpoise. Goldsmith "was a man, who, whatever he wrote, did it better than any other man could do"; he "deserved a place in Westminster-Abbey, and every year he lived, would have deserved it better" (April 9, 1778). Lord Camden, who according to Goldsmith took no more notice of him than if he "had been an ordinary man," was wrong, for a nobleman ought to have made up to such a man (April 17, 1778). And finally (among the undated remarks of Johnson's grouped by Boswell for convenience under 1780), this antithetical, summarizing declaration already mentioned: "No man was more foolish when he had not a pen in his hand, or more wise when he had."

Such was Goldsmith as seen by Johnson, such the figure known to all readers of the *Life.*

5

Today we are fortunate in having Sir Joshua Reynolds's prose Portrait of Goldsmith to place beside the figure given us by Boswell in the *Life.* Reynolds would seem to have written his character sketch about two years after Goldsmith's death, but it was not published at that time. Somehow the manuscript came into Boswell's possession and ended up in Malahide Castle, Ireland, where it lay forgotten until its discovery in 1940. The first printing occurred in 1952, when it appeared in the series of *Yale Editions of the Private Papers of James Boswell.*

It is a short composition, running in its printed form to only sixteen pages, but both in authority and vividness it is equal to Boswell's account of Goldsmith, and certainly superior to his in its acuteness of analysis. In its way it tells us as much about the Georgians' response to Goldsmith as does the *Life.* And it is more sympathetic in its point of view, Reynolds having been one of Goldsmith's closest friends. The two had met, it is believed, sometime in 1762. Before long they were seeing much of each other, and during the last ten years of Goldsmith's life are said to have been constantly in one another's company. It was to Reynolds that Goldsmith dedicated *The Deserted Village,* and we have it on Mrs. Thrale's authority that it was Goldsmith that Sir Joshua seemed to have most friendship for.

The Portrait is a careful and logical construction. And running through it, serving as the chief principle of organization, is the same antithetical concept that we have observed elsewhere. Reynolds begins with the assertion that to a biographer is given the opportunity of reconciling seeming contradictions. He then proceeds to describe the dual Goldsmiths—the genius and the weak, foolish man. In developing his Portrait Reynolds no doubt believed that he was effectively reconciling the seeming contradictions in Goldsmith's character, yet it cannot be said that he was altogether successful in this. True enough, he makes it a point to show that some of the absurdities attributed to Goldsmith were humorous remarks misinterpreted as serious ones. In any case—so he reminds us—wherever Goldsmith was, there was no yawning. Goldsmith had no wit in conversation, endeavoring instead after humor, and though he often failed in this he was happy when people laughed, even when their laughter was directed at him. But Reynolds devotes much space to enumerating and analyzing what he accepts as his subject's unquestionable defects.

Much of Goldsmith's folly was owing to his early life among mean people. He wanted always to be noticed, and would stand on his head to command attention. He would speak on matters that he had thought little about. He was envious of everyone, including Johnson as a conversationalist.

On the other hand we have the man of letters, a poet primarily but also a master of prose. It is to be observed that in speaking of Goldsmith as a writer Reynolds is still thinking, perhaps unconsciously, in terms of contrast. It is not in this case the contrast between the genius and the fool, but between two different kinds of art, one rationally calculated, the other a matter of emotion and intuition. Goldsmith's mind was entirely unfurnished. He was ignorant of all the terms of his art. More than any other man, he wrote from his feelings—which does not mean, Sir Joshua hastens to explain, that he poured forth his personal feelings, but rather that in arousing feeling in his readers he was guided not by written rules but by intuition. And it was by instinct that he knew how to order the sentiments he excited so that there was a natural chain connecting them.

Since the Portrait remained in manuscript down to our own day it has no explicit connection with the Goldsmith legend, whereas the *Life* has a very real one. One can say, however, that Reynolds reflects the general feeling of his contemporaries, and in his attempt to reconcile Goldsmith's "seeming contradictions" is really emphasizing them. Reynolds' remarks on Goldsmith as a writer are particularly interesting, for they show how easily a man of conservative aesthetic principles could be somewhat misled by Goldsmith's art. It was not an art which offended, yet it had behind it no conscious, intellectual planning. Here, one feels, Reynolds fell into one of the errors which the legend did so much to keep alive. Far more intellect went into Goldsmith's art than Reynolds and many others ever perceived, as we discover once we direct our attention to the formal aspect of his works.

VI

Comedy, Idyllic and Romantic:
The Vicar of Wakefield

1

FOR ALL ITS apparent simplicity and innocence of intention *The Vicar of Wakefield* gives rise to more questions and presents greater difficulties of interpretation than any of Goldsmith's other compositions. In this respect it serves to point up clearly and sometimes amusingly the various problems which everywhere lie in wait to worry and perplex those attempting to approach Goldsmith and his literary art in a more than superficial manner.

There are, to begin with, the minor mysteries surrounding the composition, sale, and original publication of *The Vicar*. Goldsmith, characteristically, throws almost no light on these matters; his contemporaries have left us with conflicting statements. Precisely when and where was the book written? Did Goldsmith have a real place in mind—Wakefield in Yorkshire, perhaps; or a certain village fifty miles distant from London—or was he drawing on memories of the Ireland he had once known? What were the actual circumstances surrounding the sale of the manuscript and the eventual appearance of the novel?

When we turn to Goldsmith's critics, we find that their remarks on *The Vicar* have tended from the very first to reflect a certain bewilderment. What, they ask us, is to be made of a book which succeeds so well in casting a charm on the reader and yet is full of faults? The article appearing in the *Monthly Review* in 1766 directly after the publication of *The Vicar* is in its expression of perplexity typical of any number of later critiques:

> Through the whole course of our travels in the wild regions of romance, we were never met with any thing more difficult to characterize than the Vicar of Wakefield; a performance which contains beauties sufficient to entitle it to almost the highest applause, and defects enough to put the discerning reader out of all patience with an author capable of so strangely under-writing himself.

This is not substantially different from the opinion delivered by Henry James, who spoke of the "incomparable amenity" of the book and at the same time of how little else it really had.

Other critics, especially those who are writing today, have seen in the ambiguities present in *The Vicar* the key not only to this particular work but to much that is characteristic of Goldsmith's art as a whole. The modern approach lies—some will say unfortunately—through analysis of the closest kind. Criticism of this order may at first strike us as dispiritingly complicated, but the results justify the method. Only through careful and detailed analysis does it seem possible to come to terms with a work as ambiguous in form and sustaining imagination as *The Vicar of Wakefield*. Is it too sweet in tone, too amiable in all of its implications, for modern taste? Perhaps. And yet on analysis it turns out to be not nearly so sweet as we assume. Something close to parody, if it is not actually and fully that, takes over at more than one point. The sweetness, it is seen, is mixed with sly irony. Is it a hopelessly careless piece of work, thrown together with no regard to form and structure? Careful examination opens our eyes to an underlying pattern that is contrived and highly sophisticated. But the ambiguities remain. They are an essential element of the ironic vision which has here found expression. Goldsmith's irony is never bitter. It arises out of the multiple and surprising rather than the false appearances of things. But it breathes the true spirit of comedy, for it invites us to consider the normal rhythms of life, of human experience—normal yet always unexpected in their turns—and it shows us ourselves as we appear from points of view lying outside our accustomed vanities.

2

The Vicar issued from the press on March 27, 1766. We know, however, that it had been completed, wholly or at least substantially almost four years before. Boswell's account of how Johnson came to negotiate the sale of the manuscript to a bookseller is well-known. According to Boswell (under 1763 in the *Life of Johnson*), and as has already been mentioned, one morning Johnson received an urgent message from Goldsmith requesting Johnson's immediate assistance. Johnson hurried to the aid of his friend, and found that Goldsmith's landlady had arrested him for rent. When Johnson was able to quiet Goldsmith, who had been in a violent passion, the two men began to consider what could be done to resolve this crisis. It was then that Johnson learned of a novel ready for the press. He glanced through Goldsmith's manuscript, satisfied himself as to its merit, and immediately carried it to a bookseller, who purchased it for £60. Thus Goldsmith was able to discharge his debt and gain his freedom. It is to be noted that in Boswell's version of the episode no date is given, the bookseller who purchased the manuscript is not named, and we are not told where Goldsmith was living at the time.

There are other accounts of this same affair—five more all told. These, however, only add to the uncertainties regarding what really happened, disagreeing as they do on most of the details. But when we put everything we have together, taking account of the gaps in the evidence and inevitable contradictions, we have as the probable sequence of events something like the following. Goldsmith may have begun work on *The Vicar* at any time between 1760 and 1762; there are things in the novel which seem to have grown out of the "Chinese Letters," which were appearing throughout 1760 and much of 1761. The episode involving Johnson probably occurred at Wine Office Court, and after mid-July, 1762. The bookseller who bought the manuscript was probably Newbery, who may have purchased at the time only a third share in the book, thus leaving Goldsmith free to sell another third to one Benjamin Collins, a Salisbury printer—we have Collins' record showing that on October 28, 1762, he purchased a third share—and the final third to William Strahan, another printer.

There is nothing that throws any light on the long delay in publication. Johnson's explanation (given by Boswell under 1763 in the *Life*) that Goldsmith was then relatively unknown and that "the bookseller had such faint hopes . . . that he kept the manuscript by him a long time," venturing on a publication only after the triumph of *The Traveller,* is not very convincing.

One further question remains, and unfortunately it must go unanswered. Was *The Vicar* complete when sold in manuscript, or was it finished, or revised, or in any way added to later on prior to publication? If only we knew we could perhaps dispose more readily of some of the perplexing critical problems that face us.

3

The Vicar achieved its greatest popularity after Goldsmith's death. So much is certain. During the nineteenth century it is said to have averaged two editions a year. It was translated into French repeatedly, and into most of the European and some of the non-European languages.

Opinions differ, however, as to its reception during Goldsmith's lifetime. Before the end of August, 1766, it had gone to three editions, and the fifth appeared shortly before the author's death. According to some bibliographers the number of copies involved in the early editions was relatively small, and this has been taken as indicating a lack of any great public interest. But the figures sometimes used in arriving at such a conclusion are open to dispute, and in view of the four editions which made their appearance in Ireland, an unauthorized London edition put out in 1768, and translations into French, German, and Dutch, it seems more reasonable to conclude that *The Vicar* achieved immediate popularity.

Something has already been said of the kind of critical responses which it has called forth over the years. Johnson, we know, had no high opinion of it, and is reported by Fanny Burney (in her *Diary* under 1778) to have found it "very faulty, . . . a mere fanciful performance," with "nothing of real life in it, and very little of nature." The *Critical Review*—at the time of *The Vicar's* first appearance—had been favorably disposed, though at a loss to understand why the author had thought it necessary to bring calamities so thick upon his venerable hero. The *Monthly Review,* as we have seen, found itself in even more of a quandary. Goethe spoke of it with reverence. Byron and Scott expressed only admiration. Much of nineteenth-century criticism was of the divided sort, Macaulay's remarks being in this respect typical: while the earlier chapters, he felt, have all the sweetness of pastoral poetry, the plot is one of the worst ever constructed, and the absurdities lie thicker and thicker as the catastrophe approaches. Saintsbury, writing in 1886, was exceptional in expressing a certain willingness to overlook those matters so often declared to be incredible faults. "Goldsmith never goes wrong," he wrote, "when the conventional improbabilities of its plot are once accepted." That the improbabilities could under any conditions be accepted was a new idea.

Among more recent commentators there are those who have dismissed the novel as a mere historical curiosity, an example of eighteenth-century sentimental fiction, fatuously cheerful in its pre-existentialistic innocence. Others seem merely to have taken the traditional judgment on faith: *The Vicar* is a mixture of good and bad, a curious book by a curious person. On the other hand, there has recently been an increasing inclination to trust Goldsmith's artistry and thus to accept the novel as a work which does precisely what, for sufficient reasons, it has been designed to do. It has been called a masterpiece of controlled art; it has been seen as a novel embodying elements of anti-romance; its plot and its ironic devices have been analyzed in detail. To approach the novel in this latter spirit is of course to place an entirely different interpretation on Goldsmith from the one which has generally prevailed in the past. His own century acknowledged him as one who adorned whatever kind of writing he touched. It was fully aware of the exceptional quality of his art. But it left the matter there, and proceeded to enlarge on the extraordinary contrast between the adept author and the poor Poll of the Club. It is not surprising that so many of those who have since then had occasion to discuss Goldsmith should have extended the paradox, applying it to his literary achievement, which they have accepted as being at one and the same time unassailable and yet open, much of it, to devastating exception.

4

It is important to realize that when Goldsmith turned to novel writing, certain ideas concerning the nature of fiction were already present in his mind. What these were we discover by turning to some of his early reviews and to his short narratives in the *Bee* and the "Chinese Letters," and there are other pieces dating from this general period which, though they may be contemporaneous with *The Vicar,* disclose firmly established attitudes towards fictional writing.

Taken against the background of the mid-century novels which form what we think of as the classical line—the novels of Richardson, Fielding, and Smollett—*The Vicar* seems to be a sport. We are forgetting, however, that the classical line is something largely of our own making, and that much of the fiction of the period, when full account is taken of all the works produced, does not fit into it at all. In the background there was always the romance with all the time-honored formulas of sudden disaster and unexpected deliverance and good fortune. There was the picaresque tale, the story within a story, the narrative interlarded with philosophic or political discourses, and various other types. While the masters of the eighteenth-century novel did not, of course, disregard all these fictional patterns, they did not make them their exclusive concern, and for that reason they leave us with a somewhat inaccurate impression of what the run of eighteenth-century novels was really like. To Goldsmith prose fiction meant narration in all of its long-popular forms. It was to this that he responded, and it was with this in mind that he designed and composed his own novel.

A short notice of a novel entitled *Jemina and Louisa* appeared in the *Critical Review* for August, 1759, and has been ascribed to Goldsmith. If it is not his, at least the attitude it takes corresponds, as Professor Friedman points out, with Goldsmith's views. The review gives a rapid summary of its plot. We are told how the story ends in a multitude of disasters. But consolation enough has been provided: "a great deal of money, a great deal of beauty, a world of love, and days and nights as happy as heart could desire; the old butt-end of a modern romance." As in the case of the sentimental comedy of the time, so here Goldsmith reacted to the clichés and the infantile emotionalism with humorous contempt. In fiction as well as in drama it was simplicity and naturalism which he prized above all else, and his greatest claim to originality as a novelist lies in the pictures of family life which make up the first half of *The Vicar*. Here was a new strain in fiction, a distinct contribution to the English novel. But Goldsmith recognized other kinds of narrative, and these he did not hesitate to make use of in his own work.

In the *Bee* he had the opportunity to try his hand at narrative of a special sort—something between the essay and what we have since come to know as the short story. There are four of these narrative pieces: "Alcander and Septimius," "The History of Hypasia," "A Flemish Tradition," and "Sabinus and Olinda." In all save "Hypasia" the characters are plunged from prosperity to misery only to experience at the end another reversal of fortune. We note that "Alcander and Septimius" ends with the dictum that "no circumstances are so desperate, which providence

may not relieve." There is also his ballad of *Edwin and Angelina,*
included in Chapter VIII of *The Vicar,* but possibly composed
earlier than much of the novel. It is a story of disguise, of recognition, and of reversal bringing joy after great unhappiness. We
know that Goldsmith thought highly of this composition.

What do facts like these tell us? For one thing, that Goldsmith
had as quick a sense as anyone of the fatuous character of much
popular fiction. But for another, that he could not bring himself
to disown romance. His heart still clung to it. Intellectually, instead of repudiating it absolutely, he seems to have rationalized
it. The myths which romance had taken over, the dreams of
ultimate happiness after bad fortune, were comparable to all the
other myths which had found lodgment in traditional fairy tales
and which cast a spell over the imagination of all children. Sym-
bolically they were true. The discovery scene had its analogue in
everyday experience when we discover who and what we really
are, recognition and reversal had theirs in the new understanding
of life, in the surge of energy as we are released from old fears.
The poet in his wisdom would not disdain the machinery of
romance.

Fortunately we also have the narrative pieces which Goldsmith
included in the "Chinese Letters." These, it will be recalled, have
already been discussed. Nothing could better serve to call attention to Goldsmith's remarkable control of tone. If the account
of Zelis's experiences (Letter LX) and the "Authentic history of
Catharina Alexowna" (Letter LXII) give us romance with a
straight face, the fairy tale about Prince Bonbenin bonbobbin
bonbobbinet and the green-eyed mouse (Letters XLVIII and
XLIX) and the story of Choang and his two ladies (Letter XVIII),
while not anti-romance, are anything but straight-faced.

With his sure control of tone and with his divided feelings
about fiction of the romantic kind, he was able to tell a story in
such a way that the reader is uncertain how it is to be taken. Is
it serious? Is it parody? Or is it something of both? Two of Goldsmith's essays associate themselves with *The Vicar.* "The History
of Miss Stanton" (in the *British Magazine,* July, 1760), and "The
Revolution in Low Life" (in *Lloyd's Evening Post,* June, 1762).

The latter opens with the sketch of a village which, before being wiped out to make way for a wealthy man's pleasure estate, enjoys the kind of idyllic life described in the fourth chapter of *The Vicar*. This is pastoral description, intended in all seriousness. It is in the earlier of the two essays that we have a clear example of ambivalence of intention and tone. The story here seems to be an earlier version of the Vicar-Olivia episodes in the novel. Mr. Stanton is a clergyman with a small fortune and a lovely daughter, Fanny. Mr. Dawson is the villain, who has been accepted by the Stantons as a friend, but who eventually corrupts Fanny. Mr. Stanton, learning the truth, speaks thus to his daughter:

> "Fanny, my child, my child (said the old man, melting into tears,) why was this, thou dear lost deluded excellence? why have you undone yourself and me? had you no pity for this head that has grown grey in thy instruction?—But he shall pay for it—though my God, my country, my conscience forbid revenge, yet he shall pay for it."

The denouement follows. There is a duel in which Mr. Dawson fatally shoots Mr. Stanton. Fanny, "in an agony of distress . . . fell lifeless upon the body stretched before her. . . ." Fanny's lifelessness is, however, only a figurative one. She is still alive, and Mr. Dawson, overcome by his own infamy, straightway offers her marriage. And then . . .

> The old man, who had only pretended to be dead, now rising up, claimed the performance of his promise; and the other had too much honour to refuse. They were immediately conducted to church, where they were married, and now live exemplary instances of conjugal love and felicity.

What, one asks, did the reader of the *British Magazine* make of this? For that matter, what do we today make of it?

5

The Vicar of Wakefield may be examined under three heads: the central theme, general design of the book, and the execution. The central theme is nowhere enunciated fully, yet it is at

work throughout, supporting the entire fictive structure and giving it a beginning, movement in the form of change, and a conclusion. The Vicar and his family are all central characters in the
dramatic fable that is unfolded. They are generous, credulous,
simple, and inoffensive—innocents who, when the story begins,
have never strayed far from home. They have no revolutions to
fear, nor fatigues to undergo. Their happiness is primordial. They
suffer a minor blow, but quickly settle into an equally paradisiacal
existence "in a distant neighborhood" on a little farm. But in the
presence of experience, simplicity is naiveté, and in the presence
of evil it ceases to be wholly admirable. It invites contempt, it
brings disasters upon itself, it is forced into the unsheltered world
to make its way there as best it can. The Vicar and his family are
brought low, suffering revolutions and forced to undergo un-
dreamed of fatigues. Can they, can we ever hope to find the way
home? Perhaps not. Perhaps, in time, we shall no longer want
to return, for meanwhile we have, in our lost innocence, grown
in wisdom. We have learned that the heart must be ever given
to gain that of another; we have learned the meaning of true
simplicity, forbearance, compassion. Those who tell stories can
speak of the things thus acquired as though they were "a great
deal of money, a great deal of beauty, . . . and days and nights as
happy as heart could desire," and may say that they are bestowed
by chance upon lucky heroes and heroines. The imagination
knows better. It may in a measure assent to all this, but it is not
totally blind to the irony.

Concerning the design of the novel, two things have to be said
at the very start. In the sense of plotted story it is faulty in many
obvious respects. In the wider sense of comprehensive structure,
the design has been calculated with great care, is highly ingenious,
and functions effectively.

The faults have often enough been pointed out. Something
seems to be missing between Chapter II and III, for as matters
stand the Vicar's resignation and departure from Wakefield are
not adequately accounted for, and there is an unexplained reference in Chapter XIV to the hard measures that had been dealt

him after his last Whistonean pamphlet. More than one slip occurs in connection with Sir William Thornhill. He is only thirty, which makes him, implausibly, almost as young as his nephew, Squire Thornhill. He goes unrecognized among his tenants and others who must be already familiar with him. His failure to forestall his nephew's evil designs on the Vicar's daughters seems inexplicable. Are these the negligences Goldsmith was referring to in his Advertisement to the reader? "There are," he wrote there, "an hundred faults in this Thing, and an hundred things might be said to prove them beauties." Since *The Vicar of Wakefield* is described on the title page as a tale "supposed to be written by HIMSELF," the hundred faults are perhaps merely imperfections in the way the Vicar tells his story. But it seems more probable that Goldsmith was aware of his own lapses as a novelist and was speaking of these. How, then, are they to be explained? Through carelessness and haste in composition? Or were there revisions, with certain incompatible features of an earlier version left unmodified? Since we know so little about the actual composition of *The Vicar*, we are left in the dark. Only it will not do to attribute these errors to an inherent inability on Goldsmith's part to cope with plot and structure. The denouement in the closing chapters of *The Vicar* is, merely as plotting, a masterpiece of controlled ingenuities.

The wider design of the book reveals the most exact proportioning. There are three introductory chapters and three concluding ones, the latter embodying the denouement. This leaves twenty-six chapters in between, and these split evenly into thirteen preceding Olivia's flight and thirteen from that point on to the ultimate turning of the tide. A clear principle governs this halving of the narrative. The two parts are completely different. The first consists of a sequence of comic scenes and episodes showing a certain kinship to the "Chinese Letters," save that the Vicar, replacing Lien Chi Altangi, is less of an objective observer and more of a comic chorus of one—if there can be such a thing—delivering a not always perceptive commentary on the things taking place. The latter part has been developed within the frame-

work of romantic fiction, the Vicar becoming a straight-faced narrator who is himself completely involved in the action and so
no longer in the position of an amused observer.

The memorable episodes present in the first half are all perfectly attuned to the spirit of family life as it runs on tranquilly.
The comic events are minor in nature, all circular in that they
bring in no radical changes. Goldsmith is at his happiest in these
scenes: the Vicar's calling for the coach (Chapter IV); the misadventures which overtake Mrs. Primrose and the daughters when
they set out for church on horseback; Moses dressed up for the
fair, and the way he is duped into laying out all his money for a
gross of green spectacles; how the Vicar is likewise gulled at the
fair; and the wonderful canvas depicting the entire Primrose family, the "historical piece" executed by the traveling limner but
discovered when finished to be too big to be got through any
door of the house. The midnight ball given by the Squire is an
unflawed bit of genre painting. Best of all is the description of
Olivia thumped about during the game of hunt the slipper, all
blowzed in spirits and bawling for "Fair play! Fair play!" It is a
pity that she must assume the part of the wronged woman in the
romance about to get under way.

The second half is all in the mode of the romance. The characters are thrust into the world; their experiences are violent; movement, chase, travel are forced on them. The events which come
to pass are extraordinary in themselves, and equally extraordinary
is the way in which they unfold as though all were parts of a
series which fortune had determined and which only fortune
could conclude. It may be noted that the earlier part of *The Vicar*
does not leave the reader totally unprepared for the sudden departure into romance occurring at mid-point. The daughters, Olivia
and Sophia, both have romantic names, the eldest because her
mother had been reading romances during her pregnancy and
objected to Grissel, the name originally chosen by the Vicar. And
there is the ballad of *Edwin and Angelina*, recited by Mr.
Burchell, which is full of the machinery of romance. Nevertheless
the change that puts an end to the age of innocence and brings in
revolutions and fatigues is made intentionally abrupt and shock-

ing in a dramatic way. The hardships have begun in earnest. Goldsmith proceeds to take full advantage of the loose-textured character of romantic fiction by introducing episodes allowing for distinctly different types and styles of narration. There are travel accounts: George's account of his life as a philosophic vagabond, suggestive of the picaresque tale; and the account of what befalls the Vicar as he goes forth in search of Olivia, a tale suggestive of the traditional story depicting the trials of the Christian wayfarer. The Vicar's conversation about English plays with the driver of the strolling player's cart leads into his long political discussion, vehemently delivered for the benefit of the butler masquerading as master of the house. There are prison scenes—not the first ones in English fiction. There are sermons preached by the Vicar to his fellow prisoners. The attempted abduction of the younger daughter—in eighteenth-century novels the daughters who are seduced or unsuccessfully plotted against are frequently clergymen's daughters—readies us for the melodramatic character of the final chapters. Here the dead come to life, the all-powerful disposer in the person of Sir William Thornhill stands discovered, and justice is served. In the manner of romance it is eminently satisfactory and altogether preposterous. This is comedy at the elementary level—the bestowal of prosperity greater than any enjoyed at the start. There is comedy of a subtler kind in the final glimpse that is given of Mr. Thornhill, the late villain, learning to blow the French horn as he tries to accommodate himself to his ever afterward of happiness without roguery. And there is comedy of still a different nature in the closing measures of the book, which echo the motto on the title-page—*sperate miseri, cavete fælices,* "hope on ye wretched, beware ye happy ones"—and bring the story full circle.

It is, however, by virtue of Goldsmith's execution that *The Vicar* lives. To consider the basic design exclusively is to see the novel as a work made up of largely dissimilar parts. Were it this and nothing more, were there nothing holding the parts together, it would for this reason be as gravely defective a composition as some commentators have assured us that it is. The fact however is that the book does not fall ineptly apart. The shift of pace occurring half way through is sudden, but we are not conscious of any complete change of atmosphere. We are still in familiar territory. The voices have not changed; there are the same intonations. In his Advertisement Goldsmith said this: "A book may be amusing with numerous errors, or it may be very dull without a single absurdity." What we may say is this: there is an imaginative quality present throughout *The Vicar* making it a novel that is remembered in its entirety for its own distinctive quality. The execution has justified what otherwise would be faults in the design and errors of detail.

Any elementary discussion of narrative techniques calls attention, of course, to certain obvious and readily distinguishable modes: the account rendered in the third person, the report of some witness, the story from the mouth of a participant. But in a more specialized sense, much more is involved than the particular point of view from which, at any given moment, the narration is being delivered. Always, multiple points of view are present. Thus, whether some narrator is speaking or whether the account is all in the impersonal manner, the action is bound to excite a variety of responses—it is bound, that is, to be appraised from different points of view. The reader's reactions entail his own point of view. There are separate persons engaged in the story, each of whom has a right to his point of view and sometimes asserts it. And no matter how the story is told or what it comprises, there is always the writer himself who is bringing the whole thing to pass and whose intentions constitute still another dimension—the most important point of view of all, since this is the one which controls all the others.

It is point of view in these comprehensive senses that we first become aware of as we look closely at Goldsmith's manner of execution. The entire novel is in a double sense the Vicar's story: he tells it all, and he is present as the most important character in much of it. But both his telling and his presence change in mode when we get to the second part. Throughout the course of the family comedy which comprises the earlier half the Vicar is both the narrator and a commentator on what is happening. We are aware of him as two people: a person moving as one of the characters in the story, and the person who is giving us his retrospective views about those characters, including the one who is himself. The distance between the Vicar telling and the Vicar told changes from moment to moment. Sometimes it almost disappears, and again it becomes laughably apparent. Sometimes we do not know what to think. Is the Vicar aware of his absurdities, or is he too much a humor character for that? Our doubt tells us much about Goldsmith's execution. The Vicar of the second half, however, is generally much closer to us. We share his bewilderment at the way misfortunes continue to fall, we see him as a man of fortitude and strength. The conclusion, to be sure, is different again, for here the point of view is that of melodrama, creating absurdities of its own as it lets itself go.

Trying to put into simple terms the subtleties resulting from such an interplay of multiple points of view is a discouraging business. The subtleties are so much faster than the analysis! Yet once they are understood, they seem simple enough. Much the same can be said regarding the mechanisms of irony, only here the devices are more obtrusive and consequently more ponderable. It is surprising how thick the ironies lie in both parts of *The Vicar*. Disguises make up one distinct kind of irony. People conceal their real identities, or they mask their true motives. Sir William Thornhill is for a long time merely Mr. Burchell. The two ladies introduced by the Squire; Mr. Jenkinson; the butler who sets the Vicar off on his Tory disquisition; the counterfeit friend who turns out to be a real one; both Edwin and Angelina in the ballad—all these are different from what they seem to be. Errors and deceptions—deceptions other than those of disguise—provide another sort of ironic doubleness, and these figure prominently. The Squire's deceits are a crucial part of the story, and so is Jenkinson's deception of the Squire. The deceptions suffered by Moses and the Vicar at the neighboring fair are part of the circular comedy of family life. There is the erroneous interpretation placed on Mr. Burchell's letter. Olivia is mistakenly believed to be dead. Irony of the kind associated with drama has been built into many of the scenes. The announcement of Olivia's flight from home falls upon the Vicar out of a seemingly cloudless sky. And, in one of the prison scenes, George's appearance in chains shatters suddenly and cruelly the confidence in his happiness just voiced by his father. The denouement, in the concluding chapters, is a complex of ironic disclosures and reversals.

There are, furthermore, certain ironies of language to be taken into account, but these can better be considered in connection with the last aspect of Goldsmith's artistic execution which will be mentioned: that is, the tonal variations and differences of style. Often, particularly in some of the comic episodes in the earlier half, the style is admirably colloquial and racy, as in the account of the game of hunt the slipper in Chapter XI. On occasion the Vicar commands a plain, straightforward style of narration. But he is a humor character after all, at least during the earlier chapters, and he dearly loves a pompous language. He is also sententious. In the second part he frequently, in moments of great stress, falls into the language of melodramatic romance: "Ungrateful wretch, begone, and no longer pollute my dwelling with thy baseness. Begone, and never let me see thee again. . . ." His sermons, on the other hand, are in the single, moving style which, as we know, Goldsmith urged upon Anglican preachers. The ballad and the other verses are strikingly different from one another in tone and style: a romantic ballad, a mock elegy, a masterpiece of sentimental song. A streak of outright parody runs through the denouement: " 'O goodness,' cried the lovely girl, 'how have I been deceived!'," and " 'Good heavens!' cried Miss Wilmot, 'how very near have I been to the brink of ruin!' " Goldsmith's stylistic manipulations add to and support the comic irony. They also serve another purpose. The wide range of what can be called verbal attitudes has a psychological validity. Our lived experience is equally various and has its changes.

6

The Vicar of Wakefield occupies a more or less determinable place in Goldsmith's development as a master of comedy. The comedy of the "Chinese Letters" is scenic in nature. So is the comedy of family life enacted in the idyllic setting of the little farm where the Primroses take shelter from the accidents of the outer world. Primrose is a more complicated figure, technically a more ironical one, than Lien Chi. But *The Vicar* is a fictional work, a novel with a beginning, a middle, and an end, whereas the "Chinese Letters," though it contains a framed story, remains essentially a series of essays. As a novel *The Vicar* encompasses a complete action, which leaves the characters happier at the end of their experience than at the beginning. The trials which must first be undergone seem impelled by an impersonal, brutal force. Comedy recognizes this force, and frequently allows it to govern the lives of the characters—up to a point. The final turn in comic narrative can be merely that butt end of romance, the fatuously happy ending. Again it can be more than that, and in *The Vicar* it is. For the real theme of this seemingly innocent book is discovery about life. We cannot go home and we are recompensed.

VII

Poetry's Persuasive Strain

1

WITH THE APPEARANCE of *The Traveller* late in 1764 Goldsmith all at once came into his own as a poet. The critics were for the most part unhesitating in their praise, and it was Johnson, writing in the *Critical Review* for December, 1764, who set the tone. Here, he declared, was "a production to which, since the death of Pope, it will not be easy to find any thing equal." The public response, though it was a bit slower in coming, was likewise enthusiastic. By August, 1765, four editions had been printed.

Goldsmith seems always to have thought of himself as a poet whether he was writing verse or prose, but to his readers he had hitherto been a prose man. That he was likewise a poet of unmistakable stature, came as a gratifying surprise. As Sir Joshua Reynolds tells us in his prose Portrait, Goldsmith was now "sought after with greediness." *The Deserted Village,* coming six years later, left no room for doubt in the minds of his contemporaries as to his preeminence among the poets of the time. And on the strength of the two long poems and *Retaliation,* the latter published fifteen days after his death, we can still almost agree. Today Johnson the poet seems nearly as great, and Christopher Smart, who never enjoyed much of a reputation among the Georgians, probably greater. But we fully recognize the validity of Goldsmith's poetry, and this despite the fact that *The Traveller* and *The Deserted Village* represent modes of poetic expression which are no longer ours.

It is to be borne in mind, however, that Goldsmith is not solely a poet of three poems. By the end of 1764, when *The Traveller* came out, a number of his poems had already appeared in print—in the *Enquiry*, the *Bee, The Citizen of the World,* and several periodicals—and the three poems in *The Vicar of Wakefield,* of which one is the imperishable song "When lovely woman stoops to folly," had presumably been written by this time. Several verse compositions for the theater—a prologue, epilogues, and a song—appeared before his death. On the other hand, many of his short poems and some of his longer ones were not published during his lifetime. Knowing as we now do the exact extent of his work in the medium of verse, we do not associate him exclusively with *The Traveller, The Deserted Village,* and *Retaliation,* as in the absence of any collected edition his contemporaries naturally did during his lifetime. His scope in poetry was somewhat broader than was then generally recognized. But even so, after taking into account all the verse which has now been established as his, we return to those pieces on which his reputation as a poet once rested. Their superiority to everything else is unquestionable.

2

More than once in the course of his life Goldsmith stated his own position in regard to the writing of poetry. The question in his mind was not whether he could write it—on this score he seems to have had no doubts at all—but whether he should. Could he, in view of what the publishers were paying for verse, afford to do so? Was there a fit audience for poetry—at least for poetry which made no concessions to corrupted taste? His statements are not perfectly consistent, but therein lies their chief interest, for they show us in their changes how keenly aware he was of the problems he faced as a professional man of letters dependent not upon the patronage of men of taste and means but upon booksellers and the public. His earliest remark occurs in a letter of 1759 to his brother Henry: poetry, he wrote,

> is much an easier and more agreeable species of composition than prose, and could a man live by it, it were no unpleasant employment to be a Poet.

The success of the "Chinese Letters" caused him to change his opinion somewhat. According to Lien Chi Altangi (Letter LXXXIV, October, 1760), the few poets at present in England "no longer depend on the Great for subsistence"; their patrons are the public, "and the public collectively considered, is a good and generous master." Four years later, at the time *The Traveller* was appearing, Goldsmith's confidence in the generosity of the public toward its poets had lessened. In the dedicatory letter addressed to his brother and prefixed to the poem he had this to say:

> . . . of all kinds of ambition, what from the refinement of the times, from differing systems of criticism, and from the divisions of party, that which pursues poetical fame, is the wildest. What from the encreased refinement of the times, from the diversity of judgments produced by opposing systems of criticism, and from the more prevalent divisions of opinion influenced by party, the strongest and happiest efforts can expect to please but in a very narrow circle.

He had reverted, possibly through apprehension as to the reception that awaited his poem, to the kind of pessimism concerning cultural matters that had marked the *Enquiry*. Yet he allowed the first sentence of this passage to stand when, after the success of *The Deserted Village,* a sixth authorized edition of *The Traveller* was brought out in 1770. The sentence which followed he properly enough cut out, in deference as it were to thousands of readers, but he was not ready to yield entirely, and he is reported to have remarked to an acquaintance in these later years that he could not afford to court "the draggle-tail muses," for they would let him starve, whereas by other labors he could "make shift to eat, and drink, and have good clothes." It must be said that on a different occasion, when urged to put his views on the decay of the peasantry into a prose pamphlet, he replied that it would not be worth his while to do so, since a good poem would bring him a hundred guineas—according to some reports, *The Deserted Village* had done just that—whereas a pamphlet would bring him nothing. This statement, when taken in context, is not, however, wholly out of line with the preceding one. Only two of his poems had, as a matter of fact, brought him anything to speak of, and it was an assured thing that nobody was going to pay him a hundred guineas for a sociological pamphlet on the peasantry of England.

But if he remained unconvinced as to the practical wisdom of writing verse for the Georgians, he held the clearest views about the nature of poetry. Goldsmith, we should remember, never set out to write criticism of an exact and extended nature in the manner of a Samuel Johnson. His observations on literary art occur mostly by the way, and for that reason they leave no deep impression on the casual reader. More than once we have been assured that as a critic Goldsmith is altogether negligible. This certainly he is not. There is a surprising degree of consistency about his critical dicta, and when his remarks about various aspects of literature are brought together and allowed to reinforce one another they take on a good deal of force. Thus his scattered remarks on drama reveal a very wide range of interest and concern. He touches with assurance on such matters as tragedy, comedy, sentimentalism on the stage, the conduct of modern actor-managers, and the taste of English theatergoers. We begin to see that he has a well-defined theory of the drama, or at least of comic drama. It is casual criticism, but not without importance if only because it underlies the work of the finest dramatist of the period. His poetic criticism, also occasional, is similarly significant. As a poet Goldsmith possessed more than exquisite taste and sensibility. He also had what may be defined as literary intelligence. All poetry, he firmly believed, should be governed by certain principles of artistic form and expression. These principles controlled his own poetry. In his criticism they are enunciated clearly and emphatically, though usually without much elaboration.

Goldsmith's poetic is to be seen as his vigorous response to contemporary critical theories and poetic practices. The eighteenth-century situation in poetry must be kept in mind. Unfortunately the long-standing misconceptions about eighteenth-century verse make it difficult to approach the poets of this period with sympathetic understanding. Were they genuine poets? Some surely were, and others, of whom there were too many, were only versifiers. So much is clear. What is too often missed is the considerable measure of diversity which appears in their work. They differ from one another; their materials and their styles represent distinct lines of tradition or experiment. In other words, the enterprise of poetry had not been drained of all vitality.

It is sometimes assumed that what has come to be called "poetic diction" is present as an invariable factor in all neoclassical verse. Diction of this character is not invariable, and sometimes it is not present at all. Pope, to take a prime example, uses several kinds of this highly artificial, patterned language, but not in all of his poems. When he does use it, he fashions it imaginatively to serve a specific purpose in a particular poem. But often, in his later satires chiefly, the language he employs is that of good conversation, direct and racy. The spirit of neoclassicism—neoclassicism as a matter of historical fact was originally a protest against obscurity and mannered artificialities—always admitted of simplicity. It was the minor poets of the time who turned out the dreary blank-verse epics celebrating Brittania's commercial and industrial enterprises in a language which becomes something other than English through an exaggerated and ritualistic use of poetic diction. Prior, Swift, and Parnell came far closer to the true neoclassical ideal. Their language is simple and effective English, their verse clear and straightforward, free from all stylistic eccentricities. These three served to guide more of the later writers than is usually realized.

The central tradition was, of course, that of the discursive, ethical poem in decasyllabic, five-stress couplets. Here the middle style prevailed—a style lying somewhere between colloquialism and high formality. In language and syntax the ethical poem owed something to the heritage of classical rhetoric, as appears in the figures of speech and more prominently in the arrangement of the grammatical members in certain recognized patterns devised to achieve compression, emphasis, or contract. Such poetry was saved from becoming unduly mannered because it kept well in view its central and avowed purpose: it was, before everything else, statement, and like good prose it was determined to communicate its meaning clearly. This, to place it in its proper aesthetic category, is the poetry of imitation; the thoughtful and effective representation of typical human experience.

The pressure of another style is, however, an important feature. This made its appearance in the mid-decades of the eighteenth century, developing not so much against the central style as alongside and supplementary to it. It has never been given a name, though it might well be called the aesthetic style, for it reflects better than the discursive style characteristic of the ethical poem those preoccupations because of which the Augustan period stands forth as the Age of Taste. Never had there been such widespread interest in architecture, interior decoration, landscape gardening, painting. Only the wealthy could afford Palladian mansions and fashionably landscaped estates, but the substantial middle-class was able to demonstrate in less spectacular ways that it was likewise possessed of sophisticated tastes. Along with all this went an increasing absorption in aesthetics on the part of the intellectuals. Newton and the new principles of optics had made men aware not only of the mechanism of vision but of what the human eye can see in nature and the poet reproduce in terms of the visual imagery of language. Lockian empiricism explained how our sense data are brought together by the imagination, that faculty producing our mental images of outer reality. Addison, in a famous series of essays in the *Spectator*, had undertaken to show how the imagination operates in the aesthetic field and how it informs poetic art. Mark Akenside covered similar ground in his

poem *The Pleasures of Imagination* (1742), and not long afterwards Joseph Warton was announcing in the Advertisement to his
book of *Odes on Various Subjects* (1746) that Invention and
Imagination—descriptive poetry, poetry deriving from the image-
making faculty in the poet—marked the right direction for poetry,
which had too long been restricted to the moralizing style. In
Collins this new aesthetic found its finest practitioner, and Gray
was at times to show its influence:

> Bright-eyed Fancy hovering o'er
> Scatters from her pictured urn
> Thoughts, that breath, and words, that burn.

Another approach to eighteenth-century poetry is by way of the
different types or kinds which were commonly recognized, each
kind carrying with it its distinctive manner. The ode was a well-
established type, favored by the writers of the aesthetic school.
The pastoral had by no means disappeared, and had, in fact, been
the subject of a lively critical debate. Topographical poetry and
the place poem, their prototype Denham's *Cooper's Hill* (1642),
held a special appeal for the eighteenth century, which was falling
more deeply in love than ever with the countryside and natural
scenery. And there was the ballad—the literary ballad, that is, as
written by modern poets like Prior, Gay, David Mallett, and
Shenstone, though the traditional or popular ballads were now
gaining the attention of the literati, and with the appearance of
Bishop Percy's *Reliques of Ancient English Poetry* (1765) began
to assert their own character as something distinct from the literary compositions.

Thanks to his critical comments on poets and poetry we know
precisely where Goldsmith stood in relation to the poetic trends
of his time, and what the principles controlling his own poetry
were. If the poems themselves made all this sufficiently clear his
criticism might be passed over. Frequently, however, the poems
have been taken as examples of literary art which, though not un-
premeditated—it is well known that Goldsmith slaved at the long
poems—is primarily an achievement of intuition. Even Reynolds,
who of all people should have recognized the presence of design

and intellectual control, has stressed Goldsmith's "instinct or intuition" and his "internal feeling of the right."

One of the most revealing of Goldsmith's remarks in the way of poetic criticism takes us back to the very beginning of his literary career. The *Monthly Review* for May, 1757, contained his long and careful critique of Burke's *Enquiry into the Origin of Our Ideas of the Sublime and Beautiful.* Goldsmith's entire review is of much interest, but there is one passage which is particularly relevant to his own poetry. Burke, following the empirical theory of the imagination, had made much of sight and visual imagery. Terror, he had gone on to say, is productive of the sublime, and as Goldsmith summarizes, "to heighten this terror, obscurity . . . seems necessary." This, we note, is clearly anticipatory of the artificial gloom and carefully cultivated terrors which were to mark both the novel and the drama before the close of the century. So far as Goldsmith is concerned, nothing was more alien to the spirit in which he approached literature, and he was quick to take exception to Burke on this point of obscure imagery. He did so in a footnote in which, after insisting that on the contrary it is distinctness of imagery which is productive of the sublime, he went on to suggest that there are other kinds of imagery besides the visual:

> The term *painting*, in poetry, perhaps, implies more than the mere assemblage of such pictures as affect the sight; sounds, tastes, feeling, all conspire to complete a poetical picture: hence this art takes the imagination by every inlet, and while it paints the picture, can give it motion and succession too. What wonder that it should strike us so powerfully! Therefore, not from the confusion or obscurity of the description, but from being able to place the object to be described in a greater variety of views, is poetry superior to all other descriptive arts.

Not only is Goldsmith's poetic not that of the aesthetic school, but it seems to have defined itself by way of explicit rejection of the theory which rested primarily upon images of sight. Goldsmith lived, apparently, through all of his senses. Effective description exhibited the subject clearly, not in half-light or heavy shadow; only in this way he believed could the actual, the multi-threaded texture of experience in which the object was imbedded be suggested.

Goldsmith's indebtedness to Johnson in matters of general critical theory and particular literary judgments has never been determined. All we can say is that in these respects the two were rarely far apart. Before he met Johnson, Goldsmith must have known the *Rambler* essays well, and he certainly found nothing to quarrel with in the literary principles set forth there with such power. What we should like to know is how well developed Goldsmith's critical ideas were when he first arrived in London. Had the rhetoricians and aestheticians of Edinburgh influenced him during his stay there? His dislike of the overly-elaborate in literary art, his desire for simplicity—had these been instilled in him as an undergraduate at Trinity College? Or had Johnson, by way of the *Rambler,* exercised a determinant influence? Johnson's distaste for the manner exhibited by Gray in the various odes is well known. In the *Monthly Review* for September, 1757, Goldsmith discussed the recently published volume entitled *Odes by Mr. Gray,* containing the *Progress of Poesy* and *The Bard. The Bard,* Goldsmith acknowledged, was affecting: the terror and obscurity present in it would give great pleasure "to those who relish this species of composition." But he made it clear that he himself was not pleased. This was poetry addressed to an exclusive audience; Gray's talents, "so capable of giving pleasure to all," had regrettably been exercised in efforts "that, at best, can amuse only the few." Gray should study the people, as Isocrates had urged his protégés to do.

"Let us, instead of writing finely, try to write naturally." This admonition comes at the close of the chapter "Upon Criticism" (Chap. XI) in the *Enquiry.* Earlier in this chapter Goldsmith had listed what he called the errors of present poets: affected obscurity in their odes, the tuneless flow of blank verse, pompous epithets, labored diction. Goldsmith rejected sentimentalism in literature— sentimentalism of the eighteenth-century variety—because it was unnatural, a mere fashion taken up by writers willing to swim with the current. In the same spirit he condemned those poetic styles of his day which seemed to him to depart too far from the central tradition as found in the ethical poem. He condemned such styles because they were overly contrived and because the responses they were designed to evoke from a limited group of sophisticated readers were as factitious in their way as the sentimentalism which was reducing whole audiences to tears at Covent Garden and Drury Lane. It was in the name of genuine emotionalism that he defended the poetry of the traditional line. Here human experience was represented in its many passions, and represented in a manner which insured a universal response. The two indispensable elements were true feeling and a disciplined art. "Passion alone," he wrote in a review of Langhorne's *Death of Adonis* (*Critical Review*, Nov., 1759), "will never produce a finished piece; it may, indeed, furnish the most natural sentiments, if we attend its impulses; but it is art alone that must turn them to use, and join the graces of expression." Though Goldsmith was here translating from the fifth volume of the *Encyclopédie*, his whole position was in accord with this statement. Consider, for instance, the following from *The Citizen of the World* (Letter XL):

> . . . glowing sentiment, striking imagery, concise expression, natural description, and modulated periods are full sufficient entirely to fill up my [i.e., Lien Chi's] idea of [the art of poetry], and make way to every passion.

Much more might be cited from Goldsmith's poetic criticism: "The State of Literature" in *Lloyd's Evening Post* (Jan. 29, 1762); the discussion of earlier eighteenth-century poetry in Vol. II, Letter XVI, of the *History of England in a Series of Letters* (1764), with its praise of Pope, who is said to have carried language to its highest perfection so that "those who have attempted still further to improve it, instead of ornament have only caught finery"; the letter of dedication at the head of *The Traveller;* Mr. Burchell's views on poetry in *The Vicar* (Chap. VIII); the commentary contained in the two volumes of selected poems, *The Beauties of English Poesy* (1767), which he edited, and where, speaking of

Savage's *The Bastard,* he wrote that almost all things "written from the heart, as this certainly was, have some merit"; and his *Life of Parnell* (1770).

In short, though Goldsmith achieved no distinction as a critic, he succeeded, whether this was his object or not, in illuminating through his writings the nature of his own poetic art. It was, we see, a highly regulated art, and one which conformed to the more conservative principles of English neoclassicism. The rhetoric of poetry—its phrasing and syntax, above all, its imagery—was not to be trivialized for the purpose of creating unusual aesthetic effects. The proper strain of poetry awoke the natural emotions common to us all.

3

Goldsmith was not a prolific poet. His entire verse production, as it is now represented in the Friedman edition of the *Collected Works,* consists of no more than thirty-five items, many of which are short compositions, some of them only trifles. There are the pieces—mostly epilogues—written for the theater. The majority of the shorter poems belong to the period of the prose essays and were placed by Goldsmith in the *Enquiry,* the *Bee* and subsequent essays, and *The Citizen of the World. Edwin and Angelina,* printed separately and also given in *The Vicar of Wakefield,* is Goldsmith's only literary ballad. Two of the longer compositions are unhappily distinguished by what to us is their patent inferiority: the oratorio entitled *The Captivity,* and the *Threnodia Augustalis.* A readily recognizable group comprises four of the happiest things he ever wrote. These are all social poems, varying in idiom and pace from the colloquialism of the two verse letters sent to Sir George Baker and Mrs. Bunbury, from the amusing comedies of *The Haunch of Venison, a Poetical Epistle to Lord Clare,* to the memorable wit of *Retaliation.* Finally, in a class by themselves, are the two great poems, *The Traveller* and *The Deserted Village.*

4

The facts concerning the composition of *The Traveller* and the circumstances leading up to its publication in December, 1764, have not all come to light, but many of them are known. The poem was begun in Switzerland and a part of it was at that time sent to his brother Henry—so much Goldsmith's dedicatory letter makes clear. The date would have been 1755. In one of anecdotal articles on Goldsmith in the *European Magazine* (1793), William Cooke supplied further information: the part sent to his brother contained about two hundred lines; Goldsmith did nothing with his manuscript until some years later, when Johnson urged him to consider its publication and "gave him some general hints towards enlarging it."

The ideas and themes present in *The Traveller* as we know it had been maturing in his mind for a long time. The past and present state of European culture and its probable course in the future were subjects which had always fascinated him and which must in some degree have given shape and direction to the lines composed in Switzerland. But the work of the early London years had served to extend and clarify much of his thinking within this broad eighteenth-century field of cultural history and analysis. The influence of contemporary French writers can be seen in the *Enquiry* and certain of the essays which followed. Discussions such as those by Hume in "Of the Rise and Progress of the Arts and Sciences" (in the *Essays*, 1742) and "Of National Characters" (*Essays*, 1748)—according to the latter, each nation has a peculiar set of manners—must also have influenced him. In the short series of essays entitled "A Comparative View of Races and Nations" appearing in the *Royal Magazine* in 1760, Goldsmith, drawing freely upon the theories of Buffon, had written of the different effects which different climates have on the human race, and apropos of the "polite inhabitants of the temperate zone" had described in differentiating terms the Irish, the Scots, and the English. The concluding paragraphs of the last essay of this series

(Sept., 1760) are given over to the English and directly anticipate the famous passage in *The Traveller* (11. 317-334) describing the character of the British, the "lords of human kind."

We do not know exactly when he resumed work on his poem, but there is reason to believe that he did so after his departure from Wine Office Court late in 1762. If this is the case, then the "Chinese Letters," *The Vicar,* and the essay "The Revolution in Low Life" (in *Lloyd's Evening Post,* June, 1762), all of which contain material operating in the poem, are earlier writings. "The Revolution in Low Life" describes the destruction of a village through enclosure by a wealthy London merchant, who intends "to lay the whole out in a seat of pleasure for himself." The Traveller who speaks in the poem has "seen opulence, her grandeur to maintain, Lead stern depopulation in her train," and in the spirit of the essay he deplores the increasing materialism of England, a materialism which "breaks the social tie." And the Traveller's political philosophy, chiefly his defense of royal power as a shield against the depredations of the wealthy class, is that which Parson Primrose had expressed so vehemently to the butler pretending to be the master.

There is the further question of Johnson's influence. At some time or other he gave Goldsmith direct assistance, contributing to the poem—so he told Boswell in 1783—nine lines, eight of them in the closing paragraph. The eight lines give added emphasis to one of the central concepts of the poem, namely, that in every national society characteristic virtues can be seen to balance characteristic vices, leaving a middle region, much the same in all countries, wherein we lead our private lives. Years before, Johnson had expressed something like this in his preface to his translation of *A Voyage to Abyssinia:*

> . . . wherever Human Nature is to be found, there is a mixture of Vice and Virtue, a contest of Passion and Reason. . . . [The] Creator doth not appear Partial in his Distributions, but has balanced in most Countries their peculiar Inconvenience by particular Favours.

What did Johnson mean when he remarked to Boswell, early in the summer of 1763, that Goldsmith had been loose in his principles, but was coming right? Was he perhaps of the opinion that Goldsmith had formerly been too much under the influence of the relativistic sociology of a Voltaire and a Hume, but was now, in the poem in progress, coming round to the Johnsonian view that human experience is substantially the same for all men? We should remember, however, that in the "Chinese Letters" Goldsmith had already made use of the concept of balance and the correlative idea of a governing norm.

In his "Life of Goldsmith" Bishop Percy has told how the poem was composed. "Nothing could exceed the patient and incessant revisal" bestowed on both *The Traveller* and *The Deserted Village;* to save himself the trouble of transcription, Goldsmith

> wrote the lines in his first copy very wide, and would so fill up the intermediate space with reiterated corrections, that scarcely a word of his first effusions was left unaltered.

The Traveller was completed by the autumn of 1764 and sold to Newbery for twenty guineas. Finally, after some confusion at the printer's, and after revision of proof—at which point Johnson may very well have contributed his additional lines—it was published on December 19. The reviewers promptly greeted it with enthusiasm. The public reacted somewhat more slowly, but within a year four editions were called for.

For eighteenth-century readers *The Traveller* combined something surprisingly new and something pleasingly familiar, and this fact doubtless explains much of the enthusiasm with which it was greeted. What was new was the voice, the distinctive manner. On the other hand it was a prospect poem, and this kind or type was well established, going back to *Cooper's Hill* in the previous century. Pope's *Windsor Forest* was partly a prospect or topographical poem. Addison's *Letter from Italy to Lord Halifax,* containing as Goldsmith once remarked, "a strain of political thinking that was, at that time, new in our poetry," was at least geographical. In Denham's poem the scene—the Thames, with London in the distance—is associated with the English social-political scene. In *Windsor Forest* the place serves to bring to mind a number of episodes in England's history, and these lead to the patriotic passages with which the poem ends. Addison's *Letter* opens with a survey of Italy and proceeds to contrast that decaying land with freedom-loving England. *The Traveller* is prospect poetry literally and figuratively; it is a series of verse *characters,* by means of which the different national cultures of the west are compared; it is a patriotic poem, though the patriotism is of a different order from the uncritical nationalism of Addison's *Letter;* it is an estimate of contemporary conditions, condemning much but finding consolation in the thought that nature and reason afford mankind a moral mean between deplorable extremities.

The letter of dedication, though perhaps an afterthought, is to be seen as an integral part of the composition, a kind of overture announcing the motifs which are to appear in the poem. The dedication to a brother, an obscure clergyman, and not to some distinguished patron, was in itself an act of defiance and suggestive of one of the central themes of the poem, i.e., the overwhelming importance of the middle ranks of society. The personal terms of the letter serve to establish the poem itself as direct personal expression: the "I" who is speaking in the verses is, we naturally assume, the writer who addresses his brother, and in consequence the entire piece is interiorized, the prospects and the meditations to which they give rise all taking on a subjective quality. The resentment of the new fashions in poetry—blank verse, Pindaric odes, and partisan satire—betoken a wider resentment extending to aspects of national life. The last paragraph is a direct statement of the theme that gives the poem its structure: there are contrasts between different societies; every society, examined by itself, reveals contrasting features; wherever antithetical extremes exist, there is also a point of natural equilibrium.

The poem is carefully proportioned. The first section of 104 lines—the Traveller far from home; the Alpine prospect; his emotional and intellectual reactions—is balanced by the closing section —England considered—of 122 lines. The mid-section, with its surveys of Italy, Switzerland, France, and Holland, is about twice as long, having 212 lines. It is a discursive poem, presenting a series of ideas developing out of one another in an orderly, if not always strictly logical, fashion. Readers of the time responded eagerly to this kind of poetry. And for them it *was* poetry. It was not necessary, they said, that all the ideas be acceptable so long as the statement given them was effective. It was art enhanced by being intellectualized, and though Goldsmith as we know was fully, passionately committed to the social and political views enunciated in both *The Traveller* and *The Deserted Village,* he was ready to acknowledge that the statements he was making acquired, from the fact that they were made in terms of poetry, an aesthetic value. But he did not sense the intellectual and artistic aspects as a bifurcation. The two were really one, and we can see in the symmetrical form of *The Traveller* an outward, artistic expression of the poem's intellectuality.

But it is in more subtle ways that *The Traveller* achieves a harmony of art and ideational statement. The language of the poem is constantly shifting between a rather formal style and a simple idiom of direct, personal utterance. The former is the language traditional to neoclassical ethic poetry; it generalizes, it makes discreet use of poetic diction and gradus epithets, and the syntax encouraged by the couplet form orders through parallelism, antithesis, and balance the statements being made. It is public speech, rhetorically directed. The contrasting language is singularly plain and limpid, with nothing of the ceremonial about it; it conveys the poet's emotions and invites us to share in them. On the one hand, through intellectual discourse, the apprehension of moral contrasts. On the other, the deep emotional response to the ambiguities in all human experience.

5

In the way that *The Traveller* may be described as a kind of prospect poem, *The Deserted Village* may be said to be a kind of pastoral. It conforms, at least, to that definition of a pastoral which Johnson had given in the *Rambler* (No. 37): "a poem in which any action or passion is represented by its effects upon a country life." Johnson had at the same time suggested that those wishing to arrive at the right conclusion concerning pastoral poetry should look to Virgil, and in a later essay in the *Adventurer* (No. 92) he had singled out Virgil's first and tenth *Eclogues* for praise, pointing out that both had been produced by events that really happened and for this reason illustrate the fact that we respond more strongly to truth than to the most artful fiction. As between these two pastorals his preference, he indicated, lay with the first. Whether these critical observations of Johnson's entered in any way into the conception of *The Deserted Village* no one knows, but it is an interesting fact that Goldsmith's poem, that may be said in Johnsonian language to represent an action by its effects upon a country life, should closely parallel Virgil's first *Ecologue* in two important respects. For one thing it portrays events which are affirmed to be matters of actual fact, of history. Furthermore, these events concern the dispossession of country people from their lands and homes. Virgil's first *Eclogue*, believed to have been written between 42 and 37 B.C., makes such open and direct references to recent occurrences that it is in this respect an occasional poem. After the victory at Phillippi, Octavian had proceeded to reward his veterans with lands confiscated from the original holders. Many people in the countryside near Mantua had in consequence been dispossessed, and according to some accounts Virgil would have lost his own farm had friends not intervened in his behalf. The poem is a dialogue between two shepherds, Meliboeus and Tityrus. The unfortunate Meliboeus is mourning his lot, for he is one of those whose lands have been seized and who must now emigrate to far-off places—to Africa, Scythia, Crete, perhaps Britain. Tityrus, on the other hand, whose farm has been restored to him after having been confiscated, rejoices in his good fortune. "Nos patrias fugimus. . . ." In Dryden's translation, Meliboeus in the opening passage says

> Beneath the shade which beechen boughs diffuse,
> You. Tit'rus, entertain your sylvan Muse:

Round the wide world in banishment we roam,
Fore'd from our pleasing fields and native home. . . .

Later, Meliboeus bids a pathetic farewell to the familiar scene—
to the fence of sallow trees fraught with flowers and to the flowers
fraught with bees, who

with a soft murm'ring strain,
Invite to gentle sleep the lab'ring swain. . . .

The more closely one considers the matter, the likelier it seems
that it was Virgil's pastoral which set in motion the imaginative
impulses leading to *The Deserted Village*. To Goldsmith, the
depopulation of modern villages as a result of enclosure had long
been a matter of deep concern. He had taken up the question in
his essay "The Revolution in Low Life" (1762). He had spent the
summer, he wrote, in a little village "distant about fifty miles
from town"; a rich London merchant had lately purchased all the
land for a pleasure seat, and he planned to remove the villagers.

I was grieved to see a generous virtuous race of men, who should be
considered as the strength and the ornament of their country, torn
from their little habitations, and driven out to meet poverty and
hardship among strangers.

And it could not have been long afterward that he was fashioning for his *Traveller* that prospect of England which discloses, as
counterpoise to Freedom's blessings, the opulence which leads
stern depopulation in her train:

Have we not seen, at pleasure's lowly call,
The smiling long-frequented village fall?
Beheld the duteous son, the sire decay'd,
The modest matron, and the blushing maid,
Forc'd from their homes, a melancholy train,
To traverse climes beyond the western main . . . ?

At some time, early or late, the striking analogy between what
was happening in his own day in England and the occurrences
forming the background of Virgil's poem may very well have
struck Goldsmith.

If he did in fact have the *Eclogue* in mind while designing his own poem, this would explain one detail in *The Deserted Village* which has troubled some commentators. In the letter of dedication to Sir Joshua Reynolds, Goldsmith affirmed that the miseries displayed in the poem were real; he knew them to be so from his own observations in the course of his excursions into the country. Though many of his contemporaries disputed the truth of the events he had observed, no one today denies that the enclosure movement was one of the salient facts of eighteenth-century economic history, justified perhaps by the increasingly pressing need to increase produce from the land—though Goldsmith had in mind enclosure for a different purpose—but working hardship on countless cottagers and villagers. But it is still objected that Goldsmith was in error in his belief that those forced from their homes were emigrating to distant places overseas. What was actually happening was that they were finding their way to the fast-growing urban centers where the new industries were being rapidly developed. Goldsmith was doubtless wrong about emigration—though some there must have been—but could he not have been remembering Meliboeus' plaint,

> . . . we must beg our bread in climes unknown,
> Beneath the scorching or the freezing zone . . . ?

And in still another and more important respect the Virgilian pastoral serves to place *The Deserted Village* in the right light. Is there not, it is frequently asked, more than a touch of primitivism in Goldsmith's description of the happy life enjoyed by the villagers before their eviction? Is this not Rousseauistic pre-romanticism? Crabbe, for one, rejected with contempt Goldsmith's happy swains. But what do we find in Virgil's pastoral? Not, surely, primitivistic creatures living in a Golden Age. Both the characters are farmers. To Virgil and Horace equally, the countryman represented a way of life that was anything but primitive; he cultivated the soil and in his natural and simple pleasures and pursuits added to the strength and virtue of the entire community of citizens. Goldsmith's pastoralism is really Horatian, his villagers husbandmen. They are, perhaps, overly innocent, overly helpless before the wealthy and powerful, but in eighteenth-century England simple people did, we know, sometimes suffer outrageous indignities at the hands of the privileged. *The Deserted Village* is a historical pastoral.

What we know about the composition of *The Deserted Village* comes chiefly from William Cooke's account appearing in the *European Magazine* in 1793. According to Cooke, Goldsmith was by his own confession "four or five years collecting materials in all his country excursions for this poem, and was actually engaged in the construction of it above two years." Cooke went on to describe Goldsmith's method of writing: he first sketched the design in prose, then carefully turned his ideas into verse, amplifying them but taking great pains afterward to revise lest anything added prove to be unconnected with the central design.

The poem was published toward the end of May, 1770. The reviews were laudatory, though exception was taken more than once to Goldsmith's social and economic views. Few deserted villages were to be met with, it was said, and luxury brought as much happiness into the world as it did misery. The public, however, did not evince much concern over such matters. To them *The Deserted Village* was magnificent poetry. Before the end of the year six authorized editions had appeared in England, and by the time Goldsmith died there had been some fourteen, counting piracies and a French translation. Goldsmith had become, in the words of one writer, "the foremost poet of our age."

In *The Traveller* Goldsmith had spoken out loud and clear against the growing materialism of the time, denouncing the upper-middle class—the rich men who ruled the laws which ground the poor—in the manner of some public-spirited citizen outraged to see one class endangering the welfare of the whole nation. Such a manner is by no means entirely absent from *The Deserted Village,* though it is easy to overlook those passages in which the style is that of public speech. As a matter of fact, were we to think of the entire poem as in effect an oration against the injustice of enclosure we should not be far out. The surprising fact is that Goldsmith's historical pastoral is rhetorical through-out. That is, it has been devised with great artfulness to win our attention and thereafter to appeal both to our reason and emotions. It is not a *cri de coeuer* in the way that so many have assumed it to be. In certain passages we have entirely impersonal public speech, and at these points the couplets become pointed, assertive. The dominant tone is, of course, something quite different, for the greater part of the poem is personal in accent and highly emotional. But here the poet's purpose is not to find self-expression but rather, in the manner and according to the principles of rhetoric, to sway his audience. The poet's experience becomes ours; his feelings, his passions are communicated to us; it is we who become personally engaged. Much of *The Deserted Village* is argument by pathos.[1] Comedy has been dismissed. This is more in the nature of denunciatory satire, and we are reminded that Goldsmith's Augustanism brought him closer to Swift than is always apparent. Goldsmith could no more have conceived and executed *A Modest Proposal* than Swift could have composed *The Deserted Village,* yet Goldsmith understood Swift and Swift, surely, would have acclaimed as only he knew how to do Goldsmith's appeal for social justice. These two great Irishmen were at one in their hatred of empirical materialism.

---

[1] In an essay entitled "*The Deserted Village:* Its Logical and Rhetorical Elements," appearing in *College English* (December, 1964), I have studied the poem in considerable detail. Though I do not now undertake an extended analysis, my present observations will be found to reflect some of the things I have previously had to say.

VIII

Comedy for the Theater

1

GOLDSMITH'S FIRST PLAY, *The Good Natur'd Man,* opened at Covent Garden on the evening of January 29, 1768. Everyone directly concerned was apprehensive. The rehearsals had been anything but encouraging. George Colman, the manager, had shown less and less confidence in the play, and the actors had been increasingly unhappy with their parts. To make matters worse, Hugh Kelly's new comedy, *False Delicacy,* which under Garrick's auspices had opened at Drury Lane just six days before, was having an enthusiastic reception and seemed certain to outshine and outdraw anything at Covent Garden. As for Goldsmith, the whole thing had been pretty much of a nightmare from the time, a year or so before this, when, having completed his play, he had first opened negotiations looking toward a stage production. We may assume that, as usual, he needed money badly. Would his comedy survive the ordeal of this first night? If only it received a favorable enough reception to warrant nine performances before the season closed at the end of May, he would, under the usual terms, receive the net earnings for the third, sixth, and ninth "benefit" evenings.

Goldsmith's friends had given him loyal support from the start. Johnson had been particularly solicitous. He heartily approved of the play, and it was he, it would seem, who had finally persuaded Colman to accept it for the 1767–68 season. He had, furthermore, written the prologue, he had gone to see the comedy in rehearsal, and now he and other members of the Club were accompanying the author to the opening performance.

What happened at Covent Garden that evening has often been told. One gathers that the first two acts went off well enough. But the bailiff scene at the opening of Act III, with its low characters and its low speech, nearly proved disastrous. This was not the sort of thing that audiences were accustomed to. This was *not* genteel comedy. Sentimental writing, as William Cooke was to observe in his account of this episode included in his reminiscences of Goldsmith (*European Magazine,* 1793), had then got possession of the stage:

> . . . in vain did the *bailiff scene* mark with true comic discrimination the manners of that tribe, with the elegant and embarassed feelings of the benevolent man. The predominant cry of the prejudiced and illiterate part of the pit was, "it was low—it was d-mn'd *wulgar,* &c." and this *barbarous judgment* had very nearly damned this comedy the very first night. . . .

In the end the play was saved by Shuter's fine performance in the role of Croaker, and with the omission of the controversial scene *The Good Natur'd Man* was acted ten more times that season. Thus Goldsmith had his benefits, which brought in £340. 7s. 6d. *False Delicacy,* with a total of eighteen performances that season, did much better, but Goldsmith's first venture in the theater had not by any means been an ill-starred one.

2

The drama of the latter half of the eighteenth century holds little interest for us today. Of the plays written for and produced on the English stage during the era of Garrick there are a few

which we still enjoy, but the rest strike us as poor things indeed—
the tragedies, insufferable; the comedies, fatuous. We are apt to
forget, however, what a flourishing enterprise this Georgian theater was. Drury Lane and Covent Garden, the two patent houses,
played regularly six nights a week throughout the season, which
extended from the beginning of September to the end of May.
Drury Lane held at this time over 2,000 people, Covent Garden
about 1,800, and though the average weekly attendance at the two
theaters does not seem to have approached the capacity figure,
estimates place it at close to 12,000. Probably at no other time was
the dramatic repertoire so varied and extensive. Shakespearian
drama, Jonsonian humor plays, Restoration comedies and tragedies, and all the many kinds of drama which had arisen since the
beginning of the century—the tragedy of Nicholas Rowe, ballad
opera and musical comedy, farce, and sentimental comedy—were
dutifully performed along with newly composed plays. Many men
and a few women, most of them lacking anything approaching
distinguished talent, were writing for the theater, attracted by the
small fortunes awaiting authors of successful plays. The acting, in
contrast to the playwriting, was generally distinguished, the stag-
ing and the costuming were often elaborate.

As a dramatist Goldsmith became part of an exciting world.
Actors, managers, and even playwrights were much in the public
eye, and Goldsmith found himself more of a public personality
than ever before. All sorts of people interested themselves in the
circumstances surrounding *The Good Natur'd Man* and *She
Stoops to Conquer*. As a result we have inherited a plethora of
information on this score, but it has in fact served to obscure the
really important aspects of Goldsmith's work as a playwright. His
dramatic intelligence, if we may use such a term, is much keener
and his dramatic skill greater than the traditional accounts suggest. He proved to be a born dramatist, finding late in his career
the medium better suited than any other to his gift for comic and
satiric writing. In what ways are his comedies typical of the period, in what ways do they break through the accepted formulas?
And how do they stand in relation to his own earlier essays and

fiction? In what direction were his comic sense and his comic art developing?

Goldsmith had always been interested in the theater, and had been writing about it off and on since his earliest Grub Street days. His comments are to be found in the *Monthly Review,* the *Enquiry,* the *Critical Review,* certain of the essays—particularly those in *The Citizen of the World*—in *The Vicar,* and the *History of England, In A Series of Letters.* The chapter in the *Enquiry* devoted to the stage (Chap. XII) is important. Equally important and at the same time most amusing are Lien Chi's descriptions of happenings in the London playhouse (e.g., Letters XXI, LXXIX, LXXXV, and XCVII in the *Citizen*). But it is the critique which appeared in the *Westminster Magazine* in January, 1773, just before the production of *She Stoops to Conquer*—the "Essay on the Theatre; or, a Comparison between Laughing and Sentimental Comedy"—which is best known. Those who are inclined to think of Goldsmith as a person whose geniality verged on the flaccid are overlooking his dramatic criticism. The managers, the actors, the theatrical traditions of the period, the plays themselves, and the public's taste all come in for caustic commentary. Drama, Goldsmith believed, was vitally important to the life of any civilized society, and the London theater was the most magnificent in Europe and the English people in general fonder of theatrical entertainment. But what with the arrogance of the actor-managers and the public's lack of sound taste, the English stage was scarcely in a healthy condition. According to Lien Chi (the *Citizen,* Letter LXXIX), the great secret of composing a successful tragedy seemed to be

> a perfect acquaintance with theatrical *ah's* and *oh's,* a certain number of these interspersed with *gods! tortures, racks,* and *damnation,* shall distort every actor almost into convulsions, and draw tears from every spectator; a proper use of these will infallibly fill the whole house with applause.

Comedy, however, was Goldsmith's chief concern, and in his "Essay on the Theatre" he came out roundly in favor of the traditional concept of what constitutes comedy, dismissing the *comédie larmoyante,* then so popular, in caustic terms. True comedy, he insisted, gives us a natural portait of human folly and frailty. It excites ridicule, not pity; laughter, not tears. If he had Kelly's *False Delicacy* in mind as he was writing his "Essay," he committed himself to nothing which was not perfectly in line with all of his previous critical commentary.

Both of Goldsmith's plays are at one and the same time traditional and original. He was not one to devise new forms. He used those already established—the single essay, the essay serial, the prose romance—showing his originality rather in the unusual things he succeeded in doing with the formal conventions. In superficial respects *The Good Natur'd Man* and *She Stoops to Conquer* are standard Georgian comedies, fashioned on the same last that was serving countless contemporary playwrights. With the departure of Henry Fielding from the theater and the passage of the Licensing Act of 1737, English comedy had entered upon what has been described as a long Gothic night. The darkness lasted until about 1760, when the comic theater came to life again. From that time down through the years of Sheridan's triumphs in the 1770s, two or three new comic pieces arrived annually on the stage. The writers, aside from Goldsmith and Sheridan, are no longer vivid in our memory: George Colman, the elder; Arthur Murphy; Hugh Kelly; Whitehead; Bickerstaffe; Sheridan's mother, Mrs. Frances Sheridan; Mrs. Elizabeth Griffith; Richard Cumberland. Something in the nature of a standard plot had established itself in their comedies. Two lovers, often two pairs of lovers, find themselves at the outset confronted by various obstacles to marriage. Immediately ensuing events only serve to prolong their plight. In the end, however and inevitably, fortune consents to smile on them, the obstacles vanish, and the closing scene finds them about to be happily united, prepared to live blissfully forever. It is all very cheerful and encouraging—a drama of kindness, someone has recently called it, contrasting it with our present-day drama of cruelty.

Another characteristic feature of these plays is the presence of the humorous character—more properly, the "humor" character—

no longer a figure of ridicule, no longer the object of mordant satire; someone, rather, of marked eccentricities, to be sure, but loveable through and through. The eighteenth century had discovered that Falstaff was just such a person; and the fiction of the time gave birth to Parson Adam, Mat Bramble, and Uncle Toby, not to mention Goldsmith's Man in Black and Parson Primrose.

Also distinctive is the air of naturalism. The plots were formulary, the humorous characters a fixture, yet despite such facts this was a drama of pronounced naturalism. The distance between the figures on stage and the everyday events in the lives of the spectators had all but disappeared. There was complete and willing identification with the characters and action of the drama. The good fortune that regularly befell hero and heroine at the end of the fifth act might just as well visit any of those in pit, box, or gallery.

The question is sometimes debated whether there was in fact such a thing as eighteenth-century sentimental comedy. The view most often found in the dramatic histories of this period is that something that might just as well be called sentimental comedy appeared toward the beginning of the century in the plays of Cibber and Steele. This new kind of comedy, or, if you please, an old kind with greater emphasis on certain themes and dramatic situations, was not strongly in evidence during the middle decades, though it did have a pronounced effect on French drama of these years; but in the 1760s and '70s it became a factor of great importance. In considering the English plays of this latter period we should be careful not to confuse the general air of geniality, which all of them create, with the true-blue sentimentalism found in certain ones. The sentimental comedy which Goldsmith was deriding in his "Essay on the Theatre" is easily recognized; it is highly sententious; it preaches at every opportunity; it harps on the innate nobility of human nature, a nobility to be awakened by any sufficiently emotional experience; it equates virtue with glowing sentiment, and presents as characters to be admired genteel men and women who are veritable machines of delicate, benevolent feeling. By no means all Georgian comedies, however, embody this kind of sentimentalism. Some, like *The Clandestine Marriage* by Garrick and Colman, are quite free from anything of the sort. Audiences of the period, like the dramatic critics, were clearly of two minds about the sentimental view of life and the kind of comedy in which this view was being expressed, and the dramatists were free to move in different directions. Some openly satirized sentimentalism. Others, in anticipation of Jane Austen, placed sensibility in contrast with sense. Still others, determined to have it both ways, admitted unadulterated sentimentalism into one scene only to deride it ironically or in an openly satirical manner in the next. The kind of willful ambiguity represented by the latter practice is well illustrated in *False Delicacy,* the play by Hugh Kelly which ran in direct competition with *The Good Natur'd Man.*

In the light of the characteristic comedy which developed in the 1760s, the extent of Goldsmith's conformity becomes clear. Sentimentalism is under attack in both of his plays, though in *The Good Natur'd Man,* as we shall see, a highly sophisticated form of irony is employed, for at least part of the time the satire is delivered in terms of characters, situations, and spoken sentiments which are for all the world like those of the sentimental drama which is being ridiculed. The two comedies turn on quite traditional plots, involving, in each case, two pairs of lovers who find happiness when the complications keeping them apart are at length resolved. There are humorous characters in both, and both are distinguished by a naturalism of atmosphere and voice which can easily be mistaken for the typical naturalism which then prevailed on the comic stage. It is to be observed, however, that in one very important respect Goldsmith kept clear of standard practice: he never allowed the comic distance between characters and audience to disappear.

But despite this element of conformity Goldsmith's playwriting was the culminating phase of his development as a comic writer. The anti-benevolence theme, which underlies all of *The Good Natur'd Man,* had been present in his mind from the first, as the early essays show. There had been humorous characters of rare appeal in *The Citizen of the World* and the *Vicar*. He had used the romantic plot, with its delightful absurdities, more than once. His comic vision and his ironic technique had, however, been shifting over the years. Scenic comedy, based upon ironic differences in points of view, had begun in *The Citizen of the World* to evolve into those ironies of opinion which make us aware of the natural forces acting as mediating influences. In *The Vicar*, comedy of the domestic scene and the portrait of the Vicar himself with his amusing shortcomings and his essential nobility had led, by way of the ambiguities of the romantic plot, to the voyage theme—our passage from home into the world, our ultimate enlightenment, and the things then recognized. In taking up dramatic writing Goldsmith had no intention of merely manipulating the shallow formulas of the then-popular comedy. Playwriting was a challenge to one who, though now a seasoned literary workman, had never before used the dramatic form. He was forced to shift his stance, to find new terms for the comic interpretation of experience. Fortunately, drama was by its very nature a medium which enabled him to organize his creative energies more tellingly than had any of the forms of writing he had been using in the past. New devices, new ironies, new insights —these are the important things about *The Good Natur'd Man* and *She Stoops to Conquer*. Here Georgian comedy acquired a depth to be found nowhere else, save—some might insist—in the best of Sheridan.

3

The opening night of *The Good Natur'd Man*—January 29, 1768 —has already been described. There are certain further details concerning this first play to be noted. It was written apparently in 1766 or early 1767, and from the start Goldsmith probably hoped to see it produced at Drury Lane. He had, it is true, attacked Garrick in the *Enquiry,* but since then he and the famous actor-manager, both friends of Johnson, Reynolds, and others of that

company, had often rubbed shoulders. Through the good offices
of Reynolds the two were brought together and Goldsmith submitted his play. Garrick, had he only known it, was being given
the opportunity to crown his entire career as manager by associating himself in the theater with the man one day to be recognized as the foremost dramatist of the period. It would be unfair
to suggest that Garrick dealt harshly with the play out of spite.
He was too much the professional for that. He temporized for
weeks, raising objections to the script and suggesting extensive
revisions, but undoubtedly he did so because of what he regarded
as serious dramaturgic flaws in Goldsmith's work. That summer—
July, 1667—Goldsmith finally turned to Colman, now in charge at
Covent Garden. Colman promptly accepted the play for production.

And Garrick? It became known that during the coming season
he was planning to put on a new comedy by Hugh Kelly entitled
False Delicacy. Garrick, a man of robust good sense, had frequently gibed at sentimental comedy, though as a shrewd theatrical businessman he never went so far as to exclude it from
Drury Lane. As he studied the manuscript of *The Good Natur'd
Man* he must have been struck by Goldsmith's clever satiric
strategy, which was to deliver his ridicule of sentimental comedy
through a play which was so constructed as to be in itself partly
sentimental. When Goldsmith refused to consider recasting portions of his play and then withdrew the manuscript, what more
natural than that Garrick should suggest to a more compliant
dramatist like Kelly the possibility of fashioning an amusing comedy along the lines of Goldsmith's, unactable as the latter appeared to be in its present state? To do this would not have been
underhanded in the least—not as Garrick saw the circumstances.
In his *Life of Goldsmith* Sir James Prior stated that it had been
rumoured that during the time Goldsmith's manuscript was in
the hands of Garrick or the latter's friends, Kelly had been able
to see it and had taken hints from it for his own *False Delicacy*.
"For this charge," added Prior, "there seems no foundation. . . ."
But Prior appears not to have grasped what may very well have

been the basis of such a contemporary rumor. Both *False Delicacy* and other later plays of Kelly's are sentimental and anti-sentimental by turns. Whether the formula adopted came to him from Goldsmith by way of Garrick we shall probably never know. Not that it matters much, for *False Delicacy* has little of Goldsmith's irony and none of his genuine contempt for sentimentalism.

When *The Good Natur'd Man* went into rehearsal, things began to go badly, as we have seen. And six days before it opened, Garrick presented *False Delicacy* (January 23). The public response was enthusiastic, and Kelly's play had already been performed six nights when the Goldsmith comedy opened on January 29. *The Good Natur'd Man* was not the notable success that *False Delicacy* proved to be, but on the other hand it was by no means a failure. Kelly's play received eighteen performances that season, Goldsmith's eleven. Goldsmith must have found some satisfaction in the fact that events had not fully sustained Garrick's evaluation of *The Good Natur'd Man,* but his handsome profit from the play must have been more substantial solace. Nevertheless, he had some cause to feel that fate, Kelly, and David Garrick had all united in conspiring against him. He is said to have been so envious of Kelly's success that he went about abusing *False Delicacy* in the roundest terms, declaring that so long as blockheads ruled the stage he would not write another play. There is doubtless some substance to this and other stories concerning his ungenerous attitude, but they leave out of account his legitimate reasons, some personal and others artistic, for regarding Kelly's so-called comedy with distinct coldness.

Goldsmith's friends seem to have thought highly of his play. Burke considered it to be one of the best comedies of the time, and Johnson was of the opinion (*Life,* spring of 1768) that "it was the best comedy that had appeared since 'The Provoked Husband,' " which went back to 1728. The critical comments of 1768 were on the whole mixed. Some of the reviews which appeared found more to praise than to censure. Several brought *The Good Natur'd Man* into direct comparison with *False Delicacy,* as witness this article in the *St. James's Chronicle* (January 30–February 2):

If the Drury-Lane Comedy is more refined, correct, and sentimental, the Covent-Garden Performance is more bold, more comick, and more characteristick. . . .

In January the *London Magazine* contained a "Short Account" of *False Delicacy* filled with glowing praise and pronouncing the sentiments of the play to be "such as will eminently distinguish the writer as long as virtue and morality are held respectable. . . ." The following month the same periodical took *The Good Natur'd Man* under review, the critique appearing this time in the section called "The British Theatre," which ran for a number of years beginning in 1767 and was at the start—and until a *volte-face* was executed in 1772—a vehement advocate of all that was moral, benevolent, and touching in comic drama. Goldsmith's play, the reader was assured, "no way answered the very warm expectations" which were entertained of it. The author's execution revealed, alas, his partiality for Molière and other dramatists of the previous century; humor and character are permissible when they increase our amusement and add to our instruction, but unless our passions are affected there can be no instruction.

A wide diversity of opinion marks the criticism which has appeared since the eighteenth century. Many commentators have found *The Good Natur'd Man* a badly constructed play without any dramatically controlling center, its only significance the fact that the author of *She Stoops to Conquer* wrote it. A few have pronounced it admirable despite faulty stagecraft. A whole line of critics have said that despite Goldsmith's declared views it must really be considered a sentimental comedy. Only in the course of the last thirty years or so has there emerged an entirely different interpretation of the play. Today, few who read it against its full Georgian background are likely to miss its satiric intent and its characteristic Goldsmithian irony. It is not a great play—dramatically it is much too ingenious, and the plot is overly complicated—but it is true comedy and a fitting prelude to *She Stoops to Conquer*.

There is reason to believe that some of those who saw *The Good Natur'd Man* when it was being performed at Covent

Garden missed the playwright's real interest. If they did so it is not entirely surprising. The title seemed to announce a sentimental play of the customary kind, and nothing in Johnson's rather heavy prologue served to prepare an audience for what was in store. The central plot, furthermore, dealt with the transgressions of the hero, his repentance, and his last-act reformation. True, his transgressions took the form of imprudent generosity, and his reformation lay in his renouncing ill-considered acts of benevolence, but was it not after all a touching drama of reformation? It was also generously sprinkled with admirable sentiments. Sir William Honeywood, the comic father figure, controls the lives of everyone about him with a supernal confidence in his own powers and wisdom, a confidence which is reflected in his everlasting sententiousness. And his nephew—young Honeywood, the hero of the story—shares something of his uncle's habit of speaking in pompous apothegms. The two of them provide the sentimental antiphony which brings the play to a conclusion:

> *Sir. Will.* Henceforth, nephew, learn to respect yourself. He who seeks only for applause from without, has all his happiness in another's keeping.
> *Honeyw.* Yes, Sir, I now too plainly perceive my errors. My vanity, in attempting to please all, by fearing to offend any. My meanness in approving folly, lest fools should disapprove. Henceforth, therefore, it shall be my study to reserve my pity for real distress; my friendship for true merit, and my love for her, who first taught me what it is to be happy.

If this did not wring sympathetic tears from a good-natured audience what would?

The play opens skillfully enough. Sir William Honeywood is talking to Jarvis, the faithful family servant. In Sir William Honeywood anyone familiar with *The Vicar of Wakefield* will quickly recognize Sir William Thornhill, now grown comically sententious: both have nephews in need of correction, possess apparently unlimited power over other's lives, and find great satisfaction in disclosing their true identities, hidden for a time, at moments of acute drama. Sir William Honeywood is expressing his disapproval of his nephew's hitherto incorrigible benevolence. Young Honeywood loves all the world and this is his fault—every sharper and coxcomb finds an easy entrance to his heart. But Sir William has a plan to reclaim the errant one. His nephew has just gone security for a fellow whose face he scarcely knew. The man has now absconded, and Sir William has taken up the security. "Now," Sir William announces,

> my intention is to involve [my nephew] in fictitious distress, before he has plunged himself into real calamity. To arrest him for that very debt, to clap an officer with him, and then let him see which of his friends will come to his relief.

The Good Natur'd Man is among other things a comedy of deceptions and errors, and Sir William's scheme is the first and principal deception. The rest of Act I introduces us to a pair of youthful lovers and informs us of their difficulties. Honeywood loves Miss Richland, but so do a great many others, and Honeywood is too generous to stand in anybody else's way. As for Leontine and Olivia, their situation is indeed a complicated one, for Leontine has been sent to France to bring his sister home and has brought Olivia back instead, who until a marriage can be effected must pass as the sister. Leontine's parents, Mr. and Mrs. Croaker, now make their appearance, he "a fretful poor soul that has a new distress for every hour in the four and twenty," she his exact opposite, "all laugh and no joke."

The second act completes the exposition and adds still more complications to the plot. Miss Richland learns about Olivia and Leontine, and further that Leontine, in order to hold off his father, who has been counting on a marriage between Leontine and Miss Richland, will pretend to make the latter serious proposals since he is sure that she is in love with Honeywood and will reject all other suitors. Miss Richland for her part intends, she says, to receive Leontine's proposal, thus throwing the refusal upon him. The last of the deceivers is now brought on—Lofty, who like his predecessor Beau Tibbs pretends to be on intimate terms with the great and powerful.

The ensuing complications keep the play moving at a fast pace. The funniest scene of all, which will bear comparison with the afternoon-tea scene in Shaw's *Pygmalion,* comes at the beginning of Act III. Honeywood is still in his own home but in the custody of a bailiff and his assistant, clapped on him, if the truth were known, by Sir William. Timothy Twitch is a most humane bailiff, one who by his own confession loves humanity. His assistant, little Flanigan, has a wife, four children, and a good face, but is a little seedy. When Miss Richland is announced—she has learned what has happened and has come to offer help—young Honeywood persuades Messrs. Twitch and Flanigan to pose as naval officers and Flanigan is hurriedly put into a respectable suit of blue and gold. With Miss Richland present there is conversation, in the course of which the two gentlemen, who occasionally serve in the Fleet, fall into what might be called the new small talk peculiar to the navy. "Damn the French, the parle vous, and all that belongs to them." "Give Monseers but a taste, and I'll be damn'd, but they come in for a bellyful." Miss Richland finds it very extraordinary.

There are ironies everywhere in the play. Sometimes, when a pretender like Lofty is to be exposed, or when Sir William is about to astonish everyone by revealing his identity, the audience is fully prepared for what is to happen. Again, the action takes a course which comes as a surprise to everyone. Low comedy relies heavily on ironies of circumstances—on errors, on frustrating contretemps, on disguises and deceptions. Everything seems to be conspiring against the dramatis personae, and vital energies are blocked up at all points, until benign destiny overrules chance and all suddenly comes right. But there are deeper—or higher—ironies which become apparent as soon as comedy, turning serious, lays aside its purely antic manner. There are discoveries in store for us as we live our normal lives with one another and with ourselves. So, in the play, Honeywood finally learns the truth about himself, which is that if he does indeed love the heroine he must believe so deeply and act on this clarified belief. And he learns what is the same thing in a different form: benevolence, when it is no more than a form of fashionable behavior, is ridiculous and sometimes harmful. Lofty is made to feel that he no longer desires to engage in a life of pretense. Crocker's "humor"—his gleeful predictions of disaster—vanishes in the presence of a crisis in his own family. True enough, this irony of self-discovery does not emerge with full force from the intricacies of the plot, but it is present for all that, as it had been in a different form in the *Vicar* and as it was to be in *She Stoops to Conquer.*

4

She Stoops to Conquer was the last signal triumph which Goldsmith lived to enjoy. It was an instant success. On the opening night—March 15, 1773—the audience, we are told, was kept in a continual roar, and when the play appeared in print five days later it had a spectacular sale. News of this latest theatrical event quickly spread beyond London. Boswell, in Edinburgh, learned all the facts, and just before he set out on still another trip to London he wrote Goldsmith an exuberantly congratulatory letter (March 29), noting with pride that his wife had given birth to a daughter on the very evening that *She Stoops to Conquer* had opened. Perhaps nothing gives a better sense of the excitement of the moment as shared by Goldsmith and his friends than does Boswell's account (in his "Journal" under April 7) [1] of the morning visit he paid at Brick Court a few days after reaching London. Goldsmith was still in bed, but hearing who had called he roared out "Boswell!" "I ran to him," wrote Boswell. "We had a cordial embrace. I sat upon the side of his bed and we talked of the success of his new comedy. . . ."

But if the play, once on the boards, brought glory to its author, it had entailed even more trials and tribulations than *The Good Natur'd Man,* and it was with some reason that Goldsmith wrote to one of his friends the day following the triumphant first night

[1] *Boswell for the Defence: 1769–1774* (*The Yale Editions of . . . Boswell,* *1959*).

that he had at last done with his stage adventures, having certainly lost his ease and comfort while his comedy was "in agitation." It is most unlikely, however, that he would have stuck to any such resolution, and at the close of the year we find him writing to Garrick and mentioning a new comedy, to be done in a summer or two, which he fancied would make a fine thing. And who can doubt that it would have? *The Good Natur'd Man* had taught him most of the things he needed to learn about dramatic craftsmanship. In his second comedy he was able to maneuver with ease and assurance, and this freedom gave him greater comic scope. *She Stoops to Conquer* is a triumph of effective dramatic art. Its construction, its voice are flawless, and underneath the almost farcial exterior there is deep, quiet wisdom. His unexpected death only a year later put a lamentably untimely end to his already brilliant career as a playwright. Had he lived somewhat longer it is reasonable to suppose that he would have lifted Georgian comedy to a still higher level, comparable perhaps to what is attained in the novels of Jane Austin.

The play had been finished and no doubt mostly written during the summer of 1771 while Goldsmith was living in the country. Three summers previously he and a friend had taken a cottage near Edgeware, some eight miles from London, and Goldsmith had found what he called his "Shoemaker's Paradise" much to his liking. Now he had settled down for the summer with a Farmer Selby at a farmhouse near The Hyde, on the Edgeware Road. Early in September he was writing from Brick Court, in the Temple, to Bennet Langton, a fellow-member of the Club. His letter, containing the earliest reference we have to a new play, draws an amusing picture which might be entitled "The Comic Writer at Work":

> . . . I have been almost wholly in the country at a farmer's house quite along trying to write a Comedy. It is now finished but when or how it will be acted, or whether it will be acted at all are questions I cannot resolve. . . . I have been trying these three months to do something to make people laugh. There have I been strolling about the hedges studying jests with a most tragical countenance. . . .

It was only natural that Goldsmith, in hopes of an early production of a new comedy, should again turn to Colman. The latter, however, refused for a long time to commit himself. We have the letter—conjecturally dated January, 1773—which Goldsmith wrote Colman in desperation. He begged the manager to relieve him from the long state of suspense; he agreed to make any changes Colman desired, and to make them without argument:

> I have as you know a large sum of money to make up shortly; by accepting my play I can readily satisfy my Creditor that way, at any rate I must look about to some certainty to be prepared. For God sake take the play and let us make the best of it. . . .

Whether before or after writing this to Colman he went so far as to submit his manuscript to Garrick, but the day after he did so he learned that a decision had been reached to produce the play at Covent Garden. Johnson is quoted by Boswell (*Life,* April 25, 1778) as saying that Colman "was prevailed on at last by much solicitation, nay, a kind of force, to bring it on," and Johnson is believed to have been the one who applied the force. Previously, in everything concerning *The Good Natur'd Man,* Johnson had given his friend most generous aid and encouragement, and he did so again in the case of *She Stoops to Conquer.* In the course of a letter of February 24, 1773, to Boswell he remarked that Goldsmith's new comedy was to be produced that spring, adding that no name had been yet given it. A few days later (March 4) he informed another correspondent that the play was in rehearsal.

By this time the original text had undoubtedly undergone many revisions, and as a matter of fact Goldsmith continued to make changes right up to the opening performance and in one instance afterward. There were other things as well to worry about. Actors and actresses proved difficult, some of them refusing to accept their assigned parts. Colman was persistently gloomy about the play's chances of success. A rumor was put about that the piece was exceedingly low. The rehearsals continued, however, and were attended by a number of Goldsmith's friends, including Johnson, Sir Joshua Reynolds and his sister, Mrs. Horneck and her two daughters, and the dramatist Arthur Murphy. But there was further trouble in store. Garrick, perhaps to make amends for what he had left undone a few years earlier, furnished the prologue, but a suitable epilogue had not yet come to hand. One written by Goldsmith's friend Joseph Cradock could not, for some reason, be used. Arthur Murphy submitted an outline for one to be sung by the actress playing the part of Constance Neville, but at this Kate Hardcastle—otherwise Mrs. Bulkely—insisted that she would throw up her part unless permitted to speak the epilogue. Goldsmith then had the bright idea of making a quarreling epilogue in which the two actresses could debate which would speak the closing piece, but it was now Constance Neville's turn to balk. Goldsmith set to work again, but what he wrote this time was declared by Colman too bad to be spoken. The epilogue he finally managed to produce—the one which was actually spoken—was in his words "a very mawkish thing."

Having taken care of the epilogue, the harried author had only one more problem on his hands. Before the play had gone into rehearsal Johnson had mentioned to Boswell that it had not yet been given a name. When the playbills appeared two days before the opening night they announced "a New Comedy call'd The Mistakes of a Night." Only at the last minute did someone, probably Goldsmith, find the title by which the play has ever since been known. In the epilogue which Colman had thought too bad to be spoken Goldsmith had imagined what those members of the audience who were sworn friends of sentimentalism were saying of the author of the unendurably low play they had just witnessed:

> No high-life, no sentiment, the creature
> Still stoops among the low to copy Nature.

In a moment of inspiration this had been turned into *She Stoops to Conquer,* but Goldsmith's characterization of himself as a writer who "stoops among the low to copy Nature" is in its way definitive too.

The night of the opening presentation finally arrived. It was a memorable event, and several of Goldsmith's friends who were with him on this occasion have left us their recollections of it. According to Reynolds, as reported by his protégé and biographer, James Northcote, Sir Joshua and a large party of friends planned to be present in order to support the play if necessary. They and Goldsmith first dined at the Shakespeare tavern, Johnson taking the head of the table. Goldsmith was in great anxiety, and "his mouth became so parched and dry, from the agitation of his mind, that he was unable to swallow a single mouthful." But contrary to expectation, the play was received with great applause. In his *Memoirs* the dramatist Richard Cumberland told at some length how he and other supporters of Goldsmith placed themselves at strategic points in the theater and during the performance acted as a claque, leading the laughter. Most accounts, however, would indicate that no such stratagem was required, and it seems extremely doubtful whether Cumberland was responsible in any way for the lusty response on the opening night. The story recorded by William Cooke in his sketch of Goldsmith (*European Magazine*, 1793) is easier to accept. While the performance was in progress Goldsmith was found sauntering in the Mall but was persuaded to go to the theater where his presence might prove helpful:

> He entered the stage door just in the middle of the 5th Act, when there was a hiss at the improbability of Mrs. Hardcastle supposing herself forty miles off, though on her own grounds, and near the home. "What's that?" says the Doctor, terrified at the sound. "Psha! Doctor," says Colman, who was standing by the side of the scene, "don't be fearful of *squibs,* when we have been sitting almost these two hours upon a barrel of gunpowder."

If by the fifth Act Colman was still in doubt concerning the public's reaction, no one else was. As Goldsmith wrote to Cradock shortly afterward, "The Play has met with a success much beyond your expectations or mine." There were twelve performances before the end of May, five at the Haymarket during the summer, and eleven at Covent Garden in the course of the

1773–74 season. For his three benefit nights—March 18, April 12 and 29, 1773—Goldsmith received in all £502. 18s. 6d.

With some exceptions the reviews of 1773 were highly commendatory. The *London Magazine,* which had by this time abandoned its earlier position and had become a staunch advocate of laughing comedy, found the play faulted in several respect but applauded it nonetheless as a stroke aimed at "that monster Sentimental Comedy." The *Monthly Review,* however, refused to give its approval to a play such as Goldsmith's, declaring that "what is called *Sentimental Comedy*" was "better suited to the principles and manners of the age." Individual judgments varied. Johnson's approval was unqualified: "I know of no comedy for many years that has so much exhilarated an audience, that has answered so much the great end of comedy—making an audience merry" (*Life,* April 29, 1773). Horace Walpole was forced to admit that the situation made one laugh, but found the play as a whole unendurable. "But what disgusts me most," he wrote to William Mason (March 27, 1773),

> is, that though the characters are very low, and aim at low humour, not one of them says a sentence that is natural or makes any character at all. It is set up in opposition to sentimental comedy, and is as bad as the worst of them. . . .

Fanny Burney, then about twenty and not yet the author of *Evelina,* went to see it and thought it "very laughable and comic" even though she now considered all diversions insipid "except the opera."

Though the full comic import of *She Stoops to Conquer* does not lie entirely at the surface, there is nothing in it, as there is in *The Good Natur'd Man,* to perplex or mislead an audience. One cannot properly enjoy the earlier play unless one sees through it and grasps the irony which is governing much of it. In this sense there is nothing in *She Stoops to Conquer* to be seen through. If it means more than we are immediately aware of, its fuller meanings are not contradictory to the readily apparent ones but are rather subtilizations of the obvious. The farcical elements of the play—all the bustle, the deceptions, the errors, the successive *contretemps*—are the outward evidences of that vital energy which great comedy seeks to release in us. The amusing ironies which arise when the characters act in ignorance of some or all of the immediate circumstances and are suddenly enlightened—these betoken the ironies which we ourselves experience in the course of discovering who and what we truly are.

Again Goldsmith was content to use the going formulas, and as a result *She Stoops to Conquer* is completely Georgian. There is no verbal wit here; the conversation is easy and natural, or seems to be.[2] Tone and setting are natural. The plot is a typical one, involving the affairs of two youthful couples. There are several humor characters: Mr. and Mrs. Hardcastle, Young Marlow, and perhaps Tony Lumpkin. Sentimentalism is effectively but not too obtrusively ridiculed in the alehouse scene, in the "sober sentimental interview" between Kate and Young Marlow in the second act, and best of all in those scenes which find Marlow, as a result of his as-yet split personality, suffering genteel embarrassment in the presence of women who are ladies and then displaying self-assured aggressiveness toward those who are only barmaids. The action, turning largely on deceptions and errors, was complicated enough to satisfy theatergoers of the period, who were used to this sort of thing. Mrs. Hardcastle practices several deceits, Constance Neville must pretend affection for Tony Lumpkin, and Hastings is forced to conceal the fact that he is Constance's suitor. The two central deceptions, which together serve as the backbone of the comedy, are Tony's misrepresentation of the Hardcastle house as an inn, and Kate's unmasked masquerade as a barmaid. All of these lead to ironic situations that are some-

[2] Actually, the prose given to some of the characters is a stylized one. But we are scarcely aware of the formally ordered clauses and sentences while listening to an actual performance. For example, the artificiality of the following lines spoken by Kate Hardcastle early in Act III is scarcely noticeable on the stage: "He treated me with diffidence and respect; censured the manners of the age; admired the prudence of girls that never laughed; tired me with apologies for being tiresome; then left the room with a bow, and, madam, I would not for the world detain you." In this instance the closing imitation of Marlow's embarrassed speech gives a natural turn to the whole passage.

times broadly farcical, sometimes—when human nature is displayed rather than accidental confusions—genuinely comic.

Yet all the contrivances of the plot and the artificialities by which the story is carried along do not spoil the naturalism of this, one of the few great comedies of the later eighteenth-century theater. The naturalism of which we speak occurs at different levels. The naturalism of the language has been mentioned. The Hardcastle home, its grounds, the surrounding countryside, and the people living in the neighborhood are present in a most realistic way. There is psychological naturalism, and although we do not identify ourselves with the characters on the stage—as we do, or are supposed to do in sentimental comedy—they are in no way strangers to us. Always, Goldsmith's naturalism is an expression in one way or another of that belief which underlies his comic intuition. For him, Nature is the central force. It is both accuser and healer. It brings home to us the follies we commit in our blindness; and in enlightening us, in rectifying our vision, it restores within us our life-sustaining energies. *She Stoops to Conquer* proceeds through much of the action as a comedy of deceptions. It ends as a comedy of discovery. Marlow discovers his own identity, which lies between two unnatural extremes, and simultaneously he recognizes the true Kate, who is health and sanity personified.

The End —and the Beginning

1

She Stoops to Conquer had opened in mid-March, 1773. A year later Goldsmith lay mortally ill in Brick Court, and it was here that he died on April 4, 1774. It so happens that we have an unusually full record concerning these final months of his life. During April, 1773, Boswell saw much of him, and this fact is duly reflected in the *Life*, where in the entries for this year Goldsmith figures prominently and in none too favorable a manner. James Beattie, the Scottish poet and philosopher, who was likewise in London at this time, encountered Goldsmith on more than one occasion, and in his *London Diary, 1773* recorded his impression—unflattering, to say the least—of this strangest of fellow poets. Still another informant is Joseph Cradock, who had written one of the unused epilogues for *She Stoops to Conquer* and for whose tragedy of *Zobeide* Goldsmith had supplied the prologue. In town because of personal affairs during the summer of 1773, Cradock was later to describe in his *Literary and Miscellaneous Memoirs* Goldsmith's apparent circumstances at this time and his physical and mental state. Furthermore, the illness and death of a man long recognized as one of the literary giants of the period excited wide interest throughout the Georgian world and was the occasion of various accounts and observations not only concerning the final scene at Brick Court but to some extent the events of the concluding year or so of Goldsmith's life.

It would not be accurate to maintain that the Goldsmith legend originated in this last period. The image of one whose entire conduct seemed to be governed by paradox, whose character was one amazing antithesis, had been firmly established well before 1773. And it is not, to be sure, an entirely false image. Yet it is a distorted one, and the events of the closing twelve months and particularly the manner in which these events came to be reported contributed substantially to the distortions and have been accepted as confirmation of the legend as a whole. As we examine the record today, we feel that certain of the long-standing interpretations call for some modification.

It is perfectly clear, for one thing, that Goldsmith was a sick man during this entire period. Whatever the disease was from which he suffered—there was a virulent infection in the kidneys or in the genito-urinary tract—it was by this time well advanced. In August, 1772, according to reports in the press, he had been "dangerously ill of an inflamation in the bladder" and had undergone an operation. Now he was suffering from strangury, and unfortunately relying for relief on Dr. James's Powders, a popular and much advertised nostrum of the period. "I found him much altered," Cradock tells us, "and at times very low. . . ." But on occasion the depression seemed to pass, and Cradock, who was devoting almost all his mornings to Goldsmith, would find him infinitely better. The day Cradock and his wife returned to Leicestershire they insisted that Goldsmith have dinner with them. Goldsmith joined them, but only on condition that he be excused from eating anything. Much of the irritability which frequently marked his behavior in 1773–1774 was undoubtedly the result of his steadily deteriorating physical condition. Yet of those who observed and wrote about Goldsmith not all seem to have realized as Cradock did the presence of serious illness.

And he had much to worry about besides his health. He had

never worked harder in his life than he had since about the time of his first success as a dramatist in 1768. His signal achievements had of course been *The Deserted Village* and *She Stoops to Conquer*. But most of his energy had gone into popular writing commissioned by various publishers. He had put together a two-volume *Roman History* (1769), a *Life of Parnell* (1770) and a *Life of Bolingbroke* (1770), a four-volume *History of England* (1771),[1] and an abridgment of the *Roman History* (1772). And he was still hard at work, saddled with a number of as yet unfulfilled obligations to the publishers. Since 1769 he had been under contract with William Griffin to do an eight-volume work on natural history, which he had half finished by the late summer of 1771. He had also agreed to write a *Grecian History,* and in addition to prepare a second edition of his four-volume *History of England* as well as an abridgment of this latter work. At the same time he was doing his best to interest the trade in a brand new project. Why not, he was asking, a new and completely English *Dictionary of Arts and Sciences?* And he had proceeded to round up a number of his distinguished friends—Johnson, Burke, Reynolds, Garrick, Burney—as contributors, each to take charge of matters falling within his special field of competence. As yet he had not succeeded in convincing the publishers that the scheme was worth underwriting.

But *Dictionary* or no *Dictionary,* there was only too much unfinished work demanding attention. For the past three or four years his income had been substantial; it has been estimated about £400 a year. The trouble was that he had been living quite beyond his means, receiving from the publishers very handsome advances, spending the money immediately, and thus committing himself to burdensome assignments to which he had already received payment. Such recklessness and folly were not new things on his part, but they were now beginning to take on a decidedly pathological cast. There was an element of des-

[1] This four-volume *History* is not to be confused with his two-volume *History of England, in a Series of Letters from a Nobleman to his Son,* published in 1764.

perateness in his behavior—a symptom, we may well believe, of deep-seated illness reaching beyond the purely physical. Yet in spite of everything, he did fulfill his obligations, though this fact has sometimes been left obscure even by those who have set forth in detail the works of his which were brought out by his publishers shortly after his death. The *Grecian History,* in two volumes, appeared early in June, 1774, the eight-volume *History of the Earth, and Animated Nature* at the end of June, the abridgment of the *History of England* in July, and the new edition of the *History of England* at the year's close.

Is there any justification for believing that the publishers no longer trusted him and would have refused him further contracts? Johnson, writing to Boswell in July following Goldsmith's death, may have been implying this:

> [Goldsmith] died of a fever, made, I am afraid, more violent by un-
> easiness of mind. His debts began to be heavy, and all his resources
> were exhausted. Sir Joshua is of opinion that he owed not less than
> two thousand pounds. Was ever a poet so trusted before?

Davies, one of Goldsmith's own publishers, wrote even more strongly in his *Memoirs of Garrick.* After emphasizing the fact that Goldsmith had been valued by the booksellers and that they had rewarded his labors generously, Davies went on to say that there were innumerable squabbles between the author and his publishers. Goldsmith loved a variety of pleasures, "but could not devote himself to industry long enough to purchase them by his writings. . . ." No man took less pains than he, yet everything he wrote seemed "to bear the magical touch of an enchanter. . . ." The booksellers, however, met his proposals for a *Dictionary of Arts and Science* with coldness, hesitating to enter into negotiations with "a man with whose indolence of temper and method of procrastination they had long been acquainted." It is obviously impossible at this distance in time to speak with much assurance about the gains and losses experienced by Goldsmith's publishers, but in view of the continued popularity of so many of his books— the *History of England,* for instance, and *History of the Earth,* not to mention *The Vicar of Wakefield, The Deserted Village,* and *She Stoops to Conquer*—it would seem that they generally had the better of their bargains with him. It is difficult to believe that they were prepared to cast him off.

Bad health, constant work, and worry over mounting debts must surely account for much of the querulousness which he was exhibiting in company and which was duly noted by both James Boswell and James Beattie. However, not all the bad marks which his conduct at this time was to earn him seem justifiable from our point of view today. There was, for instance, the affair involving the publishers of the *London Packet*. That paper had printed, in its issue for March 24, 1773, a personal attack on Goldsmith, grossly insulting and linking his name with that of one of the Horneck sisters. Goldsmith's behavior on this occasion struck all of his friends as lamentable because, apparently, they found it as ludicrous as any of Don Quixote's maladroit exploits. Goldsmith, accompanied by a friend, had gone to the shop of Thomas Evans, the publisher of the *London Packet*—the chances are that Evans knew nothing about the item in question—and had beaten him across the back with his stick. A struggle had ensued, in the midst of which the infamous William Kenrick, probably the real author of the objectionable paragraph, had appeared from a back room. Goldsmith retired from the encounter something the worse in appearance, but was persuaded to attend the Club dinner that evening so that he might exhibit to the entire group his wounds of honor. Evans brought a charge of assault, but this he dropped upon Goldsmith's agreeing to contribute £50 to a Welsh charity. Goldsmith was roundly abused in the papers, which rose manfully in defense of Fair Liberty and Fleet Street. The poet responded with an Address to the Public appearing in the *Daily Advertiser* on March 31. Arriving in London a few days thereafter and finding Goldsmith's Address in the newspaper, Boswell was curious to know whether Johnson had had a hand in it. Johnson's remarks in response to Boswell's probing have often been quoted:

> . . . [Goldsmith] would no more have asked me to write such a thing as that for him, than he would have asked me to feed him with a spoon, or to do any thing else that denoted his imbecility. . . . Sir,

had he shewn it to any one friend, he would not have been allowed
to publish it. He has, indeed, done it very well; but it is a foolish
thing well done. . . .

Anyone now reading Goldsmith's Address will be at a loss to
understand in what way it denotes imbecility. The press, we are
told, is rightly considered the protector of our freedom; anything
concerning the public properly admits of a public discussion.
"But of late the press has turned from defending public interest
to making inroads upon private life. . . ." The Address, in its expression of indignation in the face of specified injustice, shares
something with *The Deserted Village,* and we ought to think the
better of Goldsmith for having voiced such a protest.

In the same way the passage at words between Goldsmith and
Johnson over pickle shops (the *Life,* April 13, 1773) strikes the
present-day reader differently from the way it did Boswell, who
seems to have regarded it as an example of Goldsmith's foolish-
ness in conversation. The subject under discussion was luxury,
attacked by Goldsmith, defended by Johnson. "Let us take a walk
from Charing-cross to Whitechapel," said Johnson; here you find
the greatest series of shops in the world; what is there in any of
them that can harm any human being? "I'll accept your challenge," said Goldsmith; "the very next shop to Northumberland-
house is a pickle-shop." Goldsmith may perhaps have been
remembering that pickles had sometimes been held to stimulate
the appetite unduly and thus to lead men away from a life of
simple eating and high thinking. But after all he did possess a
comic sense, and he must have been gratified with the Johnsonian
reposte:

> Well, Sir: do we not know that a maid can in one afternoon make
> pickles sufficient to serve a whole family for a year? nay, that five
> pickle-shops can serve all the kingdom? Besides, Sir, there is no harm
> done to any body by the making of pickles, or the eating of pickles.

What charm when the philosopher stoops to pickles!

Unquestionably, though, the Goldsmith-Johnson friendship was
showing signs of real strain these days. Johnson was never more
impatient with what he regarded as Goldsmith's unpardonable

ineptitudes, and Goldsmith was increasingly irritated by Johnson's overbearing manner in conversation. Things in fact reached
the flash point just before the meeting of the Club on May 7,
1773, when Goldsmith, trying with no success to make himself
heard above Johnson's loud voice, threw down his hat in disgust,
shortly to be rebuked with a "Sir, you are impertinent." But their
friendship, after all, was of too long and sturdy a growth not to
weather moments like this of mutual ill temper. When the Club
assembled later on that day, there occurred a touching reconcilia-
tion (*Life*, May 7, 1773). Both men were to some extent to blame
for the tension that had been developing between them. On Goldsmith's side there was constant, nagging worry over money matters, and the deeper he found himself in debt the more desperately
he hoped for sudden rescue by way of a pension from the King.
Sudden deliverances happened in fiction; and they happened in
real life—to other people. The thought of Johnson's pension of
£300 yearly, bestowed in 1762, became a source of constant vexa-
tion. When Johnson showed no interest in a project for building
a third theater in London solely for the production of new plays,
Goldsmith retorted, not without some justification, "Ay, ay, this
may be nothing to you, who can now shelter yourself behind the
corner of a pension" (*Life*, under May 1781; Boswell had, however, been told of the episode shortly after its occurrence in 1773).

But it was really James Beattie—James Beattie, Professor of
Moral Philosophy and Logic in Morischal College, Aberdeen,
author of the *Minstrel* (Book 1) and of the *Essay on Truth in
Opposition to Sophistry and Scepticism*—who galled the pension-
less Goldsmith past endurance. The man himself was agreeable
enough. But the adulation he was receiving on the occasion of his
1773 visit to London, the honorary degree conferred on him at
Oxford, and the pension with which George III was happy to
reward one who in his opinion had confuted at a single stroke of
the mind Descartes, Locke, Berkeley, Voltaire, and David Hume—
all this was too much to be borne with any semblance of mag-
nanimity or even affected indifference. Though Goldsmith's de-
pendence upon the reading public was absolute, it had never

interfered with his intellectual and social independence, and this he had no intention of yielding, no matter what the circumstances. According to one story in circulation, he had formerly been offered a stipend to write in defense of Lord North's ministry but had declined. It was only now that he was becoming aware of the presence of the Georgian Establishment. This was to be distinguished from the Commercial Interest, which in an already dominantly middle-class civilization controlled economic life. The Establishment—though the term is ours, not Goldsmith's—stood for conventional and dull propriety in the things that pertain to the arts and the mores of the nation. Beattie and his pretentious, shallow, and entirely successful *Essay on Truth* suddenly became symbols of the present deplorable state of polite thought and learning in Great Britain.

In the light of what we know from other sources about Goldsmith's affairs and state of mind during 1773, Beattie's *London Diary* makes amusing reading. Beattie had arrived from Aberdeen early in May. A month later he was sitting for his portrait to Frances Reynolds, Sir Joshua's sister, and on June 9 he recorded that at Reynolds's house he had met much agreeable company, including Garrick, Richard Burke, Beauclerk, and Goldsmith. Goldsmith had been very entertaining and merry after supper. A few days later Beattie and Miss Reynolds had driven to Richmond, where Sir Joshua now had a summer villa. Much company was on hand, and Goldsmith, Burke, and Johnson were among the guests. Burke and Johnson both spoke of the *Essay on Truth* with strong approval. Beattie talked to Burke about ways and means of procuring a royal pension. Miss Reynolds talked to Beattie about Goldsmith. Goldsmith, it seems, Beattie noted in his *London Diary*,

> not only is, but even acknowledges himself to be, envious of all contemporary authors whose works are successful, and has several times spoken wt. some peevishness of the attention that has been shown to me in England. "Why should he have a pension?" (he said one day in a company where I happened to be mentioned)—"For writing the minstrel? Then surely I have a better claim." One of the company

told him, that my claim was founded on the Essay on Truth, a work of public utility, and which had been attended wt. danger or at least no small inconvenience to the Author.

The defender of truth, having put his life or at any rate his convenience in jeopardy by reason of his attack on infidelity, was not disposed to forgive Goldsmith his lack of appreciation. "He was a poor fretful creature," wrote Beattie fifteen years later, "eaten up with affectation and envy." Furthermore, Goldsmith's conversation seemed to make no sense. A strange mixture it was of absurdity and silliness—"of silliness so great, as to make me sometimes think that he affected it." Beattie endorsed everything which Mrs. Piozzi had said about Goldsmith.

Goldsmith's final protest against the adulation of James Beattie was made to Sir Joshua apropos of the latter's portrait of Beattie, executed at this time. Beattie, dressed in his Oxford gown, looks out at us with an expression conveying both surprise at his own rise to fame and complete self-satisfaction. He is firmly clasping the *Essay on Truth* while above him the Angel of Truth is pushing three infidels down to the lower region. Some said that two of the spurned figures bore resemblance to Hume and Voltaire. This is perhaps questionable, but apparently Goldsmith believed or chose to believe that Sir Joshua had at least intended to depict Voltaire, and according to Northcote *(Life of Reynolds)* Goldsmith had spoken his mind. "It very ill becomes a man of your eminence and character, Sir Joshua," he is quoted as having said,

to condescend to be a mean flatterer, or to wish to degrade so high a genius as Voltaire before so mean a writer as Dr. Beattie; for Dr. Beattie and his book together will, in the space of ten years, not be known even to have been in existence, but your allegorical picture, and the fame of Voltaire will live forever to your disgrace as a flatterer.

Voltaire or not, the Establishment has been deservedly rebuked for absurdly overestimating the *Essay on Truth*.

Yet despite all his trials and tribulations, Goldsmith still had his high moments, sometimes when he was writing, and again when he was briefly carefree and among friends. At the end of

December, having borrowed £60 from Garrick, he treated himself to a holiday at Barton in Suffolk with the Hornecks—Catherine Horneck, the younger of the sisters, had recently married Harry Bunbury, the caricaturist and brother of Sir Charles, who now owned Barton—and proved to be the most delightful of guests, as Mary Horneck, later Mrs. Gwynne, was to testify years afterwards.

And it was in the course of the winter of 1773–1774 that he made one of a group of men who liked to meet from time to time in one of the coffeehouses for dinner. Burke, Garrick, Reynolds, and the comedian Samuel Foote were among those sometimes on hand. It was at one of these foregatherings that Garrick and Goldsmith found themselves committed to writing each other's mock epitaphs. Garrick, glib with a pen, immediately produced his famous distich,

> Here lies Nolly Goldsmith, for shortness call'd Noll,
> Who wrote like an angel, but talk'd like poor Poll.

The lines must have produced in Goldsmith an exquisite shock as he recognized in a flash the shape and substance of what was to prove to be his final achievement as a comic master. Shortly he was at work composing bit by bit but with classic assurance his *Retaliation,* that incomparable portrait gallery of Georgian personalities.

2

What with bringing *Animated Nature* to completion, grinding out his promised *Grecian History,* readying a second edition of the four-volume *History of England,* and preparing an abridgment thereof, Goldsmith had little time during this period preceding his death for the kind of writing he should have been doing. There are four essays contributed to the *Westminster Magazine,* two appearing in the number for January, 1773, two in the one for March. And there is *Retaliation,* published in its still unfinished form some days after his death.

Retaliation is further demonstration of Goldsmith's remarkable versatility. In *The Traveller* he had written wonderful verse paragraphs in which he had anatomized various European countries, treating each one like a living person, a distinctive character. Never before, however, had he undertaken to compose verse *characters* about actual people who—though at the time they did not know this—sat for him while he worked. The series of portraits which he thus produced have lost nothing down through the years. Here is Burke,

> Who, born for the Universe, narrow'd his mind,
> And to party gave up, what was meant for mankind,

and who,

> too deep for his hearers, still went on refining,
> And thought of convincing, while they thought of dining. . . .

Two of his portraits are also dramatic criticism. Richard Cumberland, author of such touching plays as *The Brothers* (1768), *The West Indian* (1771), and *The Fashionable Lover* (1772), is treated with the kind of ironic touch that had become Goldsmith's cachet. Cumberland is described as "the Terence of England, the mender of hearts"; his gallants are all without faults, his women all divine. Where has our dramatist caught this malady?

> Say was it that vainly directing his view,
> To find out mens virtues and finding them few,
> Quite sick of pursuing each troublesome elf,
> He grew lazy at last and drew from himself?

Are these closing couplets compliment or disparagement? Cumberland himself, in his *Memoirs*, expressed gratitude for this epitaph which his fellow dramatist had bestowed on him. Mrs. Thrale, on the contrary, insisted that the portrait expressed the ill will Goldsmith entertained for a rival.

The *character* of Garrick is the cleverest of the series. It is comment both on the man and on the theater, and shows throughout a good-natured, perfectly poised ambiguity of judgment:

> On the stage he was natural, simple, affecting,
> 'Twas only that, when he was off, he was acting. . . .

He was a glutton for praise, swallowing all that came his way and mistaking for fame the puffing of dunces like Hugh Kelly. Yet he saw to it that both he and the dunces profited—he was "be-roscius'd," they were "be-prais'd." The two couplets with which the *character* ends are an inspired bit of generous malice: when Garrick's spirit flies into the hereafter,

> Those poets, who owe their best fame to his skill,
> Shall still be his flatters, go where he will.
> Old Shakespeare, receive him, with praise and with love,
> And Beaumonts and Bens be his Kellys above.

Retaliation as we have it ends with the unfinished sketch of Reynolds:

> His pencil was striking, resistless and grand,
> His manners were gentle, complying and bland. . . .

The portraits have all been executed with so much naturalness of effect that we almost lose sight of their intellectuality and high wit. Goldsmith's art—and his artfulness—is at its finest here. Ludicrous as his behavior so often was in the company of his fellows, he was anything but an introvert. No self-centered malcontent could have appraised his companions with such zestfulness and unhindered objectivity.

There could have been no more *Retaliations*. The poem as a thing to do, as a thing done, is definitive. Have we any way of guessing with any degree of probability what direction Goldsmith's comic artistry might have taken if he had not succumed to disease at the premature age of forty-three? In a hurried note written three months prior to his death he had mentioned to Garrick a new comedy, to be ready in a season or two, which he believed would be worth Garrick's acceptance. ". . . I fancy," Goldsmith had added, "I will make it a fine thing." We shall never know more than this about what would have been his third comedy. "A fine thing," if a still finer thing than *She Stoops to Conquer,* would not only have established him as indisputably the greatest of the century's playwrights but would have come as an all-important addition to the too-few triumphs of the later Georgian theater. Of the essays in the *Westminster Magazine,* one—

"The History of a Poet's Garden" (January, 1773)—suggests a certain line of nondramatic writing which would have suited Goldsmith's talents exactly. The best-known of these four later essays is, to be sure, the "Essay on the Theatre" (January, 1713), but it is doubtful whether he would have written much more criticism as significant as this. "The History of a Poet's Garden," on the other hand, may well be taken as signaling the imminent return of Lien Chi Altangi, or at least of someone much like him. Only this time Lien Chi would not have been content to remain in London. He would have traveled widely through England and Scotland. He might even have made sightings in Ireland. The result could very well have been a book of sketches combining all the better features of Defoe's *Tour Thro' . . . Great Britain,* Christopher Anstey's *New Bath Guide,* and Arthur Young's *Tours.* Can there be any doubt that it would have been a worthy sequel to *The Citizen of the World?* Goldsmith's essay has to do with the Leasowes, the well-known estate in Worcestershire which had belonged to the poet William Shenstone, who had died some ten years before the appearance of this sketch. Shenstone had devoted the latter years of his life to turning his small piece of property into a model of landscape gardening, and visitors had come from far and wide to view the walks and the stream, the cunningly arranged vistas, and the statuary by means of which chosen spots in the garden were appropriately sentimentalized. Visitors, among them Goldsmith it would seem, still came, but what changes had this once-beautiful garden suffered! Shenstone had himself been to blame for what had first happened to spoil the beauty of the place, for yielding to the pride he took in his achievement he had thrown his estate open to the public, who proceeded to break his hedges, trample his lawns, and deface his statues and urns. He had been obliged to close the grounds to visitors. Nature had repossessed the place and in time had repaired the damage. At this point he had died, and the estate had been purchased by a Mr. Truepenny, described as a wealthy button-maker, who had gone to work to demonstrate that his taste and genius were equal to his fortune. A different style of landscape gardening had been introduced, the natural wilderness favored by Shenstone giving place to a regularity of treatment appealing to one in the button trade. But Truepenny had in time sold the Leasowes to a traveled ship's captain, and the captain was also a man of taste but with a great passion for the Oriental style. The garden finally took on the appearance of an East-India village, lacking only the proper inhabitants. Thus the whirligig of Taste with its varying vanities to enliven the peace of the Georgians. Goldsmith's last essays show no falling off either in spirit or execution.

3

Throughout the summer of 1773 Goldsmith had remained in town instead of seeking quiet and country air at Farmer Selby's as he had sometimes done in the past. But March of the following year found him once more at Selby's house, where apparently he was resolved to work without interruption on the poem which engrossed him. It was not long, though, before another attack similar to those which he had previously experienced sent him back to Brick Court in the Temple. It was Friday, March 25, and the Club was meeting that evening, but Goldsmith did not put in an appearance. He tried to doctor himself, but late at night grew alarmed and sent for a physician, William Hawes, over whose protest he insisted upon taking a dose of Dr. James's Fever Powders, which he believed had brought him relief in the past. Dr. George Fordyce, recently admitted to the Club, was now called in. The following day Goldsmith's condition was worse, and shortly a third physician, Dr. John Turton, a friend of Johnson's, was asked to assist, replacing Hawes.

During the ensuing week it was clear that Goldsmith was sinking. He scarcely recognized Bishop Percy when the latter visited him on Sunday, April 3. Though his patient was obviously dying, Dr. Turton was at a loss to undertand why his pulse was in such great disorder. It was important in these cases that a man be at peace with himself and the world. Could it be that Goldsmith was not? Turton settled the matter once and for all by putting the

direct question to his patient. "Is your mind at ease?" The Comic
Spirit, though not now in attendance, must surely have overheard
the not-surprising answer: "No, it is not."

Death came on Monday, April 4, early in the morning.

4

So the end. But not to the legendary figure. Each year from
then on through the rest of the century and beyond the Goldsmith
of fable acquired fuller dimensions. Men and women who had
known him came forward with their recollections of him and
their anecdotes about him. Writers undertook to set before the
interested public his singular character and the facts of his life.

He had died, so Johnson believed, in fear of distress, having
raised money and squandered it "by every artifice of acquisition,
and folly of expense," and Sir Joshua Reynolds and Dr. Hawes,
who had taken charge of matters, discovered that Goldsmith had
left only debts behind him. At first it had seemed proper that he
should be buried in the Abbey with public pomp and circum-
stance, and a list of distinguished pallbearers had been drawn up,
but there were second thoughts when the true state of his affairs
became clear. It was decided, as Reynolds' biographer James
Northcote put it, to have him buried in the plainest manner and
to apply what money could be procured to a memorial. On Sat-
urday, April 9, he was laid to rest in the Temple Burying Ground.
The service was private, attended only by a handful of people,
one of whom was the playwright Hugh Kelly, who wept as emotion overcame him. At the last moment the coffin was opened so
that a lock of hair might be obtained, in response to the belated
request of Mary Horneck.

Obituary poems were soon appearing—a *Monody*, a *Tears of
Genius*, a *Druid's Monument*. William Kenrick, alone in his glee,
was unable to forgo this opportunity of defaming once more the
man he had so long pursued. He likewise resorted to verse:

> Share, earth-worms share, since now he's dead
> His meagrim, maggot-bitten head.

Goldsmith's furniture and books from Brick Court were sold at auction. *Retaliation* appeared, to be followed by the *Grecian History,* the *History of the Earth, and Animated Nature,* the abridged *History of England,* the recently revised *Enquiry into the Present State of Polite Learning in Europe,* and the second edition of the *History of England.* Dr. Hawes published an *Account of the Late Dr. Goldsmith's Illness,* which turned into a discourse on the dangers, benefits, and proper uses of Dr. James's Powders. The proprietors of the famous Powders, disturbed at this mention of possible dangers, issued a public statement controverting Hawes. Hawes responded, and a battle was on, lasting for months.

By the summer of 1776 the plans for a memorial had matured. Sir Joshua had chosen a spot in the Abbey in the Poets' Corner, and the sculptor Joseph Nollekens was executing a medallion portrait of Goldsmith with a tablet beneath to bear the epitaph being prepared by Johnson. Johnson submitted his composition to the other members of the Club, who good-naturedly drew up a Remonstrance in the form of a Round Robin, in which they expressed the hope that Johnson would consent to revise his memorial phrases somewhat and to render the whole in English instead of Latin. Johnson's reply quickly settled the matter. He would never consent, he said, to disgrace the walls of Westminster Abbey with an English inscription.

The epitaph in English would not, perhaps, have been the offense Johnson professed, but inevitably it would have been something different in voice. One can only feel surprise at the failure of the Club to recognize that the lines as composed by Johnson have the finality of a masterpiece. Here, in the cadenced words ("ingenio sublimis, vividus, versatilis; oratione grandis, nitidus, venustus"—"in genius lofty, lively, versatile; in style weighty, clear, engaging"), the true character of Goldsmith, Goldsmith the assured literary artist, has been immortalized. On Johnson's part, the inscription was a magnificent act of controlled sympathy and imaginative insight.

Appendix

Notes on Some of Goldsmith's Miscellaneous Writings

In the nine chapters comprising the foregoing study no attempt has been made to account for all of Goldsmith's published work, and in consequence certain items of secondary literary importance have not even been given passing mention. Something, however, deserves to be said, if only in an informal and cursory way, about the following:

I. the interesting pamphlet on the Cock Lane Ghost, *The Mystery Revealed;*

II. the biographical pieces, the finest of which—*The Life of Richard Nash*—is very nearly one of his major compositions;

III. the historical writings;

IV. Goldsmith's work as a popularizer of scientific subjects, if solely for the reason that his easily overlooked *History of the Earth, and Animated Nature* turns out in its improbable fashion to be one of his most delightful books.

In such writing as this it is Goldsmith the professional hack—a magnificently paid hack, to be sure—who is constantly in evidence. Though it has always been acknowledged that these commissioned works of his are all marked by a wonderfully easy-flowing, graceful, agile style, it has been customary to regard them—at least the histories and *Animated Nature*—as almost valueless in other respects. Goldsmith has been put down as one who had the knack of compiling popular treatises on subjects about which he had little or no real knowledge, doing so quite irresponsibly, relying as he went along upon other men's works for all his information and pillaging unmercifully.

Such a characterization fails, though, to take certain factors into account. The ground rules for a mid-eighteenth-century hack writer were not ones which had been dictated by the intellectual world of humanistic scholarship and advanced scientific inquiry. They were entirely practical, meant to insure large sales to a large and indiscriminate reading public. The fact is that Goldsmith turned out exactly the sort of things he was hired by the booksellers to produce. It was the great age of compilations, and it was pretty much taken for granted by the public at large that an established man of letters, such as he, was at liberty to make use of all available publications in gathering his data. He could borrow at pleasure from other books, he could draw on multiple sources, selecting and arranging in his own way such materials as were pertinent to the task in hand. He was not called upon to be original. He was asked only to present his subject in accordance with the standard lines of treatment and in an agreeable, easy manner. Goldsmith gauged his operational level with the unerring sense of the practiced professional writer. Furthermore, he used sources that were respectable. He used them, too, more intelligently than he has usually been credited with having done, and more than once he frankly acknowledged that he was attaching his name to writing which was in truth little more than compilation.

Such considerations as these do not, needless to say, enhance in any way the value of these popularizing items of his when they are judged solely on the basis of the materials being presented. Yet some of these works are not, for various reasons, to be dismissed out of hand. They have a place, if only a minor one, in any full accounting of Goldsmith's career as a writer. The *Life of Nash,* though much of it is undoubtedly compilation, is nevertheless a work of art in its own right and a fine example of the new mode which had begun to reshape biographical writing. The histories of England, in addition to the fact that they were widely read well into the nineteenth century, throw light on some of Goldsmith's central throughts. As for *Animated Nature,* it is a veritable *carnaval des animaux*—natural science popularized and, perhaps we may say, now and again ironized by a most accomplished narrator, who may or may not have believed that cows, at three years old, shed their horns as no less an authority than the eminent Buffon had once affirmed.

The notes which follow have been arranged under the four heads mentioned above and will serve to call attention to the more important points which have been developed in the modern criticism and scholarship concerned with these secondary writings. Each of the four divisions carries its own bibliographical listing of the more significant items of recent commentary.

I. *The Mystery Revealed; Containing a Series of Transactions and Authentic Testimonials, Respecting the supposed Cock-Lane Ghost; Which have hitherto been concealed from the Public*

This pamphlet, published toward the end of February, 1762, can pretty safely be attributed to Goldsmith, though such interest as it holds for us today owes much less to Goldsmith's probable authorship than to the celebrated affair that is here being dealt with. When the pamphlet appeared all London was talking about the Cock Lane Ghost, and the principals in this bizarre happening were known by name in every household in the metropolis—William Kent; Fanny Lynes, who to all intents and purposes had been Kent's second wife, though a recognized marriage was barred because she was his first wife's sister; Richard Parsons, in whose house in Cock Lane, near Smithfield, the Kents had occupied a rented room until departing for other lodgings; Elizabeth Parsons, the ex-landlord's eleven-year-old daughter; and most famous of all, Scratching Fanny, the invisible but highly communicative ghost of the now deceased Fanny Lynes.

The material events were as follows: Kent had lent Parsons £12. Parsons would not repay and Kent had brought suit. The Kents had moved to other quarters. Fanny, pregnant, had contracted smallpox, died after a short illness, and had been buried in the vault of St. John's, Clerkenwell. All this had taken place some two years before the Ghost of Fanny had, according to Parsons and his supporters, manifested herself to Elizabeth Parsons. Fanny communicated by scratches and knocks, and the Parsons devised a simple system by which they could put questions and the Ghost could reply with a "yes" or a "no." Yes, she was Fanny Lynes. Yes, she had lived with Mr. Kent. Yes, she had been ill with smallpox. But yes, Mr. Kent had poisoned her with arsenic. The interrogations were often conducted by the Reverend John Moore, lecturer of St. Sepulchre's. Needless to say, the séances became one of the attractions of London. The liveliest contemporary account is Walpole's in a letter to George Montagu (Feb. 2, 1762). Walpole, the Duke of York, Lady Northumberland, and others, had gone to the wretchedly small and miserable house in Cock Lane in a hackney coach. It was raining torrents. The Lane was mobbed with people. Thanks to the presence of the Duke of York, Walpole & Co. were admitted to the crowded chamber—fifty people, no light but one tallow candle, the child lying in bed awaiting the coming of the ghost. They stayed on till half past one but nothing out of the ordinary happened. Walpole's explanation of the whole thing was simple, and probably largely true: Parsons, a drunken parish clerk, had set all this on foot out of revenge; the Methodists had adopted it; and now the whole town of London thought of nothing else.

It was not all a joke, however. Kent lay under public accusation, charged with murder by a ghost and an eleven-year-old medium. Responsible citizens felt called upon to stop such dangerous nonsense, and the Reverend Stephen Aldrich of St. John's took the lead, organizing a committee of investigation which included Samuel Johnson among other notable men. These eminent gentlemen examined Elizabeth Parsons, and later proceeded in the dead of night to the crypt of St. John's where, as they had been given to understand, Fanny's ghost had promised to attend them and make her presence known by knocking on her coffin. They called on the spirit to make good her promise, but according to the *Account* of the proceedings drawn up by Johnson and published in *Lloyd's Evening Post* at the beginning of February, "nothing more than silence ensued."

Johnson's *Account* and Goldsmith's pamphlet were not the only noteworthy by-products of this nine days' wonder of 1762. Addison's old comedy of *The Drummer, or, The Haunted House* was revived and brought up to date by means of a new prologue "Occasioned by the Cock Lane Apparition." Garrick's farce, *The Farmer's Return from London,* put on at Drury Lane, made sport of the Ghost. Hogarth put her into his *Credulity, Superstition, and Fanaticism.* And Charles Churchill, now triumphantly impertinent, lost no time in turning her to satiric advantage in his poem *The Ghost* (I and II, March, 1762): give us an entertaining sprite, one who does not appear to the eye but only talks by sounds and signs; one who knocks so gently that no lady could be affrighted in the darkest night—

> Such is our Fanny, whose good will,
> Which cannot in the Grave lie still,
> Brings her on Earth to entertain
> Her friends and Lovers in Cock Lane. . . .

Later on in the poem comes the account of how Pomposo, otherwise Samuel Johnson, and his group of investigators made trial of the spirit.

Goldsmith's pamphlet may well, one feels, have been commissioned by Kent to serve as his public defense against the charges eminating from Cock Lane. It begins with a clear and rapid account of the events leading up to the activities of the supposed Ghost, and then proceeds to describe the subsequent occurrences in a manner that leaves no room for doubt as to their proper interpretation. The pamphlet is forcible argumentation, ending with a strong expression of contempt for the sort of mass credulity which had just been witnessed.

It should be mentioned that Kent took action against those superintending the accusations. Parsons, his wife, and the woman who had professed to decode the messages were all found guilty when brought to trial the following July and received varying sentences.

Helpful notes on the Cock Lane Ghost are given by Douglas Grant in his edition of the *Poetical Works of Charles Churchill* (Oxford, 1956).

The most recent treatment of the whole episode is also by Douglas Grant: *The Cock Lane Ghost* (London and New York, 1965).

II. *Biographical Works*

Biography in Goldsmith's time was coming strongly into its own. There was a new interest in people as individual human beings, and this was kept within bounds because of a prevailingly naturalistic, unsensational approach. As in Hogarth's portraits in oils so in a fine biographical study like Johnson's *Life of Savage* (1744), interest in the particular and a rich sense of our common humanity are harmonized in a manner that is uniquely of the eighteenth century. Johnson himself was a prolific biographer, and his discussion in No. 60 of the *Rambler* (October, 1750) and No. 84 of the *Idler* (November, 1759) of the purposes, the importance, and the art of biography contributed greatly toward setting the tone and style of Georgian biographical writing. The slightly more than half of a century which followed the *Life of Savage* saw the appearance not only of Johnson's *Lives of the Poets* (1779, 1781) but of William Mason's "Life of Gray" (1775), Thomas Davies's *Memoirs . . . of Garrick* (1780), Mrs. Thrale's *Anecdotes of . . . Johnson* (1786), Sir John Hawkins's *Life of . . . Johnson* (1786), Arthur Murphy's *Essay on the Life of . . . Johnson* (1793), Gibbon's *Autobiography* (1796), and—the zenith in biographical art—Boswell's *Life* (1791). Such a roll call only accounts for a few of the better-known, full-length works; the periodicals were full of biographical notes and brief sketches of famous people, living and dead.

Goldsmith wrote a good deal of biography sooner or later, but only in his *Life of Nash* and—perhaps we should add—in the *Life of Parnell* was he sufficiently committed to the task in hand to produce other than decidedly mediocre work. The biographical items by or in some fashion associated with Goldsmith can be listed as follows:

1. 1758: *The Memoirs of A Protestant, Condemned to the Galleys of France, For His Religion. Written by Himself . . . By James Willington.* The original work is in French, the author a Jean Marteilhe. It is an autobiographical account of the indignities and barbarities endured by the writer, a Huguenot, after being captured in 1700 and sentenced to the galleys. For some reason known to himself, Goldsmith did not put his own name down on this translation, but used that of a contemporary of his at Trinity College, Dublin. Goldsmith's own Preface shows him in complete accord with the new biographical principles of his day: "No Events are here to astonish . . . Our Reader must be content with the simple Exhibition of Truth, and consequently of Nature; he must be satisfied to see Vice triumphant, and Virtue in Distress; to see Men punished or rewarded, not as he Wishes, but as Providence has thought proper to direct; for all here wear the Face of Sincerity."

2. "Memoirs of M. de Voltaire." This appeared in the *Lady's Magazine*, February-November, 1761.

See p. 18 of the present study.

3. 1761: A translation of the *Mémoires de Milady B.* by Charlotte-Marie-Anne Charbonnier de la Guesnerie.

No copies of this item, published by Newbery, seem to have come down to us.

4. 1762: *Plutarch's Lives, Abridged from the Original Greek, Illustrated with Notes and Reflections.*

Seven volumes of these *Lives* were put out by John Newbery from May to November, 1762. Goldsmith apparently did the first four volumes and part of the fifth. In his Preface Goldsmith discusses biography, which "since the days of *Plutarch* [has] been considered as the most useful manner of writing, not only from the pleasure it affords the imagination, but from the instruction it artfully and unexpectedly conveys to the understanding." He ends by quoting in full Johnson's *Rambler* No. 60.

5. 1762. *The Life of Richard Nash, Esq.; Late Master of Ceremonies at Bath. Extracted principally from His Original Papers.*

See the discussion below.

6 and 7. In 1763 Newbery was crediting Goldsmith with a "Life of Christ" and a "Life of the Fathers," sometimes referred to in the Newbery records as translations. The "Life of Christ," no copy of which has survived, was very likely an abridgment of William Reading's *History of our Lord and Saviour Jesus Christ* (1716, 1717). The "Life of the Fathers" is *An History of the Lives, Actions, Travels, Sufferings, and Death of the most eminent Martyrs*, etc. (1764), an abridgment of the seventeenth-century works by William Cave.

1763: It may be noted that in March, 1763, Goldsmith agreed to do a two-volume *Chronological History of the Lives of Eminent Persons of Great Britain and Ireland,* to be published by James Dodsley. Little came of this work, and in lieu of it Goldsmith seems to have made an abridgment of his first *History of England,* which Dodsley inserted in a new edition (1765) of a work he had previously published, *The Geography and History of England . . .*

8. 1770: *The Life of Dr. Parnell.*

This had first appeared as an introductory piece in an edition of Parnell's poems put out by Tom Davies in June, 1770. The following July it appeared separately.

As mentioned above, the *Life of Parnell* is now the only one of Goldsmith's biographical pieces other than the *Life of Nash* which retains real merit. Goldsmith had at his disposal first-hand materials concerning Parnell furnished by Sir James Parnell, the poet's nephew, and by a Mr. and Mrs. Hayes, the poet's relations, and in a concluding footnote he acknowledged this assistance. He seems also to have drawn on his father's and his uncle Contarine's personal recollections of Parnell.

Any interest we have in this *Life* today is likely to be confined to the two paragraphs of critical remarks coming toward the end of the biography. Parnell is here described as "the last of the great school that had modelled itself upon the ancients, and taught English poetry to resemble what the generality of manking have allowed to excel." He was careful in the choice of his subjects, happy in the selection of his images. His poetical language is correct, belonging as it does to that period which brought it to its highest pitch of refinement, from which it has ever since "been gradually debasing." Parnell conceived the language of poetry to be the language of life, conveying "the warmest thoughts in the simplest expression."

9. 1770: *The Life of Henry St. John, Lord Viscount Bolingbroke.*

This first appeared, late in 1770, in a new edition of Bolingbroke's *Dissertation upon Parties.* A few days afterward it was issued separately. It is mostly hack work, borrowed in great part from the fifth (1760) volume of *Biographia Britannica.*

Returning, now, to the *Life of Nash.* Richard Nash, who had reigned at Bath as master of the ceremonies since early in the century, died in February, 1761. The precise circumstances which resulted in Goldsmith's becoming the author of the *Life* of this well-known personality can only be inferred. Most of Goldsmith's older biographers have assumed that he visited Bath in the summer of 1762, observed the city and the Nash memorabilia at first hand, and then wrote his book from a personal viewpoint, claiming, when it served his purposes to do so, a closer acquaintance with people and past events than he actually could have had.

But as has more recently been brought out, it seems unlikely that Goldsmith visited Bath prior to the virtual completition of the biography. What probably happened is that Newbery, who was one of the eventual publishers of the *Life,* had commissioned Goldsmith to work up a full-length biographical sketch of Nash, arranging matters so that Goldsmith could have access to important Nash materials in the hands of George Scott, who was acting as Nash's executor. In the second edition of the *Life,* which appeared early in December, 1762, less than two months after the first edition, Goldsmith inserted an opening Advertisement in which he stated that he had George Scott's permission to assure the public that all the significant Nash papers had been "communicated to the Editor of this Volume . . ." We are to think, then, not of Goldsmith as the author—his name did not appear—but as the "editor." The *Life* is a compilation—besides the Nash papers Goldsmith used, for almost a tenth part of his book, the *Essay towards a Description of Bath* (2nd. ed., 1749), by John Wood—and it should be approached as such. The person who is addressing us need not and probably should not be thought of as Oliver Goldsmith. Taking the work in this way, we are not less aware of Goldsmith's biographical artistry.

The *Life* has a roughness of texture which adds greatly to its vivid, impressionistic quality. The truth, we are persuaded, has been left to make its own impression; it has not been touched up by the writer so as to present a finished, varnished appearance. It is not difficult to understand why the *Life* sold, as one of those concerned put it, "in a most extraordinary Manner." Everything pertaining to Bath was of interest to those who had ever visited the famous spa, and perhaps of still greater interest to those who had not. Nash had been a renowned personality for half a century. The *Life* offered itself at just the right moment as an authentic account of a famous figure and of the scene he had presided over with such effect.

But the critics of 1762 were not overly impressed. "A trivial subject, treated for the most part in a lively, ingenious, and entertaining manner," observed the *Monthly Review,* and added: "Mr. Samuel Johnson's admirable Life of Savage seems to have been chosen as the model of this performance." Today, the triviality of the subject, the ingenious manner, and the Johnsonian approach are the very things which excite our admiration. Nash was much of a fool, occasionally a scoundrel, frequently a kindly and charitable person, and something of a social genius, organizing the daily manners and customs of Bath. The Palladian squares and façades that spring up everywhere, thanks to John

Wood, father and son, and to the encouragement of residents like Ralph Allen, Fielding's friend, were the outward token of this social order. Life at Bath was trivial, but it proceeded like a minuet. In a peculiar way Nash had possessed true imagination.

Editor Goldsmith proved by the manner in which he composed his materials that he fully understood the principles underlying the new biography: truth, attention to apparent trifles, instruction without sanctimonious moralizing, establishment of an emphatic response, the balancing of a man's vices against his virtues. Nash, we are told, was of the middle ranks. He was possessed of both vices and virtues, these being equally apparent to the public eye. He had "too much merit not to become remarkable, yet too much folly to arrive at greatness." In other words, a sometimes admirable, sometimes reprehensible, sometimes ridiculous personality. Goldsmith keeps the antithetical qualities in balance throughout the *Life,* and it is round the contrasts involved that he arranges his data.

Stylistically, this balancing is often echoed in prose which takes on the movement of a minuet. Were the ceremonies introduced by Nash absurd affairs? No:

> The natural gradation of breeding begins in savage disgust, proceeds to indifference, improves into attention, by degrees refines into ceremonious observance, and the trouble of being ceremonious at length produces politeness, elegance and ease. There is therefore some merit in mending society, even in one of the inferior steps of this gradation; and no man was more happy in this respect than *Mr. Nash. . . .*

Two details of a different nature should be mentioned. In 1762 Goldsmith was presumably at work on *The Vicar of Wakefield,* and *The Vicar* and *The Life of Nash* are found to have a few moments in common, for the story of how Nash succeeded in bringing a colonel *M——* and a Miss *L——* together after they had been separated by various unfortunate circumstances is essentially the same as the episode in *The Vicar* in which Arabella Wilmot recognizes in the strolling player acting the part of Horatio in Rowe's *The Fair Penitent* her lover George Primrose. It seems likely that *The Vicar* was in this instance drawing upon the *Life.* The theme, in an elementary form, which was later to serve Goldsmith in *The Good Natur'd Man* can also be traced back to the *Life of Nash,* where in the story of Miss Sylvia S—— it has been taken over, as we are informed by Goldsmith, from Wood—i.e., from Wood's *Essay towards a Description of Bath*—and from "another memoir" mentioned by Wood.

The entire subject of biography in Goldsmith's period has been admirably treated by Donald A. Stauffer in *The Art of Biography in Eighteenth Century England* (Princeton, N.J., 1941). Goldsmith as a biographer has been discussed by Joseph E. Brown in "Goldsmith and Johnson on Biography," *MLN*,[1] *XLII* (1927), 168–171; and by Frances M. Haydon in "Oliver Goldsmith as a Biographer," in *South Atlantic Quarterly*, XXXIX (1940), 50–57. In his edition of the *Works* Arthur Friedman furnishes Introductions and some notes for most of the biographical items listed in the present Appendix. Wardle's *Oliver Goldsmith* is extremely helpful in identifying these items and placing them within the chronology of Goldsmith's life. In connection with items 6 and 7 in this Appendix, R. W. Seitz may be consulted: "Goldsmith's *Lives of the Fathers*," *MP*, XXVI (1929), 295–305. A recent and valuable discussion of the Nash biography is Oliver W. Ferguson's "The Materials of History: Goldsmith's *Life of Nash*," *PMLA*, LXXX (1965), 372–386.

III. *Historical Writings*

More than a little can and as a matter of fact has been written about Goldsmith as a historical writer. The histories of his which we hear most about are four: *An History of England, in a Series of Letters from a Nobleman to his Son* (1764), *The Roman History . . .* (1769), *The History of England, from the Earliest Times to the Death of George II* (1771), and *The Grecian History* (1774). But these do not cover all of his work, as the full bibliographical listing given below shows. He was as extensive a writer—or shall we say compiler—of historical items as he was of biographical, and shortly after the Royal Academy of Arts was instituted by the King in 1768 Goldsmith was named honorary Professor of History therein.

Quite as important as the new biographical art was the new history which was likewise establishing itself in the eighteenth century. History, Bolingbroke had declared, is "philosophy teaching by examples how to conduct ourselves in all the situations of private and public life," and in France, under Voltaire's inspiring leadership, historical writing was coming to reflect an ideology—the earliest one in that sequence of ideologies which have worked so strongly in the modern world. History, it was held, should perform in the name of philosophy, teaching the principles of Nature and Reason, declaring the concepts of Liberty and Humanity, and thus civilizing all societies. Human nature was assumed

---

[1] For this and similar abbreviations in the bibliographical notes included in this Appendix, see the table below on page 197.

to be substantially the same at all times and places, but the appearance of great figures and the different effect of varied climates and religions precluded uniformity in historical developments. History was not a specialized discipline so much as an enterprise to be engaged in for the intruction of rational men. It should alert them to the empirical facts about their social and political institutions, while at the same time it pleased through effective presentation and a readable style. Voltaire's *History of Charles XII* (1731) had been the first of his brilliant series of works, which came to include his *Siècle de Louis XIV* (1751) and his history of Europe from Charlemagne to the Renaissance (the *Essai sur les moeurs et l'esprit des Nations,* 1756).

Though England was eventually to produce, in Gibbon's *Decline and Fall of the Roman Empire* (1776–1788), the greatest of all eighteenth-century historical works, the earliest historians, English and Scottish, who had appeared during this period revealed little of the ideological edge which we find in Voltaire and his school in France. Hume, whose *History of England* (from Julius Caesar to 1688) appeared in eight volumes in 1763, had issued the earliest part of this work in 1754. William Robertson's *History of Scotland during the Reigns of Queen Mary and King Jame VI* had come out in 1759, Smollett's *History of England . . . to 1748* (4 vols.) in 1757 and the *Continuation* (5 vols.) in 1761–1765. Goldsmith admired Voltaire greatly and had been influenced in more ways than one by the latter's liberal and empirical rationalism, but in Goldsmith the historian we find one who was essentially the compiler, producing for his publishers a salable commodity which, by virtue of a pleasing style and the kind of exposition which could be readily followed, could hold its own with the historical works of contemporary British writers like Hume, Robertson, and Smollett. On the appearance in 1771 of his *History of England, from the Earliest Times* he was, as he put it, "abused in the newspapers for betraying the liberties of the people." "God knows," he wrote to Bennet Langton, "I had no thoughts for or against liberty in my head." His whole aim, he avowed, was only "to make up a book of a decent size that as Squire Richard says would do no harm to nobody" (Letter of September 7, 1771). How he worked was described by William Cooke in the sketch of Goldsmith appearing in 1793 in the *European Magazine:*

> His manner of compiling [the *History of England in a Series of Letters*] was as follows: he first read in a morning, from Hume, Rapin, and sometimes Kennet, as much as he designed for one letter, marking down the passages referred to on a sheet of paper, with remarks. He then . . . spent the day generally convivially. . . .

and when he went up to bed took up his books and paper with him, where he generally wrote the chapter, or the best part of it, before he went to rest. This latter exercise cost him very little trouble, he said; for having all his materials ready for him, he wrote it with as much facility as a common letter.

The sources he drew on are known, and he made no effort to conceal the fact that he was a compiler—in the Preface to the *History of England, from the Earliest Times* he refers to himself as such and writes that the books "which have been used in this abridgement are chiefly Rapin, Carte, Smollett, and Hume."

Are Goldsmith's histories of any general value? On this question Samuel Johnson was apparently of two minds. He is reported by Mary Hamilton—in her diary—as having said in May, 1784, that though Goldsmith wrote the history of England "he knew nothing more of it than turning over two or three English Histories & abridging them. . . ." Yet eleven years previously he had assured Boswell, to the latter's amazement, that even as a historian Goldsmith stood in the first class—before Hume, Robertson, Lord Lyttelton. "I have not read Hume," Johnson continued; "but, doubtles, Goldsmith's History is better than the *verbiage* of Robertson, or the foppery of Dalrymple" (*Life,* April 30, 1773). And today opinion is still divided. In an essay on Goldsmith included in his *Men and Places* (1963), Dr. J. H. Plumb has pronounced Goldsmith's *Animated Nature,* both his histories of England, and his *History of Rome* to be worthless and unreadable. On the other hand Mr. Terry Coleman, writing in the *Manchester Guardian* on the occasion of the three-hundredth anniversary of the publication on June 26, 1764, of the *History . . . in a Series of Letters,* while fully acknowledging that the book is not a piece of scholarship, hails it as "that marvelous thing, an historical work that stands reading." And it is possible to say more than this in its behalf, as what is to follow in the present notes will suggest.

Goldsmith's historical work includes these items:

1. 1761: In this or the preceding year Goldsmith began a history of the Seven Years War. Prior, in 1837, was the first to print it, giving it as *Preface and Introduction to the History of the Seven Years' War.* Its real title, however, was *A Political View of the Result of the Present War with America,* as the manuscript in the Huntington Library shows. It is a compilation derived from articles, including two by Johnson, which had appeared in the *Lady's Magazine* in 1756–58.

1762: It is possible that in this year he revised for Newbery a work by Mrs. Sarah Scott which appeared early in 1762—a *History of Mecklenburgh.*

2. 1764: Beginning on April 2, 1764, Newbery and other associated publishers put out some twelve volumes of *A General History of the World From The Creation to the Present Time,* by William Guthrie and John Gray. For this Goldsmith wrote the Preface, having received payment for it during the preceding years. He made generous use of Vol. V of the *Encyclopédie.*

3. 1764: *An History of England, in a Series of Letters from a Nobleman to his Son.*

This appeared in two volumes late in June, 1764. See the discussion below.

4. 1765: *A Concise History of England; Or, The Revolution of the British Constitution.*

This was issued by Dodsley in March, 1765. Dodsley included it as a second part in *The Geography and History of England Done in the Manner of Gordon's and Salmon's Geographical and Historical Grammar,* a book he had first published many years before. Goldsmith's *Concise History* is really an abridgment of his *History of England, in a Series of Letters,* and was apparently done in lieu of the *Chronological History of the Lives of Eminent Persons of Great Britain and Ireland* which he had been under contract to write for Dodsley.

5. 1768: *The Present State of the British Empire in Europe, America, Africa and Asia.*

This was published by a group of booksellers. Goldsmith compiled it from various sources, taking a hundred pages almost directly from Burke's *Account of the European Settlements in America* (1757). The fact that Goldsmith's fee for this assignment was, so far as we know, only a small one suggests that he was commissioned to make up a book out of recently published materials.

6. 1769: *The Roman History, from the Foundation of the City of Rome, to the Destruction of the Western Empire.*

In his Preface, Goldsmith refers to "the present work (or rather compilation)."

7. 1771: *The History of England, from the Earliest Times to the Death of George II.*

This four-volume work, published by Thomas Davies, appeared early in August, 1771. In the Preface Goldsmith stated that the books "used in this abridgment are chiefly Rapin, Carte, Smollett, and Hume." Hume particularly he had taken for his guide, but he was careful to point out in the paragraph which followed that he did not share Hume's ambiguous attitude toward religion. "The Second Edition, Corrected," which seems to have received Goldsmith's attention, appeared after his death, late in 1774. *The History of England, from the Earliest Times* is briefly discussed below in connection with the *History . . . in a Series of Letters*.

8. 1772: Toward the close of this year appeared *Dr. Goldsmith's Roman History Abridged by Himself for the use of Schools*.

9. 1774: *The Grecian History, From the Earliest State To The Death of Alexander the Great*.

This appeared posthumously in June, 1714.

10. 1774: *An Abridgement of the History of England*.

This, an abridgment of the four-volume work of 1771, was published posthumously in July, 1774.

The only historical writings deserving much attention are the *History of England, in a Series of Letters* (hereafter referred to as the *Series of Letters*) and, by virtue of its association therewith, the later *History of England, from the Earliest Times* (or, simply, the *History*). Both works have been studied for what they reveal concerning Goldsmith's political opinions, which have sometimes been held to have undergone certain changes—largely as a result of his personal experiences—between the earlier *Series of Letters* (1764) and the later *History* (1771). These matters aside, the *Series of Letters* proves to be essentially a commentary on the English constitution and as such has a somewhat greater significance, at least in respect of the development of Goldsmith's general thought, than has always been discerned.

Goldsmith is of course to be put down as a Tory, but having done that we have not done much. We should not make the mistake of reading into the political structure of the 1760s and 1770s a clearly defined two-party system. Goldsmith's protestations in his letter to Langton of 1771, apropos of his *History*, may be accepted as perfectly valid: his aim had been to produce a book that "would do no harm to nobody"; he is now being set down as an arrant Tory, a betrayer of the liberties of the people; but any part of the *History* might well establish him, he declares, as a sour Whig. Perhaps Goldsmith had Swift in mind, for the great Dean had maintained that despite his association with the Oxford-Bolingbroke Tory administration, despite his long war against Walpole & Co., his fundamental principles had always been Whig. He was right to the extent that from the first he had emphasized 1, the whole people as the ultimate source of political power, and 2, the theory that rational liberty could be preserved in the state only by maintaining a balance between the separate interests represented by Crown, Lords, and Commons. In *The Citizen of the World* Goldsmith had applied a concept of balance to opposing views of luxury, etc. In *The Traveller* he had extended this concept to the contradictions to be observed in national culture. In the *Series of Letters* he made the theory of a balanced constitution his central theme and organized his whole historical statement round it. As a political theory this was, of course, anything but new— it is usual to trace it back to Polybius. Swift had given it the clearest of statements. Bolingbroke, in the *Craftsman,* had written about "that balance which has been so much talked of": "it is this division of power, these distinct privileges attributed to the king, to the lords, and to the commons, which constitute a limited monarchy." In *L'Esprit des Lois* Montesquieu had called the three powers the legislative, the executive, and the judiciary, and had warned that liberty is endangered when these different powers are united in the same body; and J. L. De Lolme, Montesquieu's follower, had asserted in his *Constitution of England* (1771; Eng. tr. 1775) that British freedom was the result of an "equilibrium between the ruling powers of the state." All of this was easily said, but in actual practice who or what really constituted the different powers, how were they to be kept properly divided, and who was to effect the balance? George III and the Interest of the Crown, as well as the forces that thought of themselves as being in opposition, were equally unclear on these constitutional questions.

Goldsmith's Toryism was principally a distrust of the upper-middle class, of the men of aggressive wealth. And for him the three powers consisted of the King, those whose minds were swayed by wealth with double force, and the commonalty or—as we would say—the substantial middle-class. Goldsmith was in advance of most of his English contemporaries in perceiving that the forces that needed to be kept in balance were really social and economic rather than purely political in the older sense. "I'm for Monarchy to keep us equal," he once remarked to Burke (Boswell's "Journal," April 30, 1773).[2] Otherwise he decried party spirit. "Party," he asserted in the Dedication prefixed to *The Traveller,* "entirely distorts the judgment, and destroys the taste. When the mind is once infected with this disease, it can only find pleasure in what contributes to encrease the distemper."

It may be, as Seitz held in his interesting article on "Some of Goldsmith's Second Thoughts on English History," that for personal reasons —his lack of a royal pension bearing heavily on him—he injected into his *History* a somewhat different tone from that to be found in the *Series of Letters.* Did he show less tendency, in 1771, to fly to the throne for protection, a greater readiness to criticize English monarchs, and at the same time more hostility toward the Whigs of history? But if there are such differences of emphasis, one feels that they may well signify no

---

2 "Journal" for 1773 (*The Private Papers of James Boswell from Malahide Castle,* VI, 130).

more than such differences of style and presentation as can be expected in easy, popular writing of this kind. "God knows I had no thoughts for or against liberty in my head." Political reasonableness, informed and disciplined liberty—these lay in an area where the extremes of party and dogmatism were held in compromise.

On eighteenth-century historical writing in general, J. B. Black's *The Art of History; A Study of Four Great Historians of the Eighteenth Century* (London, 1926) is a useful guide. Also helpful are Thomas P. Peardon's *The Transition in English Historical Writing, 1760–1830* (N.Y., 1933), and James W. Johnson's informative article on "Swift's Historical Outlook" *(Journal of British Studies,* IV [1965], 52–77). Goldsmith as a historian is discussed in broad terms by L. M. Angus-Butterworth, "Goldsmith as Historian," *South Atlantic Quarterly,* XLVIII (1949), 251–257. Friedman's notes and commentaries on the historical pieces *(Collected Works)* and Wardle's running discussion of them pretty well summarize the important matters brought out in recent scholarship and criticism, but two important articles should be mentioned: R. S. Crane and J. H. Warner, "Goldsmith and Voltaire's *Essai Sur Les Moeurs,"* MLN, XXXVIII (1923), 65–76; and R. W. Seitz, "Some of Goldsmith's Second Thoughts on English History," *MP,* XXXV (1938), 279–288. To consider Goldsmith as historian quickly involves us in both his political and social views, and for this reason reference may here be made to the following: The Rev. Father Paschall, O.S.F.C., "Goldsmith as a Social Philosopher," *The Irish Ecclesiastical Record,* Fifth Series, XXXV (1930), 113–124; Robert W. Seitz, "The Irish Background of Goldsmith's Social and Political Thought," *PMLA,* LII (1937), 405–411; Howard J. Bell, Jr., *"The Deserted Village* and Goldsmith's Social Doctrines," *PMLA,* LIX (1944), 747–722; and Richard Clements, "The Social Teachings of Oliver Goldsmith," *Social Service,* XXI (1947), 87–90.

IV. *An History of the Earth, and Animated Nature*

It has been customary to laugh at any mention of poor, simple Goldsmith's compilations of philosophical-scientific materials, the largest of which was *Animated Nature,* often asserted to be a completely worthless treatise. The fact that he had had some scientific training, or had at least exposed himself to lectures of a scientific nature, after he left Trinity College, Dublin, is seldom remembered. To be sure, "scientific training" in the 1760s did not ordinarily amount to much by our standards, but the fact remains that Goldsmith was knowledgeable in the fields then being cultivated by eighteenth-century science. There is evidence, according to Winifred Lynskey, whose studies of Goldsmith's scientific thinking are authoritative and revealing, "that Goldsmith was a skillful and conscientious compiler and that he had a varied knowledge of the eminent scientific works available in his day."

The materials Goldsmith used, the scientists and naturalists whose books he abstracted and summarized as he synthesized modern views, are known: Brookes, Buffon, Derham, Pennant, Plucke, Swammerdam, Willughby, etc., etc. The general information which Goldsmith purveyed accorded with the established views of the qualified men of the period. If Goldsmith's science was entangled with assumptions about Divine purposes manifesting themselves in the universe of Nature, that was because he was only following standard theory—the design argument kept peace, at least in England, between God and his theologians on the one hand and scientists—who were sometimes theologians as well— on the other.

Some five items account for most of Goldsmith's known works of the sort here under discussion:

1. 1760: "A Comparative View of Races and Nations," a series of four essays appearing in the *Royal Magazine* in June, July, and September, 1760.

Much here is owing to Buffon's *Histoire naturelle*.

2. 1761: Four essays in the *Public Ledger* in August and September, 1761: "New Fashions in Learning," "Avenbrugger's Discovery of Percussion," "The Progress of the Arts in Switzerland," and "South American Giants."

1762: It is probable that toward the end of 1762 Goldsmith began, for Newbery, a compilation ultimately known as *A Survey of Experimental Philosophy*. See No. 5 below.

3. 1763: *A New and Accurate System of Natural History. By R. Brookes.*

This, a six-volume affair, was put out by Newbery. Goldsmith, who apparently revised the text, wrote a Preface to the whole work and probably the Introductions to the first four volumes.

1766: Goldsmith made a translation of Formey's *Histoire Abrégé de la Philosophie* which Francis Newbery published in 1766 as *A Concise History of Philosophy and Philosophers*.

1773: At this time Goldsmith was hoping to edit a "Dictionary of Arts and Sciences." The project came to nothing.

4. 1744: *An History of the Earth, and Animated Nature.*

This appeared posthumously, in eight volumes, at the end of June, 1774. Some informal notes on this are given below.

5. 1776: *A Survey of Experimental Philosophy, considered in its Present State of Improvement.*

It is *Animated Nature* which invites almost exclusive attention. The modern reader who can bring himself to dip into this forbiddingly massive work has a surprise in store. It is one of Goldsmith's most charming performances. Is it, we ask, popular science masquerading as a comedy, or is it a comedy in the form of a natural history? Whichever way it goes, there is a tincture of irony. Authorized scientists and naturalists can have no possible interest in any of it; for them, as scientists, the science of yesterday holds as such no significance. But humanists—and scientists are often humanists in their off hours—are permitted the historical perspective, and one of the things coming into view for them is the following:

The literary mind from at least the time of Francis Bacon was following new scientific enquiries with much eagerness, but it often experienced a certain bewilderment in the presence of the conflicting theories of one sort or another being advanced. The angel Raphael in *Paradise Lost* owes something to Milton's own scepticism—a scepticism strictly within bounds—when he warns Adam that God was likely to confound all men's astronomical explanations. And Swift's Aristotle, speaking in the Vision of the Dead in *Gulliver's Travels*, Part III, prophesies that the new science of the seventeenth century will someday seem obsolete. In the middle of the eighteenth century a sharp and prehensile mind like Goldsmith's was as much aware as ever of the contradictory theories advanced by specialists. In the field of natural history, much ground had been secured in taxonomy and systematics through the notable efforts of men like Ray, Réaumur, and Linnaeus, and the problems of nomenclature, identification, and classification had been effectively dealt with. But as to the origin of the earth there was still no conformity of opinion, and in biology some of the experts were more inclined than others to account for the differences between the species—the species were generally assumed to be fixed—on the traditional basis of teleology. Goldsmith, we may be sure, would have accepted with enthusiasm the modern scientific frame of reference in which all the uncertainties in scientific thinking become a function in the overall enterprise. As it was, seeing himself as a popular writer standing outside recognized professional circles and only seeking to purvey information to the reader as pleasantly as possible, he would naturally feel at liberty, in the interest of effective presentation, to handle his material with a certain freedom of interpretation.

Goldsmith's friends spoke of *Animated Nature* more than once. We have Boswell's amusing passage (*Life*, April 10, 1772) about the visit he paid to Goldsmith when the latter was staying at Farmer Selby's and working on the natural history: "He was not at home; but having a curiosity to see his apartment, [Mr. Mickle and I] went in and found curious scraps of description of animals, scrawled upon the walls with a black lead pencil." Boswell reports, as of a year later, Johnson's often-quoted comment: "Sir, [Goldsmith] has the art of compiling, and of saying every thing he has to say in a pleasing manner. He is now writing a Natural History and will make it as entertaining as a Persian Tale" (*Life,* April 30, 1773). And in a footnote apropos of the Goldsmith Epi-taph Johnson composed in 1776, Boswell added this: ". . . I have heard Johnson himself say, 'Goldsmith, Sir, will give us a very fine book upon the subject; but if he can distinguish a cow from a horse, that I believe, may be the extent of his knowledge of natural history.' " Boswell him-self was later to express his delight in the work: "I read a good part of Goldsmith's first Volume of the *History of the Earth* with pleasing wonder," he noted in his "Journal" for 1779.[3] And we have Goldsmith's own revealing remark made to his friend Joseph Cradock and given in the latter's *Literary and Miscellaneous Memoirs:* "I never took more pains than in the first volume of my 'Natural History'; surely that was good, and I was handsomely repaid for the whole."

The work begins in the then traditional manner with a "history of the earth," i.e., a summary of cosmological theory, and it is to be noted that in this initial section Goldsmith has not excluded the attitude asso-ciated with the Newtonian physico-theologists. When he comes to the world of "animated nature," however, his interest and delight in plain natural history assert themselves so strongly that there is less room for those final causes which the design argument had been wont to invoke. The hand of Providence is assumed to have been everywhere, but Gold-smith chooses to explain the varieties within the animal kingdom in accordance with a chain of being—a gradual system—rather than in terms of telelogical ends and means—and Winifred Lynskey points out that his emphasis on the great-chain-of-being concept was in this respect exceptional among those writing on natural history.

Goldsmith's controlling attitude finds expression in his general Pref-ace. Discovering, ascertaining, and naming all the various productions of nature constitute the difficult part of natural history. But describing the properties, manners, and relations which these productions bear to us is amusing and "exhibits new pictures to the imagination, and im-proves our relish for existence, by widening the prospect of nature around us." Once the difficult part is mastered,

> nothing but delight and variety attend the rest of [one's] journey. Wherever [one] travels, like a man in a country where he has many friends, he meets nothing but acquaintances and allurements in all

3 *The Private Papers of James Boswell from Malahide Castle,* XIII, 263.

the stages of his way. The meer uninformed spectator passes on in gloomy solitude; but the naturalist, in every plant, in every insect, and every pebble, finds something to entertain his curiosity, and excite his speculation.

Gloomy solitude tomorrow; today the comedy of Nature, improving our relish for experience. Studying natural history, a man "turns all nature into a magnificent theatre, replete with objects of wonder and surprise, and fitted up chiefly for his happiness and entertainment. . . ." The author acknowledges that he has "been content to describe things in his own way," and has "formed a kind of system in the history of every part of animated nature. . . ." And having dealt with the history of the earth in Part I, he turns thereafter to the creatures and the real show begins. Good Comedy may grow old but it never dies: the animals still proceed by twos into the Ark, and after the flood they amuse us in the circus ring and in the zoo. Some are friendly, some are noble, others contemptible. We judge "our humble partners in creation" from our own fully prejudiced point of view. The horse is "this noble animal"; the ass "is, in a state of tameness, the most gentle and quiet of all animals"; the stag "is one of those innocent and peaceable animals that seems made to embellish the forest, and animate the solitude of Nature." Unfortunately, animals of a cat kind are said to constitute "a bloody and unrelenting tribe, that disdain to own [man's] power, and carry on unceasing hostilities against him." The dog, on the contrary, is "the most intelligent of all known quadrupeds," the acknowledged friend of mankind. On the squirrel our teller of Persian tales has lavished all his art. The squirrel is a beautiful little animal, leading "the most frolicksome, playful life," and his tricks and habitudes "may serve to entertain a mind unequal to stronger operations." Among his habitudes, we have just been told, is his manner of crossing a body of water. This is quite extraordinary and it takes place in Lapland:

> Upon approaching the banks, and perceiving the breadth of the water, they return, as if by common consent, into the neighboring forest, each in quest of a piece of bark, which answers all the purposes of boats for wafting them over. When the whole company are fitted in this manner, they boldly commit their little fleet to the waves; every squirrel sitting on its own piece of bark, and fanning the air with its tail, to drive the vessel to its desired port.

It is Buffon embellished *con amore* for minds unequal to stronger operations.

And so on, through Birds, Fish, Frogs, Lizards, Serpents, Insects, to the Zoophytes.

There is an informative monograph on *Animated Nature* by James H. Pitman, *Goldsmith's "Animated Nature": A Study of Goldsmith,* Yale Studies in English, LXVII (New Haven, 1924). Exceedingly valuable are four articles by Winifred Lynskey: "Pluche and Derham, New Sources of Goldsmith," *PMLA,* LVII (1942), 435–445; "The Scientific Sources of Goldsmith's *Animated Nature,"* *SP,* XL (1943), 35–57; "Goldsmith and the Warfare in Nature," *PQ,* XXIII (1944), 333–342; and "Goldsmith and the Chain of Being," *JHI,* VI (1945), 363–374. See also Buffon's Place in the Enlightenment" by Otis Fellows in *Studies on Voltaire and the Eighteenth Century,* XXV (1963), 603–629; and Jacques Roger, *Les Sciences de la Vie Dans La Pensée Française Du XVIIIe Siècle* (Paris, 1963).

Bibliographical Notes

ABBREVIATIONS:

CE	=	Collage English
ELH	=	Journal of English Literary History
JHI	=	Journal of the History of Ideas
MLN	=	Modern Language Notes
MP	=	Modern Philology
PMLA	=	Publications of the Modern Language Association of America
PQ	=	Philological Quarterly
RES	=	The Review of English Studies
SEL	=	Studies in English Literature
SP	=	Studies in Philology

1. EDITIONS The *Collected Works of Oliver Goldsmith,* edited by Arthur Friedman (5 vols.; Oxford: The Clarendon Press, 1966) now supersedes all others. Two older collected editions are, however, still useful in various ways: *The Works,* edited by Peter Cunningham (4 vols.; London, 1854); and *The Works,* edited by J. W. M. Gibbs (5 vols.; London, 1884–86; New York, 1901–08). For Goldsmith's correspondence, *The Collected Letters of Oliver Goldsmith,* edited by Katharine C. Balderston (Cambridge: Cambridge University Press, 1928) is standard. There are many partial editions, selections, etc., valuable for the notes

and editorial commentary which they contain. Some of these are noted below in the appropriate subsection under Section 5 ("Scholarly and Critical Materials"). The following may be mentioned here: *The Miscellaneous Works,* with a biographical introduction by David Masson (London, 1869); *Goldsmith: Selected Works,* chosen by Richard Garnett (London, 1950); *Oliver Goldsmith: The Vicar of Wakefield and Other Writings,* edited with an introduction by Frederick W. Hilles (The Modern Library; New York, 1955); and *A Goldsmith Selection,* edited with an introduction by A. Norman Jefferes (London, 1963).

2. DISCUSSIONS OF THE CANON AND TEXT   On all questions pertaining to the Goldsmith canon the Friedman edition of the *Collected Works* embodies the cumulative results of modern scholarship, and this it also does in connection with textual problems. Also to be consulted, in regard to matters of attribution, is the statement given by R. S. Crane in Section 4 ("Separate Publications") and Section 5 ("Spurious, Doubtful, and Lost Works") of his Goldsmith bibliography in the *Cambridge Bibliography of English Literature,* Vol. II (Cambridge, 1940). Temple Scott's *Oliver Goldsmith, Bibliographically and Biographically Considered* (New York, 1928) is interesting and sometimes helpful.

3. BIBLIOGRAPHICAL AIDS   R. S. Crane's Goldsmith bibliography in the *Cambridge Bibliography of English Literature,* Vol. II (Cambridge, 1940) covers biographical and literary studies of Goldsmith into 1937. *The Supplement* to the *CBEL* (Vol. V [1957]), carries this listing into 1954. *English Literature: 1660–1800. A Bibliography of Modern Studies As Compiled for "Philological Quarterly"* (4 vols.; Princeton, 1950–62) covers the period from and including 1925 through 1959. For 1960 and subsequent years there are the annual eighteenth-century bibliographies appearing in *PQ,* Vol XL (1961) *et seq.* The annual "International Bibliographies" appearing in *PMLA* cover the Goldsmith studies from 1956 onwards.

4. BIOGRAPHICAL MATERIALS   Goldsmith's own autobiographical notes, dictated to Bishop Percy on April 28, 1773, will be found on pp. 13–16 of Katharine C. Balderston's *The History and Sources of Percy's Memoir of Goldsmith* (Cambridge, 1926). The account of Goldsmith by his sister, Mrs. Hodson, is given by Katharine Balderston as Appendix III ("Mrs. Hodson's Narrative") in her edition of the *Collected Letters of Oliver Goldsmith* (Cambridge, 1928). Of early biographical accounts, the one by William Cooke in the *European Magazine* for Aug., Sept., and Oct., 1793, is of special importance. "The Life of Dr. Oliver Goldsmith," by Bishop Percy and others, appearing in Vol. I of *The Miscellaneous Works of Oliver Goldsmith, M.B.* (London, 1801) has great authority. In connection with this "Life" one may consult Katharine C.

Balderston's *The History And Sources Of Percy's Memoir of Goldsmith.*
The Life by Sir James Prior (2 vols.; 1837) is valuable not solely because
of Prior's first-hand knowledge of things and people connected with
Goldsmith. John Forster's *The Life And Times Of Oliver Goldsmith*
(2 vols.; 1854) provided at the time of its appearance a comprehensive
biographical summary, and for this reason is still significant. Many
other biographies have appeared since then and are duly listed in the
standard Goldsmith bibliographies. The last of these is Ralph M.
Wardle's admirable *Oliver Goldsmith* (Lawrence, Kansas, 1957), which
now takes its place as the standard biographical work, up-to-date and
authoritative in practically every respect.

Under biographical materials can also be included those items by
Goldsmith's contemporaries which bear in some way upon his personality and the events of his life. Here first place must be given to Boswell's *Life of Johnson* (1791), associated with which are the materials
we now have in the *Private Papers of James Boswell from Malahide
Castle* (18 vols.; privately printed: Mount Vernon, New York, 1929–34)
and in *The Yale Editions of the Private Papers of James Boswell* (10
vols.; New York, 1950–66). See also Frederick A. Pottle's *James Boswell.
The Earlier Years: 1740–1769* (New York, 1966). Of first importance also
is the prose Portrait of Goldsmith by Sir Joshua Reynolds, given in
Portraits by Sir Joshua Reynolds, edited by Frederick W. Hilles (*The
Yale Edition of the Private Papers of James Boswell;* New York, 1952).
Among other items the following are of more than passing importance:
James Beattie, *London Diary, 1773* (Aberdeen, 1946); George Colman,
the younger, *Random Records* (1830); Joseph Cradock, *Literary and
Miscellaneous Memoirs* (1828); Richard Cumberland, *Memoirs* (1807);
Thomas Davies, *Memoirs of the Life of David Garrick, Esq.* (1780); Sir
John Hawkins, *The Life of Samuel Johnson* (1787); Arthur Murphy,
Essay on the Life of Samuel Johnson (1792); James Northcote, *Life
of Reynolds* (1819); Mrs. Thrale, *Anecdotes of Johnson* (1786) and
"Diary" (*Thraliana,* edited by Katharine C. Balderston [2nd ed.;
Oxford, 1951]); and Horace Walpole in his correspondence. See also
the material given in the *Johnson Miscellanies,* edited by George Bir-
beck Hill (1897).

5. SCHOLARLY AND CRITICAL MATERIALS   The listing which follows is a
highly selective one.

(a) General Aspects of Goldsmith: Austin Dobson's work deserves,
both because of of its range and its excellence, a place of its own.
Dobson was at one time or another a Goldsmith editor, a biographer,
and a critic, as the following books and essays of his show: 1883, an edi-

tion of *The Vicar of Wakefield;* 1885, a facsimile reproduction of *The Vicar* of 1766; 1887, *Selected Poems;* 1888, *The Life;* 1889, *Poems and Plays of Oliver Goldsmith* ("Everyman's Library"; 1910); 1890, an edition of *The Vicar* with a discussion of the work of its different illustrators; 1891, an edition of *The Citizen of the World;* 1892, some essays on Goldsmith in *Eighteenth Century Vignettes;* 1906, *The Complete Poetical Works.*

There are two outstanding critical works of recent date: Karl Eichenberger, *Oliver Goldsmith: Das Komische in den Werken seiner Reifeperiode* (Schweizer anglistische Arbeiten, Bd. 35; Bern, 1954); and A. Norman Jefferes, *Oliver Goldsmith* ("Writers and Their Work," No. 107; London, 1959). There are many shorter critical items of recent date, among them these: R. W. Chapman, "Oliver Goldsmith," in his *Johnsonian and Other Essays and Reviews* (Oxford, 1953); Richard Church, "Oliver Goldsmith," *Criterion,* VIII (1928–29), 437–444; Boris Ford, "Oliver Goldsmith," in *From Dryden to Johnson* ("Pelican Guide to English Literature," No. 4; London, 1957); W. H. Graham, "Oliver Goldsmith," *Contemporary Review,* CLXXXI (1952), 304–308; R. Wyse Jackson, *Oliver Goldsmith. Essays towards an Appreciation* (Dublin, [1951]); F. L. Lucas, "Oliver Goldsmith," in his *The Search for Good Sense. Four Eighteenth-Century Characters* (London, 1958); C. G. Osgood, Jr., "Notes on Goldsmith," *MP,* V (1907–08), 241–252; Virginia Woolf, "Oliver Goldsmith," in her *The Captain's Death Bed and Other Essays* (London, 1950; first ptd. in the *Times [London] Literary Supplement,* March 1, 1934).

(b) Goldsmith's Essays: On all problems of canon and text in connection with Goldsmith's essays, see Arthur Friedman's edition of the *Collected Works,* particularly Vols. I and III. There is a selection of Goldsmith's essays by A. H. Sleight (London, 1925). On the eighteenth-century essay in general, see Bonamy Dobrée, *English Essayists* (London, 1946; Walter Graham, *English Literary Periodicals* (New York, 1930); George S. Marr, *The Periodical Essayists of the Eighteenth-Century* (London, 1923); G. M. Segar, *Essays from Eighteenth-Century Periodicals* (London, 1947); and Melvin R. Watson, *Magazine Serials and the Essay Tradition,* 1746–1820 (Louisiana State University Studies No. 6; Baton Rouge, 1956).

(c) *The Citizen of the World:* There is a full-length monograph by Hamilton J. Smith, *Oliver Goldsmith's The Citizen of the World* (Yale Studies in English No. 71; New Haven, 1926). See, too, Smith's essay "Mr. Tatler of Pekin, China: A Venture in Journalism," in *Essays in Criticism by Members of the Department of English, University of*

California (Univ. of California. Publications In English, Vol. I; 1929). An edition of the *Citizen* by Austin Dobson appeared in 1891, another by Richard Garnet in 1904.

(d) *The Vicar of Wakefield:* The editions which have been published since the earliest one made its appearance on March 27, 1766, are legion. Noteworthy for one reason or another are the following: London, 1883, with a preface and notes by Austin Dobson; London, 1885, a facsimile reproduction of the first edition of 1766, with an introduction and bibliographical note by Dobson; London, 1890, with a preface by Dobson discussing the illustrations for *The Vicar* made by different artists; New York, 1900, with an introduction by Henry James; London, 1904, containing twenty-four colored illustrations by Thomas Rowlandson; London, 1926, with the Rowlandson illustrations and an introduction by George Saintsbury; London, 1928, with an important introduction by Oswald Doughty; New York, 1951, with a valuable critical introduction by Frederick W. Hilles; New York, 1964 (Bantam Books), with introduction, notes, and a selection of commentaries by Robert Donald Spector.

The circumstances concerning the composition of *The Vicar* and the events leading up to its publication have been the subject of much discussion. See, particularly, Oswald Doughty's introduction to his edition (1928). Friedman in the *Collected Works,* Vol. IV, summarizes the known facts rapidly and admirably.

Modern criticism is extensive. Interesting items include the following: George Saintsbury, introduction to his edition (1926); Oswald Doughty, introduction to his edition (1928); George Orwell, "Money and Virtue," *Tribune,* Nov. 10, 1944, pp. 15–16; D. W. Jefferson, "Observations on 'The Vicar of Wakefield,'" *Cambridge Journal,* III (1949–50), 621–628; Richard Church, in his *The Growth of the English Novel* (London, 1951); Frederick W. Hilles, introduction to his edition (1951); Morris Golden, "The Family-Wanderer Theme in Goldsmith," *ELH,* XXV (1958), 181–193; Lionel Stevenson, in his *The English Novel. A Panorama* (Boston, 1960); Morris Golden, "The Time of Writing of *The Vicar of Wakefield,*" *Bulletin of the New York Public Library,* Sept., 1961, pp. 442–450; Leo Lowenthal, in his *Literature, Popular Culture, and Society* (Englewood Cliffs, N.J., 1961); Robert D. Mayo, in his *The English Novel in the Magazines, 1740–1815* (Evanston, Illinois, 1962); Sheridan Baker, "The Idea of the Romance in the Eighteenth-Century Novel," *Studies in English Literature* (Tokyo), English number, 1963, pp. 49–61; MacDonald Emslie, *Goldsmith: The Vicar of Wakefield* (Barron's Studies in English Literature; Great Neck, New York, 1963); Robert Donald Spector, in his edition (1964), in which are reprinted Curtis Dahl's "Patterns of Disguise in 'The Vicar of Wakefield'" (1958),

Morris Golden's "Image Frequency and the Split in *The Vicar of Wake-field*" (1959), and Michael E. Adelstein's "Duality of Theme in 'The Vicar of Wakefield'" (1961); Harrison R. Steeves, in his *Before Jane Austen. The Shaping of the English Novel in the Eighteenth Century* (New York, 1965); and Robert B. Pierce, "Moral Education in the Novel of the 1750's," *PQ,* XLIV (1965), 73–83.

The illustrations for *The Vicar* which have been executed over the years by a great number of artists are in themselves something of a commentary on the protean character of the novel. The six plates after Thomas Stothard in the 1792 edition of *The Vicar* are dignified in air without too much idealization. Rowlandson's work for the 1823 edition is controversial: pronounced a mass of "coarse rotundities" and "a pictorial outrage" by Austin Dobson, they were reproduced in an edition of 1904 and again in one of 1926, the latter by Saintsbury, who remarked that it is by no means "improbable that Rowlandson has presented a country parson, a country parson's wife, and a country parson's family, not at all unlike what such people actually were a little after the middle of the eighteenth century." Other illustrators have been Cruikshank (1831), Mulready (1843), and John M. Wright, a pupil of Stothard's, whose work was reproduced in an edition published in 1911. The range of interpretation has been great, running from the matter-of-fact, through the robust, to the delicate, the sentimental, and the anemic. A modern film director of imagination might well give us a version of the novel displaying an enigmatic quality behind all of its sudden changes.

(e) Poetry: All the poetry, together with textual notes, is given by Friedman in the *Collected Works,* Vol. IV. Still valuable, because of the introductory essay and notes, is Austin Dobson's *The Complete Poetical Works* (London, 1906), an extended and revised version of his 1887 edition of *Selected Poems.*

There is a *Concordance to the Poems* by William D. Paden and Clyde K. Hyder (Lawrence, Kansas, 1940).

There have been many modern editions, some complete, others selective. Those which are of most interest by reason of the editorial criticism they contain are the following: Austin Dobson, *Poems and Plays of Oliver Goldsmith* (1889; reprinted 1910 in Everyman's Library); Thomas Seccombe, *Plays and Poems* (London, 1912); William H. Hudson, *Johnson and Goldsmith and Their Poetry* (London, 1918); W. H. Garrod, *Oliver Goldsmith. [Poems And Plays.]* (London, 1924); Padriac Colum, *Oliver Goldsmith: Essays, Poems, Letters and Plays* (Dublin, [1928]); A. S. Collins, *Goldsmith. The Vicar of Wakefield and The Deserted Village* (London, 1929); and of unusual distinction, Alan Rudrun and

Peter Dixon, *Selected Poems of Samuel Johnson and Oliver Goldsmith* ("Arnold's English Texts"; London, 1965).

In the way of commentary and criticism of one sort or another, the following may be mentioned: John Aiken, *Essay on Song-Writing* (1772), and "On The Poetry of Dr. Goldsmith" (in *Poetical Works of Oliver Goldsmith*, 1796; reprinted in Lucy Aiken, *Memoirs of John Aiken, M.D.* [1823]); Robert A. Aubin, *Topographical Poetry in XVIII-century England* (New York, 1936); Wallace C. Brown, *The Triumph of Form. A Study of the Later Masters of Heroic Couplet* (Chapel Hill, N.C. 1948); James E. Congleton, *Theories of Pastoral Poetry in England, 1684–1798* (Gainsville, Florida, 1952); Donald Davie, *The Late Augustans: Longer Poems of the Later Eighteenth Century* (London, 1958); T. S. Eliot, "Johnson's 'London' and 'The Vanity of Human Wishes,'" (Introduction to Haslewood Books edition, 1930; reprinted in *English Critical Essays. Twentieth Century*, "World's Classics," 1933); Boris Ford, as under 5a above; Albert B. Friedman, *The Ballad Revival* (Chicago, 1961); Frederick W. Hilles, as under 1 above; Kenneth Hopkins, *English Poetry: A Short History* (London, 1962); F. L. Lucas, as under 5a above; Ricardo Quintana, "*The Deserted Village*: Its Logical and Rhetorical Elements," *CE*, Dec., 1964, pp. 204–214; Virginia Woolf, as under 5a above.

(f) Plays: There are many editions. The latest is Friedman's *Collected Works*, Vol. V. Other editions of one or both of the plays include the following, which are noted because of their editorial commentary: Austin Dobson, *Poems and Plays of Oliver Goldsmith* (1889; Everyman's Library, 1910), and his Introduction to *Oliver Goldsmith.* [*Good Natur'd Man, She Stoops to Conquer, An Essay on the Theatre, etc.*] (1905; "Mermaid Drama book," New York, [1958]); Katharine C. Balderston, *She Stoops to Conquer* (Crofts Classics; New York, 1951); Vincent F. Hopper and Gerald B. Lahey, *She Stoops to Conquer* (Barron's Educational Series; Great Neck, New York, 1958).

Recent critical items: R. Quintana, "Goldsmith's Achievement as Dramatist," *University of Toronto Quarterly*, XXXIV (1965), 159–177, and "Oliver Goldsmith as a Critic of the Drama," *SEL*, V (1965), 435–454; A. Norman Jefferes, *A Critical Commentary on Goldsmith's "She Stoops to Conquer"* (Macmillan Critical Commentaries; London, 1966).

(g) Biographical Writings: See bibliographical notes in the Appendix under Biographical Works.

(h) Historical Writings: See bibliographical notes in the Appendix under Historical Writings.

(i) Philosophic and Scientific Compilations: See bibliographical notes in the Appendix under *An History of the Earth, and Animated Nature.*

(j) Miscellaneous Aspects of Goldsmith: Several items pertaining to Goldsmith's political and social views are cited in the bibliographical notes in the Appendix under Historical Writings. To these should here be added: W. F. Gallaway, "The Sentimentalism of Goldsmith," *PMLA*, XLVIII (1933), 1167–81.

Important is Austin Dobson's "Goldsmith's Library," in his *Eighteenth Century Vignettes* (1897).

Still useful, though somewhat outdated in certain respects, is Arthur L. Sells, *Les Sources Françaises De Goldsmith* (Paris, 1924).

Goldsmith as a critic is discussed by W. Vaughan Reynolds, "Goldsmith's Critical Outlook," *RES*, XIV (1938), 155–172.

On Goldsmith's prose style, see the following: John Arthos, "The Prose of Goldsmith," *Michigan Quarterly Review*, I (1962), 51–55; and D. W. Jefferson, "Speculations on Three Eighteenth-Century Prose Writers," in *Of Books and Humankind. Essays and Poems Presented to Bonamy Dobrée* (London, 1964), pp. 81–91.

Index

G. is used as an abbreviation of Goldsmith. G.'s works appear under his name. Items in the bibliographical portions of the Appendix and in the Bibliographical Notes are not included.